Also available at all good book stores

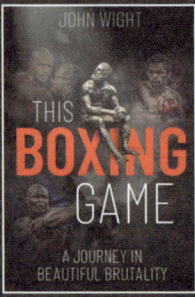

9781785316272

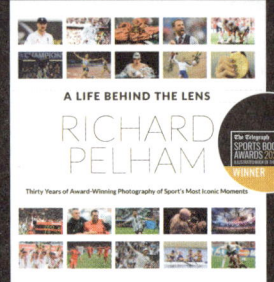

9781785315466

9781785316173

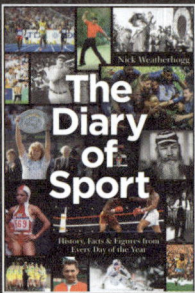

9781785316289

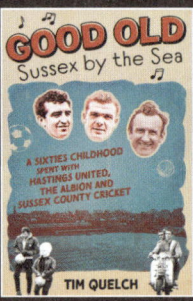

9781785316197

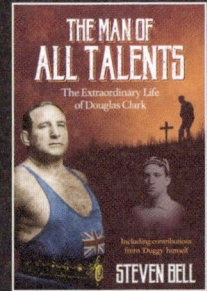

9781785316821

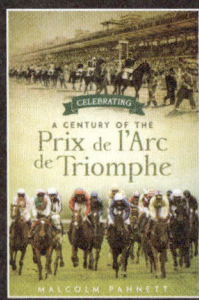

9781785317248

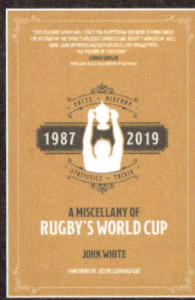

9781785315619

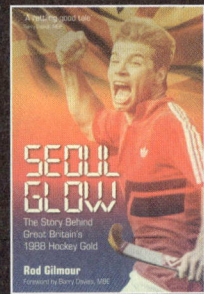

9781785314315

Interviews

with

Inspiration

JAMES WILLSTROP

Interviews

with
Inspiration

Heroes and Icons...
and What Drives Them to Succeed

First published by Pitch Publishing, 2021

Pitch Publishing
A2 Yeoman Gate
Yeoman Way
Worthing
Sussex
BN13 3QZ
www.pitchpublishing.co.uk
info@pitchpublishing.co.uk

A CIP catalogue record is available for this book
from the British Library.

ISBN 978 1 78531 823 8

Typesetting and origination by Pitch Publishing
Printed and bound in India by Replika Press Pvt. Ltd.

Contents

Introduction. 9

Jessica Ennis-Hill. 15

Tony Smith 26

Jonah Barrington 40

Julian Barnes 64

Katherine Grainger 82

Alexander Hanson 96

Jonny Wilkinson 126

Alison Rose. 145

Alistair Brownlee 157

Ali Jawad 173

Stefan Edberg. 179

Stuart Pearce 198

Denise Gough 212

James Brining. 229

Steve Redgrave 238

Chris Hoy 258

Simon Stephens. 265

Rich Landau and Kate Jacoby 285

Ramy Ashour. 303

Dominic McHugh 312

Malcolm Willstrop 327

Vanessa Atkinson 337

David Campion. 344

How do you measure achievement?

I can't measure achievement in my own work because I can't look at it that way. If I read a book, go to a play, see a painting or hear a piece of music that makes me expand the parameters of my response, makes me think differently, more completely about something, then that's a useful experience. Otherwise it's merely decorative and a waste of time.

Edward Albee (2005)

Introduction

THIS BOOK is ostensibly bound by interviews with characters who have been a source of interest and inspiration – in varying degrees and from all manner of worlds – to many people, but certainly to me. They come together in this book for different reasons: primarily, I've been interested or moved in some way by what they have done. There's a personal aspect at work, which I won't apologise for, but it's why you will see areas studied that interest me. I've been a professional squash player in my time, so naturally there are squash people involved, but not too many.

If the characters don't draw you, the reader, in by name alone, then I hope all is not lost and that the content itself can supersede the superficial draw of the character in terms of fame. I've tried to bring out of the interviews everything that can engage anyone in a broader sense. If I've got this right, then a ball-sport-hating mathematician should annex something enlightening from what Jonny Wilkinson says about playing world-level rugby or maintaining balance in his life while doing so; and I hope I've worked cleverly enough in order that someone who has never read a novel in their life can be pleasantly informed by what Julian Barnes says about writing them.

There were obvious constraints on who would be interviewed. I aimed for diversity of subject and character, but to an extent I was governed by who agreed to an interview or turned me down. There were many of the latter, which is why I must say now, I'm profoundly grateful for all the people in this book who very selflessly and patiently gave me their time. I'm not famous and I'm a dreadful networker, so drawing them in was challenging. Had I had a name in modern-day celebrity society, attached to the BBC or David Beckham, I would have had people lining up. The famous could near bring back the dead for an interview, but, when you're an unknown, people understandably are reluctant. Indeed, there were pools of heroes I fantasised about speaking to but there was only so much chasing around and waiting for agents I wanted to or was able to do.

At stages I was urged by experts in the industry to scrap the format and try to deliver something with more arc, more thesis, but I was fairly set on not attempting to write another 'How people find greatness' books. I'm not armed for it, and lack the will to get to know enough, or the capacity to be academic. Why would I be academic anyway, when as a squash player I was fortunate enough to reach the top of the world in squash and had been through it all? Surely, I should lean on the fact I could talk about it in real, perhaps romantic, terms, rather than through figures and research and statistics. And to chew it all over in its finished format with some of the people I've admired was a lively thought.

And I love reading interviews. I go back to things like *Lunch with the FT* or Richard Eyre's *Talking Theatre* interviews and evince little nuggets of pleasure and knowledge every time. I'm a slow reader who finds long linear stories challenging, so great sprawling novels can be problematic. I love books I can dip in and out of, start at the end or in the middle of, or where I can jump to a particular interview. One interview is a good length for a sitting, and if I put the book down for a few weeks it doesn't mean I've lost the plot and can't return to it. I hope there will be others who are the same and can appreciate the format. I may have tree-chopped any chances of a bestseller in the first move of the chess board, but hey ho, at least I can serve my instincts.

Added to all this was the selfish and ambitious conceit I have to aspire to writing scripts for film or the stage, so I'm energised by the dance of dialogue, the interplay between people through words; exploring just what a good simple conversation can throw up.

Speaking of format, standing contrapuntal to the dialogue sit my own interjections, which could bugger the whole thing up and prove to be a particular annoyance, but I couldn't help it, and if nothing else it may add a little chiaroscuro to this bible of wisdom you have in your hands.

I hope I've succeeded in revealing to the reader, without any filler, how some of the greatest athletes, writers, actors, chefs, surgeons, etc. reach their level and achieve brilliance.

I'm guarded about using the word 'brilliant'. I did try for another, yet in this case it does just seem right. When writing the book, I often found myself talking about 'success', but success can mean anything. To be truly brilliant is to add colour and contrast and to steal the breath of the voyeur; to move an audience, reader or partaker profoundly; to change something inside another person. As Edward Albee said, to 'expand parameters'. In fact, it might not always be successful at all. Brilliance leaves a footprint, certainly in the minds of people, whereas success, which can't be quantified easily, doesn't always do the same. Apart from the word 'brilliant' being hideously overused, it's actually, I feel, an adjective that does justice to its meaning the way I'm using it.

Having had a life in sport, why then delve into other worlds, rather than focus it all on sport? Simply put, I've had a lot of sport in my life, and I think that many of us are invested in drawing on the comparisons that exist between different forms of expertise in all areas. There are parallels that exist between many disciplines and they stimulate intriguing questions and answers. As a professional squash player, it would have been intensely narrow-minded of me to study only squash all my life, and I'm a huge subscriber to the fact that inspiration can come from all sorts of places. The outside world, life itself, is a great source of illumination for us, and perhaps the world of sport, culture and the arts is an obvious specific prism for accessing this.

It's curious to think about what we consider artistic. Sport is an art form yet it's often not deemed so in the way music or dance or literature is. Neither too is being a physiotherapist or doctor. We could do to rethink this: these people perhaps accomplish the most basic artistic sentiments of all by actually saving lives or helping people to walk again. In the end, the artist rouses emotion or changes something in people, and all of the people in this book do or have done that in some way by the sheer standard and poetry of what they do.

I've learned things about my squash career by doing an acting class, reading a book, or so often simply by listening to what people have to say. I've certainly found morsel after morsel in these interviews to help me look afresh at the way I play squash at high levels. The more knowledge we take on from anywhere, the broader and wider our horizons become in our own worlds.

Every question or answer that I have included in this book I included because it has the potential to offer any reader – whether from a sport, business, arts, culture, music, finance, politics or any other background – insight into what makes high-class, brilliant performance and how we might learn about advancement.

After all, there's some basic urge for all humans to want to better another or themselves, to want to improve at something, however seemingly insignificant. By dipping into the words on these pages I hope to simply entertain the reader, yet I would be doubly encouraged to feel that they can gain inspiration and knowledge, and initiate ideas about how to discover.

As I got further into this, the question wasn't just: how do these people become successful? It was asking what success means to these different people and what it does to them. Is success about the inspiration it gives to others? Or is it simply about winning the gold medal? How do people going to great lengths to achieve in their field retain balance and stay healthy, and what's the cost of this so-called 'success'?

I've tried to preserve the charm, humour and sheer entertainment value I shared with these people, the idea being to fascinate, titillate and entertain more than be academic, knowing or statistical. I felt that witty anecdotes should get the nod over passages of research.

And aside from all the brilliance, I hope the book can take you a little deeper and touch on the effects of it all and what goes on away from the disciplines themselves: the emotions, difficulties, obstacles, the perspective we all find in our worlds from pursuing something. Brilliance isn't everything – sometimes just getting by is the biggest thing – but it's an intriguing part of the tapestry for all of us in one way or another.

Jessica Ennis-Hill

I INTERVIEWED Jess at the EIS in Sheffield, her training base. At London in 2012 she became Olympic Heptathlon Champion under outrageous amounts of scrutiny and pressure. Her time since will have been much less her own, as in subsequent years she found herself assuming the position of the darling of British sport.

Although she must have had her fill of the same old interviews at the time, Jess was engaging and interesting on every question. After our interview she gave her time and patience to a fan who had somehow managed to track her down, even though we had found a quiet corner of the building. This attention is a by-product of her London achievement that she has since had to balance.

—

JW: Can you explain what made you an Olympic champion?

JEH: It's very hard to say it's one thing. I think there's maybe a certain ability that I was born with, so a slight genetic element, but without having the environment that I had – the upbringing, the coaching the people around me, the facilities – that ability would never have surfaced. They all came together to allow me to bring that talent out. A combination of all that, mixed with previous competitions that I had done,

15

championships, disappointments, injuries, all the things that I ever experienced, just fused and I brought them all together for those two days in London.

JW: You had a horrendous low in 2008, having to miss the Beijing Olympics because of a metatarsal injury. Do the setbacks improve you?

JEH: Yes, through injuries and setbacks and those occasions when you feel you're there and you're not quite there, you can learn so much. You have that horrible, disappointed feeling when you're coming away from championships. Those are the moments where you learn more about yourself, through enforced breaks. You're forced to take a step back and work things out from different angles and perspectives. You go away and focus on things that you really need to focus on, and you must find that mental strength to put things back together. I definitely learned a lot from my injury in 2008. It made me appreciate my ability and what I had achieved so far, and also made me more hungry to go on and achieve more.

JW: Can you give me an idea of how much you think that innate talent has got you where you are?

JEH: I don't know whether you can be specific on that. I was a really active child and I loved athletics as soon as I came down to sessions. My coach, Toni [Minichiello], said that he could see that I had natural running ability from a young age. But if I hadn't been put into the right environment, not been coached by him and allowed to develop into the heptathlete that I am, and then worked so hard, I wouldn't have achieved all this. It takes both.

JW: I've heard you talk about how frustrating it is to miss even single sessions. Every session you do is vital, so much work, hour upon hour …

JEH: You have to have the wherewithal to do those tough sessions and it's been instilled in me from a young age by Toni. You break your body down because that's the foundation that you need when you're competing in the summer. That understanding that it's going to hurt and be painful but that it will make it easier when you come to compete.

JW: Do you have ways of dealing with the toughest sessions you have to do when they are impending?

JEH: Yes, I have to mentally prepare, so if it's a tough 800m session I have to make sure that I know what the session is and start thinking about it beforehand. I hate the pain of running the 800 or those kind of running sessions. I go within myself a little in the lead-up to them. That's my way of dealing with it. I'll never not finish a session and will always give it absolutely everything.

JW: People don't have any idea how hard you had to go to create that performance in August 2012 …

JEH: No, probably not. You have to kill yourself on the track or the court because you know that your competitors and rivals are doing the same thing.

JW: I loved the description of the Sunday morning session in your book, where you would look at people heading off for their nice day of rest and you would have an horrific session to put yourself through. Those are the tough days.

JEH: It's a big sacrifice and it consumes your whole life for a long time. But it's that short period of time where you have that opportunity and where you have the talent, so why not try giving it absolutely everything? You just get on with it.

JW: Great writers tend to read or will have read the best writers. Great musicians would watch the best musicians to learn. Would you say that watching others has been a big part of your learning?

JEH: To be honest, as I was growing up I wasn't sport mad. I loved watching athletics. I enjoyed doing it, less so watching. I just wanted to do everything. As I get older, I do enjoy watching some of the great athletes compete, whether it's the heptathlon, pole vault, the long jump … just seeing someone who can execute their event perfectly is inspiring and gives you goosebumps.

JW: What about all the advisory services that are such a part of sport today? Have you bought into them?

JEH: That part of it is one of the biggest things. It's very important to tap into everything you can. Athletics is an individual sport, and you see the athlete go and perform alone on the track, but the people around me – Alison Rose, Derry Suter, my coaches – they spend so much time on me. They are not the ones competing but they are the ones behind the scenes doing everything so that I can step on the track in the best possible shape. They are a huge part of what I've achieved.

——

There's been a significant transition over the last three decades. Sport is now not just about a coach and a player, and neither is it about training for hours and hours on end aimlessly and brutally. It's more about seeking the advice from all the different experts who can advise on the complex science of training: psychology, nutrition, coaching, physiotherapy, physiology and more. It becomes about training smartly, sensibly, not for hours and hours on end, but for however long it takes to train optimally. Jess has people working with her of whom she seems proud and grateful, and every time she wins, she knows that small group have facilitated the achievement, and I'm sure Jess would agree to some extent that they own a part of it. They deserve a little of that gold medal.

After the biggest achievements in my sporting career, the only thing I wanted to do was thank and share it with those who helped me most. I wanted them to have some of the adulation. I wouldn't have become world number one without a handful of very special people who run my sessions, be my friend, keep me fit and motivated, and give me their time on a weekly basis. After winning a silver and bronze medal in Glasgow at the 2014 Commonwealth Games, I wanted to literally give my medals to Alison Rose (also Jess's physio). Six weeks prior to the games, a doctor told me I might not play professionally again. My hip was shattered, I needed an operation and Alison worked indefatigably to get me to Glasgow and beyond. I wouldn't have been at those games if it were not for Alison. Forget the medals; I wouldn't have realised the whole experience, which was one of the most enjoyable sporting experiences of my career, made much more so by the threat of not playing. The athlete's existence is somewhat selfish, and they need extremely selfless people around them to enable them to compete and be successful.

—

JW: People say that it's the hours that you put in, but what about the quality of what you're doing? Is it better to spend less time doing something better?

JEH: I think in previous years it's always been flat out. You've got to put a lot of effort in … maximum quality.

JW: Two days of solid competing is tough, so you must need to be very intense in training to replicate that sensation …

JEH: I have to train at a much higher level than I'm competing. I had my injury, though, in 2008 and that made me realise and appreciate how important recovery and rest really is. Before then I was less willing to rest. I wanted to lose no time and would train all the time, making sure I was ready. But now I appreciate that having those days off, especially as I'm getting older, is really important to let the body recover from what it has done. Then you can push harder again. As

I'm getting older things are changing and Toni and I have to make sure we get good quality sessions and that I'm not getting injured.

JW: So, you try not to worry about getting loads of hours in, more about just getting it right?

JEH: Yes. It's picking up a few points here and there now, not putting 200 to 300 points on my PB unfortunately. So, it's quality we're looking for.

JW: Your relationship with Toni can be quite volatile I've read, but then many coach-player relationships tend to be. Is that sort of conflict likely to be part of any successful process when you're working so hard to achieve at the highest level?

JEH: I think every coach and athlete are different. It's such a unique relationship and you spend so much time together, wanting something so badly, and it's frustrating for me when I don't perform the way I want to in training. It's equally frustrating for Toni at times and we sometimes clash. We might not communicate with each other in the best way, and that's when he might storm off and there might be tears. I think it's part of having success. We've worked hard for all that success! And it makes it exciting.

———

That success that athletes strive for at high levels rarely seems to be found at the end of a smooth path. People talk about high achievers being difficult to work with. Is this because they were snotty during practice or challenged things in business meetings? Are we describing the Michelin starred chef, the one with high blood pressure on television becoming angry when his chefs overdo the peppercorn?

When there is collaboration it is almost impossible to avoid some form of conflict. If the chef lets the sauce issue go because he doesn't want to be difficult to work with then his product is not how he wants it and his standard falls short. So he'd rather be difficult to work with but really really good.

When building towards high standards, constant questioning and criticism is necessary and it will probably mean someone might get upset somewhere along the line. When aiming for high levels, there's bound to be a certain ruthlessness required in getting there. As much as Jess and Toni love each other, this relationship naturally has a fractious element. They are constantly trying to overcome challenges and problems together so there is no way that this process could be easy.

When I am training it is, I guess, my work. I try to balance the intensity as much as I can so it is not all completely over-revved and lacking in enjoyment and spontaneity, but undoubtedly there is an element of intensity that I've sometimes struggled to contain because I'm trying so hard. I don't consider myself to be the most endearing person on the training court when working with my coaches, though there are compatriots of mine who from what I've heard and seen could be far worse!

But the training session is the time of the day where I can do something to improve the way I play. I don't want the time to be wasted and I feel like I've sometimes let myself down with regards to my attitude to others, be it coaches or training partners.

I was so keyed up one day that I had a go at someone filming me on a mobile phone. It was a silly and pompous reaction and I regretted it, but I suppose the training court is where the day job unfolds; I'm trying to focus hard on the work and sometimes that difficult side comes out, certainly in the relationships I have with the people who I'm working with. I don't want to waste time practising badly and in the past I would have let nothing come in the way of that. If it meant being a bit rude then I guess I was. With age I've implored myself to lighten up. If something disrupts the session, or I'm not happy with a practice, or god forbid if we all start joking about a bit, then let's embrace that. It's only life. We are all just playing at being kids anyway. It's only a game and lots of people in the world have real problems. So enjoy it, for crying out loud.

I do recall those sessions which have gone less well, where in the aftermath I talk or argue it through with Malcolm. They often turn in to endless analyses on how to keep improving, how to work things out. The petulance and conduct at times during training I have not been particularly proud of, but then maybe I needed some of this to reach the level I did.

Maybe a certain standard in training is necessary and maybe I shouldn't have to apologise for it, if I too have been difficult to work with. Brian Clough definitely wouldn't be apologising, I'm sure. Malcolm Willstrop either. But maybe I am doing, a bit.

——

JW: How important is the downtime in what you do?

JEH: It's crucial for me, having the balance. Athletics is a huge part of my life, but I have to have separation and to be able to switch off from it. I like to go home and not talk about athletics. We see friends, have the dog so we take her out, and switch off completely. It was quite hard during Olympic year because of the stress of training and everything going on in the media. I do find that if you've got some separation it helps.

JW: The problem with what you did in London is that you have two specific days on which you have to produce that incredible form and performance. It's one thing being great generally at what you do, but it's another doing it at the right time. Is there a calculated psychological process that you have in order to post that performance at that very particular time, or do you just take the Olympics as any other event?

JEH: Toni would always say in the lead-up that these are the same girls that I've competed against in World and European championships. It's the Olympics, it's in London, but it's still the same event. Go out and do what you've always done, was the message. It's difficult not to dress the Olympic thing up so much and think you've got to make all these changes and do all these amazing things to be successful. But if you trust in what you do and keep repeating it, then that's the best way.

JW: So, it's just about concentrating on the process rather than the occasion?

JEH: Yes. I didn't think about the occasion. I didn't think about how many people were watching, the whole drama of it all, I just focused on one event at a time.

JW: There was stuff in your book about the illnesses [in the lead-up to London, her brother-in-law visited her house with a cold and Jess wasn't too happy with that]. That tendency towards being obsessive; many athletes will go to all lengths to avoid illness. I find quite a lot of high performers show this side …

JEH: Well, you make so many sacrifices and particularly in athletics. You have one or two championships that year and it's that one occasion where all that training you've done is for that one specific time … and something so silly as picking up a cold can completely ruin that. During Olympic year I was so worried. It was kind of out of my control in a way. You can control your training and the things you do but if you go out or a family member comes round with a cold, you can pick it up and it can affect your chances.

JW: They wouldn't even think. In all likelihood they have a job where it doesn't really matter if they pick up a cold.

JEH: Yes. My brother-in-law just came round and said, 'Oh I've got a really awful cold. Sorry, I hope you don't get it!' I was like: 'Thanks a lot!'

JW: Do you think you could have been very, very good at something else?

JEH: I'm not sure I would. I think I was lucky to fall into athletics. I enjoyed it and was good at it.

JW: But the in-built drive and dedication to succeed might have taken you so far at a lot of things, surely?

JEH: Without a doubt I would have known how to apply myself at whatever I did. I went to university, but athletics was always a priority, so maybe if athletics hadn't been there I would have applied myself more in a different area and done well.

JW: I read about you being very calm when competing and how a few people close to you tried to encourage you to be more outwardly emotional. You stood against that and said it wasn't your way. Athletes are criticised nowadays if they are not showing outward passion, but you, along with athletes like Roger Federer for example, have proved that you can have an inner intensity and perform well. People think that because you're quiet, you don't feel passionate, and that you don't care. Do you think that attitude has been a help on the track?

JEH: Yes. I would have been trying to be someone that I wasn't had I changed. Toni would always say that I didn't look like I was trying, and he asked me to be more aggressive, but that just wouldn't work for me. I'm not the kind of athlete that slaps herself and gets herself fired up like that. I can get myself fired up and be equally as ready as the next person, but I just do it internally. That's what works for me. Carolina Klüft was an amazing athlete and was just the opposite. She would really get herself fired up outwardly, but there's no point in me trying to copy what she did for the sake of it. So, I've always looked calm, but the adrenaline and fire is on the inside. I want it as much as anyone else.

JW: How tough is being a world-class athlete? People see the glamour side of it. But what's it like to dig yourself into the ground on a regular basis. Does the toughness of it get to you at times?

JEH: When you want something so badly you put pressure on yourself and you spend so much time at the track, making all these sacrifices and it does affect the different parts of your life, and sometimes you have those days where you think: 'What am I doing this for? Is it even going to work out? Will I achieve what I want to achieve?' Before the London Olympics I just wanted someone to tell me what was going to happen. But you've just got to keep believing in yourself and get on with it. You're in a unique position that not many people get to realise: having your hobby as a job and career, travelling the world doing all these amazing things. There are difficult times during the process, but then you consider the good times and keep it in perspective. And it's such a short time that you have, where you're nailing your body into the ground. Early thirties and I'll be retired, by which time I hope I can relax and forget the pain of the sessions!

——

It strikes me how cut-throat sport can be. Jess is certainly an outstanding, world-class athlete, but that Olympic gold was always going to take her to another stratosphere. It would earn her more money, more fame, and she would have achieved the ultimate accolade and could take that and say it for the rest of her life. Is there any wonder she became protective and strung up about catching a cold? Everything has to go right for that day. And if it doesn't go right, then life-changing events don't happen.

Tony Smith

I FIRST met Tony when he brought his Leeds Rhinos team to play squash at my club Pontefract in the mid-noughties for a break from the pitch during a heavy season of rugby league. He and my dad Malcolm regularly, among much waspish banter, swap ideas on sport. Tony's record is one for which many rugby coaches would give a limb. He steered Warrington to three Challenge Cup victories, in 2009, 2010 and 2012; the last silverware they had won prior came almost 60 years before. He won two Super League titles with Leeds Rhinos and he has coached England. I've visited Tony's training sessions at Leeds and Warrington in the past and loved gleaning insight into the workings of his teams.

Tony often cites a new ethos or slant that he's pursuing, which may or may not benefit the development of his squad. One of the signs of a great coach is an inclination to engage with new or different ideas. Tony may not act on each and every piece of advice or information he receives, but his astute ability as a coach means he will assimilate and decide which of it to use. It's a true sign of an insecure and narrow leader who instantly dismisses new ideas or doesn't listen and attempt to learn or absorb. The moment a coach is derisory regarding anything scientific or new-fangled means that they believe they are threatened, and that they misguidedly feel that they can cover everything. Of course, they can't, no one can. An expert coach is an expert delegator. Excellence is a game of fine lines, and they can be crucially determining in sport. Not every new science is right for everyone, but to be dismissive is dangerous.

I've loved picking Tony's brains about the whys and wherefores of cultivating elite performance over the years. When I realised this book was starting to take shape, I knew he would be one of my first interviews, should he agree.

—

JW: Can you sum up why you win big rugby league titles?

TS: [He laughs] I think I maybe have a talent to coach. I think I can communicate, though, most of all. I've been fortunate to get some of the more talented players to coach for me, which makes me appear more successful! If I can get my players to think I'm a good coach, then I'm a good coach.

JW: The first job you had was at Huddersfield, and the team was relegated immediately. You went unbeaten the next year in National League One. But then, as is often the case in rugby league, you had to win a Grand Final to achieve promotion. That must have been serious pressure.

TS: It was an enormous match. It's a one-off game, and everything we had done that year didn't matter – we were undefeated. It was about people's livelihoods! That was the most pressure I've ever felt and that was my least enjoyable year. Our team was too good. The relegation the previous year shaped my coaching career. I lost 13 matches in a row with Huddersfield but kept my job, which would be unheard of now. I believe that still stands as a record number of defeats for a coach without being sacked. That period reinforced my coaching philosophies, though, and it was vital to my development as a coach. The team was actually losing but getting better, and I was happy.

It wasn't quite as dark a time as might be imagined. It's easy to envisage a big dark cloud hanging over the place every Monday morning, but it wasn't like that. I knew I had to exude confidence and cool as the leader of a group.

—

'The team was actually losing but getting better, and I was happy.' I felt a knowing pang. My own biggest successes in squash are simply the by-product of a thousand other defeats.

There's no doubt that any person attaining high achievement will be well versed in the art of accepting and absorbing rejection or failure. One of the great modern examples of an athlete who overcame considerable failure was Kelly Holmes, who won double Olympic Gold in the 800m and 1,500m in Athens in 2004. Prior to this incredible achievement she had been labelled injury-prone, a runner-up. It's hardly a bad thing to be in the latter category, despite journalists often insisting so. We all know what happened next.

There are posters dotted about the EIS training centre in Sheffield, which are strategically placed to inspire the athletes as they train. One of them features Holmes on the podium after winning two gold medals at the Athens Olympics. Above her teary-eyed profile float the words: 'There's no such thing as failure, only failure to try, try and try again.' Some of these dictums can be overstated and syrupy, but this one I like for its simplicity and truth. She proved that consistent searching, probing and graft can prevail. But hell, she did have to endure some disappointment in order to finally bathe in her vat of gold.

Katherine Grainger won three consecutive silver medals in three different Olympic Games before winning her gold medal in London in 2012. These athletes are so inspirational that they are unclassifiable and unique. When I've gone to the bottom of the well in training for weeks and months on end, and all roads still lead to failure (which they have done time and time again), consolation and inspiration comes in the form of Grainger and Holmes.

To be successful it's necessary to endure and react against failure. And very often. Think of the archetypal figure on our sporting horizon in this century whom, if such a thing does exist, practically screams the word talent: Usain Bolt. As much as he makes a good case for the existence of raw, innate ability, he has still actually lost many, many times. He has trained many, many times. Despite all the finger waving, dancing and camera-thieving, he has felt disappointment frequently in the past and has learned and responded. We wouldn't know it when he was in full flow, winning everything.

—

JW: That one-off, sudden-death situation is tough. Just recently I found myself playing the deciding rubber to win the World Team Championships for England. So much riding on one performance, and I felt incredibly nervous. I can lose to anyone in one match! It wasn't just about me, that was the problem. My team-mates could call themselves world champions forever if I won that match. So, what do you say and do as coach in a one-off Grand Final to bring the best out of your players on that very occasion, in that very specific 80-minute period?

TS: It's not normal, but we try to normalise it! I tend not to build it up too much. I try to be as calm as I can be and get the team focusing on the things we focus on throughout the year. They still have to pass the ball and make tackles just like they would in any other match. Why change too much when it works all year round? It's hard to blank out the 80,000 people and the enormity of it all, but after soaking that up it's time to do the little things well. Some big matches, I'll reflect and think I got it just right; other times it was wrong. I'm not sure it's an exact science. Each final is different.

—

There seems to be no right or wrong in terms of preparation, but the best seem to be able to make that massive, one-off occasion feel like any other match in their heads. Olympic champions are amazing animals because very often they only get a couple of chances a lifetime to achieve what they deem their pinnacle. The amount of training and effort that goes into performing to gold medal level is scarily disproportionate to the time taken to achieve what they want on a few days in August.

Clearly, champions seem to dedicate their mental energy to the process, rather than concentrating on the outcome, the title, the trophy, the prize. It's very much a buzz phrase in sports psychology, but as a philosophy it's strong. There's just no point in wasting energy thinking about the dream, the achievement, for too long. By doing that you're constantly building the thing up to be this monumental task, which can get out of hand and be a completely overbearing emotional obstacle. It's easier to negotiate winning a world title or Olympic title when it's broken into more simple steps, into a process.

When I'm asked by young players how I handle pressure on big occasions and play the big matches, this is the best advice I can think to offer.

—

JW: How much do you think that talent is a factor for the top-class players that you work with?

TS: It varies with different players in our sport. Innate talent definitely exists, you can see it. Some players will squeeze everything out of themselves and be very driven. Now if they do that and have some talent, then they are world class. There are some players who don't squeeze every ounce out but are talented. They can be good, very good, but they could get so much more. Everybody has to work a certain amount, however talented they are. I like the ones who like to work hard. I LOVE the players who are talented AND work hard. There's an example of a player I've coached, Kevin Sinfield, who leaves nothing out there but also has that talent, and these players are very rewarding to work with.

JW: Do you feel that you've worked hard to become a world-class coach? Have you had to graft, or was that natural?

TS: Yes, I do graft. You don't just walk into winning Challenge Cups. I had an older brother to learn from. I could watch him, worked under him, and found my work ethic from him. I also saw the mistakes. I saw him work hard and not get the right balance with family and life. There have been times when I've overworked and I didn't have the balance. I constantly work at this. There are some people who sacrifice everything for trophies, and I don't find that healthy. I need family and outside life to be in order. I've had to work long hours, don't get me wrong, but I think I've found a better balance. I wouldn't pay that price if I had to sacrifice my life outside rugby for the sport.

———

My dad Malcolm always liked to say that to perform well in top-class sport it's important to have clarity and be happy, to be settled personally. I've produced some of my best performances when in tatters emotionally, and I know others do, so I'm not sure it's completely right as a blanket statement, but I agree it has to be helpful. It seems that some degree of personal balance is important when we're aiming high. This might not mean balance in the conventional way, but perhaps it equates to whatever 'balance' means to an individual. Some people find it through someone close, some seek assurance from the exact opposite, solitude. However a person feels most comfortable spending free time seems to create ideal scenarios for producing high-quality output.

The time away from the discipline is almost as important as the discipline itself, especially when you're older and have specialised for so long. After playing competitive squash for over 20 years, the breaks, the rests become indispensable, like gold dust. When a great athlete is working so hard to strive to such extraordinary levels, that rest, that enjoyment, whether it be walking the dogs, reading books, spending time with those they love, is as important a part of the process as the endless hours of practise and effort.

——

JW: The players must get that balance right too. How can you as a coach affect that?

TS: I'm always trying to help the players with this. I think one of the most important things to have as a coach is empathy and understanding, and to communicate and observe the players. You get a feel for how your players are doing, whether they are tired or not. I'm always watching the players even if I'm not coaching – how they move in between stations in training for example. I ask the staff to listen to the banter; whether the players are chirpy or not! Some days it's flat. This can tell me a lot.

JW: Rugby lads often like a drink. Can that enjoyment help them?

TS: Yes, having a drink can be fine, possibly a good thing, if done at the right times and in the right quantities! When I came here, I talked to the players: what sort of standards do we want to set? If we want to be world class, we have to work to world-class standards. Does that mean never drinking? Absolutely not. I've just given the players five days off and we have a two-week break, so now might be a time for them to fill their boots! But in two weeks' time, leading into the finals, it's not. A social event can be helpful in letting an athlete relax if that's what they enjoy. I may have to get heavy if things are way out of whack, but this rarely happens.

JW: Successful people seem to be guided by routine. It's often highly structured. Even many writers, who you might think would work strange hours or need to wait for a big moment of inspiration, seem to have routines. Do you stand by a set routine?

TS: It varies. We're all creatures of habit, and we've all got little elements of OCD. One of my players has severe OCD. Structure in preparation is good. We have fairly strict outlines of our weeks of training, which are planned, but there always needs to be an element of adaptation if things don't go the way you want. You need to be able to overcome things that are not part of the routine. Not everything will always go to plan.

JW: Many players have rituals and obsessive tendencies. Maybe it's something to do with the intensity of athletes …

TS: I try to encourage my players not to get too bogged down in these things. Some players do their structures and still lose, but they continue to persist! Some routines can actually not help. But you're right, sportsmen and women do tend to be meticulous, and if they are not OCD or superstitious, they tend to follow routine quite strictly.

JW: How much importance do you put on bringing in different people to help the team?

TS: A lot. For instance, the area of sports science has changed so much in the last couple of decades. We're learning so much about training and injury prevention. But it's important that I involve all the different aspects that affect performance, whether it be nutrition, psychology, physiotherapy, etc. I find all this fascinating information for the coach to decipher. I encourage the players to use as many different facilities as possible to make them become better players. I won't, though, let the sports science department run the team. I love info filtering in. Sometimes I say, 'Thanks for that,' and walk away. But I ask a thousand questions. We may have gone a little too scientific sometimes.

We have specialists in many areas who we use to consult as well, from outside the club. As a coach I can't do everything, and I can't provide that knowledge. We have medical staff, coaches, psychologists.

JW: You're tremendously dignified in your interviews after matches. It would be easy to lose your cool in that direct aftermath, especially after a loss. I find this part incredibly difficult; perspective at that point isn't easy.

TS: I try to think about how people can react to that. I want my team to give the best performance they can, and if it's not good enough then we hold our heads up and move on. If I'm going to project any negatives, then they won't be until I get home and am alone. At the matches, in the view of the public eye, in front of the press, I try to present a level and dignified persona. It's easier at the match. When you get home, that's when it's tough. I can do what I like after that in the privacy of my own home.

JW: When I've a bad loss, I've taken it out on Vanessa and Malcolm, and sometimes I regret it later. Do you have that outlet at home!? How important is the support from friends and families away from the field?

TS: Well yes, Lisa is invested in this life as well and she will happily give me opinions and talk things through with me. She will tell me if she thought a performance was poor and I'll be like, 'Okay, okay, I know.' I don't rant and rave too much when I get home. I'll get home and stay apart for a while, go quiet, and Lisa understands. She gives me that space.

There's nothing wrong with a bit of 'mourning'. Sometimes it's good to have that period of suffering. There's nothing wrong with that because it gives you the impetus and the desire to improve.

The lowest I felt after a match was at Huddersfield. Hunslet, two divisions below us, beat us in the Challenge Cup. I went home that night and couldn't sleep. At 2.30am the next morning I was in the stadium and I moved the whole office around. I carried on all day. This wasn't normal behaviour for me. It was an extreme day and I let myself get very low. Even losing a Grand Final was never as bad as that.

—

I once played a match in a tournament in Sheffield, lost, stormed out to my car and drove. I drove down the M1, then thought, 'What am I going south for?' so drove back up the M1 and wound up in Scarborough, a Yorkshire seaside town. Festering in stale sweat, I eventually slept in a car park, then drove to York and binged on cake. After cosseting my misery, I decided to continue west towards Halifax around lunchtime, where my brother David lives and works. By mid-afternoon my gloom had abated somewhat, and I regained some clarity. I was able to see that my behaviour had been that of an unqualified, self-pitying arse. Now in my mid-thirties I can barely believe I was this desperate to win squash matches when things like the Holocaust exist. What on earth was I doing? It's a game of squash. Having said all this, I can probably see that my mid-thirties' attitude probably wouldn't have got me to achieve what I did. There's a ruthless narrow vision that I think I had, which is necessary and unnecessary, damaging and enriching, all at the same time.

It's sinister to think what made me like this but there's a certain something that happens after those losses in a physical sport. The blend of the adrenaline, the disappointment and lack of oxygen to enable clear thinking clearly coalesced in this instance to turn me dark, and I was doing things that weren't helpful to anyone.

I once went for a walk after a loss in Qatar and fell asleep on some steps, a couple of miles away from the stadium. I had actually made myself bored of sulking. I've smashed rackets, cried, shouted, walked through fields and towns, all in reaction to bad performances or results.

I'm more measured now, but even as late as 2013 I had an episode where I decided to walk miles to the hotel from the Queen's Club in London after a loss in the World Series Finals and sulk on my own for five hours, ignoring everyone.

I look back on these episodes with regret – they affect other people, they are unhelpful and stressful, and all because of what?

Even though I'm working against these explosive reactions, I do understand it's a natural emotion that I won't always be able to repress. To an extent, this disappointment I feel is healthy, a driving force to some extent. Perhaps it's necessary to feel dejection so that there's the motivation to work harder and harder, so that you do everything you can not to experience the same thing again.

But is this sort of mania a common thing, even a bad thing for achievers? Is it necessary for them to have this inner fire in some way, to drive themselves? Maybe so. Perhaps it's important to temper the periods of 'mourning', as Tony calls them. I spent far too long dwelling and being negative and sad. If I had my time again, I would work hard to put these 'mourning' spells to much better use, psychologically more than anything else. It was never a problem physically. I wouldn't ever just sit on my arse in a stew. If anything, I would be straight back on court or in the gym working, probably too soon. But now I would look to have a plan to get over this quickly and look to the future with positivity rather than being pessimistic and down on myself. I would ask myself about all the positive aspects of the losing performance and really encourage myself when I could. I would always look at the negative stuff with a dose of positivity now. After all, if this is a weakness for me, doesn't that give me the positive of knowing I've got something to work off and improve? All these questions could have formed a positive mental response after these failures, rather than this desperate sort of sulking that would fold in on me.

I'm sure there's not a sportsman on earth who has experienced top-level failure and not been overcome with acute disappointment. Sometimes it lasts for days and weeks, but to recover and respond successfully we need to really look at how these failures affect us and how we use them. Sulking and wallowing, I now know, just doesn't help anything. Talking, communicating, interrogating, asking and spinning the situation positively does.

I don't know whether I was actually doing all this training to win. In fact, I'm sure I was doing it to NOT lose. The elation of success, as good as it is, never quite reaches the same depths as this desperate sort of dejection that shadows failure.

Interesting to hear Tony has had similar emotional events.

—

JW: How do you sleep?

TS: Pretty well. There's the adrenaline thing, which sometimes gets me thinking at night, but generally I'm okay. I sometimes struggle going into a big match because there are inevitably men in that squad to whom I'll have to deliver bad news. And that's not funny. I feel for those people badly. I try to make it an inclusive squad effort, but delivering news to people you like and have worked with for years, telling them that they won't be playing in a Grand Final is one of the worst aspects of coaching. People always say what a great week the Grand Final week is. For a coach? It's actually not good.

JW: The Huddersfield period was a process for you, and no doubt you're going through processes with your team all the time. Developing, improving, failing, winning, failing again. The Andy Murray example is a good one, a British sportsman who hit the mark later in his twenties, later in his development. I always sympathised with him when the press criticised because they don't understand. They get used to things being done overnight, to deadlines, and champions don't work like that and they don't appear overnight. A lifetime's work is what makes Murray win a Wimbledon title.

TS: I agree. I'm fascinated by how my own career has developed, how much I've learned and gained. Whatever happens, I want to learn from it, whether it's good or bad. It doesn't prevent mistakes; we will always make them, but we learn. There are some fantastic examples of perseverance and Andy is one of them. He has had the weight of a nation on him. The other thing I would say is, somebody achieving THEIR optimum is a great achievement. If Andy never won a major but reached the number three ranking in the world, how good is that? Let's salute that.

JW: Absolutely. Couldn't agree more. People criticised Tim Henman gratuitously for never winning a Grand Slam, and it used to drive me mad. How many of us can claim to be the fourth best at what we do in the world? Like you said, losing in a Grand Final isn't such a big disappointment; it's a remarkable success.

TS: It brings great pleasure to win. We and our followers want to win. Of course, we want to win. But come on, we just have to look over the fence to see some grotesque suffering. What am I really suffering after a win or a loss? There are people out there that never get the chance to lose a trophy.

The media lose perspective of what's important. Sport gives enjoyment to people. Yes, there are cameras, and we win and lose trophies and money, but it's just a sport in the end. If the athletes perform as well as they can, then that's it.

JW: Can you remember your greatest match or moment in rugby league?

TS: I can remember a player, Franny Cummins. He had an ongoing record of appearances for Leeds. When I came in as coach, I broke that sequence by not picking him for a game. It was a massive thing. I just thought others were playing better. He had been there breaking this record for some time and I just came in and did that. Consequently, you might have thought some issues would have arisen, but we got on especially well after. He didn't make the Grand Final that year; I didn't pick him. And what he did is etched in my memory. He was in his suit, and the vision I now have is of him sprinting on to the pitch at the final whistle after we had won to celebrate with his team-mates. That epitomised his attitude. He was part of that team, even though he wasn't playing.

My other memorable moment was when a young man, Richard, who had Down's Syndrome, came to Warrington. He used to work with our janitor. He wouldn't talk or acknowledge anyone at first. He was shy and withdrawn. After a while he would start talking to me in my office about the games. And a lovely memory was when we played the Grand Final and I spotted him in the crowd. It wasn't about the Grand Final, it was about how he had developed through his association with the sport and the club. I felt we had an impact on the guy. He had been included. He's a bigger success than any trophy.

Jonah Barrington

HIS NAME is synonymous with squash. The man affected its growth on so many levels. He reconstructed the template for squash training, and he opened the game up to an audience in the UK, which saw the sport segue seamlessly from its amateur to its professional era. Many people believe that squash wouldn't exist in its present form had Jonah not done what he did. The 70s squash boom was his doing. Suddenly it became *le dernier cri* of sports in the UK. Films and stage plays of the time portrayed it, and almost everyone played it.

He's known for his achievements (especially after coming to the game so late in his life), winning six British Open titles. He was and is acknowledged as having a ferocious appetite for implausibly brutal training and was the first person in squash who could see that this sort of application to physical advancement would make him better.

This sounds ridiculous now. In this scientific age, athletes leave no stone unturned, and training for a sport is a much more exact process. Back then, people laughed at him for doing sit-ups and press-ups after matches. He decided he wanted to be the best squash player on the planet, and would do anything to achieve that; he didn't give a toss what people thought.

He was born in Ireland but has lived most of his life in England. At one point in his early development he had to decide whether to continue to play for Ireland, for whom he was the country's number one, or for England, where he 'languished' at number four. Looking back on this decision later in his life, he quipped, 'The decision wasn't of much consequence really. I wasn't going to be anybody's number four for very long.' A typically articulate, witty and bloody-minded riposte.

Jonah didn't have a mobile phone, so I rang his home. He responded after I left a message, to which he left another voice message, believing me to be his gardener, imploring me to look at the guttering under the spare room. Surely the great Jonah has people making these calls for him. I tried a couple more times and missed him; for one of those a lady answered, saying, 'Sorry, can you ring back? He's on the rowing machine.' He can't still be training? Isn't it time for him to be wearing slippers and poring over cryptic crosswords?

When I finally did catch him, we had a full-blown 40-minute conversation over the phone. Straight into the squash we dived, head first, chewing the fat on the best players and the Olympic bid. Having not seen or spoken to him for a while, there was much to talk about. He was as effusive and ebullient as ever, and in many respects our interview had already begun.

Over the years he has cultivated a very rare ability to speak lucidly. He's one of the most interesting talkers, so refreshingly free of cliché. I could have reclined in his Glastonbury cottage, purring like a satisfied cat alongside his slumbering geriatric dogs, and listened to him all day. Indeed, the words printed on this page won't do his deliverance justice. Transcribing interviews is enjoyable when you're interested in the content, but it can be laborious and time-consuming. With Jonah's recording, I laughed the time away, loving his animated talk, full of variety, light and dark, wit and knowledge. He talked about his rowing machine ('the sodding thing!'), his quite horrific training regime back in the day and his take on talent with such colour and vivacity that I've tried to transcribe much of the interview exactly as Jonah conveyed it in speaking, and to capture each intonation, each ebb and flow carried in his statements.

We immediately talked about all manner of things, and my hour and a half recorded interview was merely a segment. I needed somebody to follow us around all day to record everything as he poured out endless musings with utmost ardour. All those questions I had written beforehand were pointless and I should have known I wouldn't have to work hard to extract fascinating information.

—

JB: The first input I had was from Jack Giles. He saw me running around like a demented hyena at the RAC in London. He said, 'You can get a lot better, but you have to control what's going on in your head.' He immediately had an influence. I wanted to listen and learn.

JW: I was reading about you walking around London after matches. Do you think the top people in their fields tend to show this kind of tendency?

JB: What I did do, James, was to get out of the door of the club and run when I'd had a disaster. I couldn't be in the changing room. It was therapeutic recovery. It was manic, but it made a difference and settled me down. When I lost to Geoff Hunt [Jonah's great Australian rival] in the Amateur Championships I was absolutely desolate afterwards. The match was coming under my control and he mentally changed tack. He suddenly didn't hit one error. I was hunting the victory but was too far ahead of myself. I was at match point, yet a million miles away from winning the bloody match. You've had that sort of experience, in a British Open. It took me a long time to get over that. I tended to brutalise myself afterwards.

JW: Looking back, do you think that was unhelpful?

JB: Well, I know much more about sports science now. I think in many ways I was lucky that I didn't know much about the scientific aspect in a way because, as it happened, I was very lucky with my body. I deserved to have problems a lot earlier. There was very little separation between sessions; they came thick and fast and I didn't work on the basis of one hard, one easy. When I think about it there must have been just dozens and dozens and dozens of occasions where something could have happened, and I could have been set back. Players today are so conscious and aware. If athletes get injured now, they can almost diagnose it. I never thought like that at all. But this is a very professional age.

In any sport like squash that demands so much in so many different ways, there needs to be an understanding of how the body works, what recovery there needs to be. Every single asset to squeeze everything out of yourself. The guys who don't make it don't ever understand this or recognise this like the very best players do. It's what makes a 'world-class player'. It's very difficult to join them unless you understand what it takes. Ramy Ashour is a very particular talent. He had significant injuries and operations. But he has great talent, AND the attitude of a champion. I don't care how talented anyone is, they won't make it without having the vision and the mentality of a champion.

It's only in this last period that players have been able to take on board all the many advisory services. Jahangir and Jansher Khan were monster players. [Jahangir and Jansher were two of the game's greats. Jahangir is known for one of the most incredible sporting achievements of all time: he went unbeaten in competitive match play for five and a half years.] If they had been in this era with all the extra knowledge ... how good? In any era, they would have made more of the advantages and they would have been world class. They both started to get injuries early though. All the players in that era ran into physical problems. There's an abundance of knowledge now and you would have to be ignorant not to access that. That would have made a difference to me. But at that time, I had a clear-cut idea of what I wanted to do, and that was to make myself fitter and stronger than anyone in my generation.

I think what many people didn't realise was just how much time I spent hitting the ball, practising. I practised more than anybody else. I didn't talk much about it to anyone. I knew that there was a psychological factor, which preyed on the minds of other players, because they probably knew how ferociously hard I was training.

JW: So, they knew you had done all that work ...

JB: Yes, but I never talked about the practice. I did so much practice.

JW: Do you believe talent is a big factor where excellence is concerned?

JB: Yes. Someone can come along and change things, but they all have to practise. Essentially, I tell my kids, 'Don't think Ramy Ashour doesn't practise mate!' He will have hit thousands and thousands of balls. They talk about 10,000 hours, don't they? Some people who talk about that don't believe in genius though. I disagree, because when you're talking about Mozart, somebody who is composing at five years old, you're talking about a particular genius.

They still must go with it in terms of work ethic. Muhammad Ali had the most extraordinary talent, but he had a terrific training schedule, and when you put that together with the inherent talent you have something that's so different. But those hours have got to go in.

10,000 hours

There is a common philosophy in sporting circles that is talked about and mused upon, which advocates the 10,000 hour rule, conjecturing that world class ability comes from a minimum of 10,000 hours of practice.

In all honesty it's probably not a bad benchmark; by the time we've finished with this book I feel quite sure I'll be able to prove that an inordinate amount of time needs to be expended in any discipline to achieve world class status. Regardless of how innately talented we think my interviewees might have been, they probably won't be saying they achieved greatness by sitting on their backside and just letting the talent do it all.

But undoubtedly, the 10,000 hours theory has to be far too simplistic. We live in a world that appreciates boxes or compartmentalisation. It's lovely and rounded to make a statement to declare 10,000 hours of practice equals world class.

In all honesty? Everything is far too random, each different discipline far too deep in complexity for it to be quite so simple. It needs to be more detailed and specific than that.

For people who lap up this kind of clean statement, the first thing I tend to say is: 'Practice what? And how, and at what age is best?' For example, suppose a person decides he wants to be a good squash player and does his 10,000 hours. For a start, it will take a while, but if he will practise just one shot in solo fashion, let's say, static straight drive hitting, then that is just one tiny dimension. There is no way he will find himself a world class squash player after those 10,000 hours. It would have been ten thousand hours of the wrong practice, or of too much of the same practice. He would never have built court or spacial awareness through playing or interacting, or doing different routines and practices, he would have little strength, agility or general fitness. He would have done some good practice, but would be nowhere near world class with such a limited and narrow form of practice.

10,000 hours related to age

I spoke to my dad Malcolm at length about age and development recently. He is one of squash's acknowledged coaches world wide, and being conscious of bias, I still have no problem stating that one of his greatest strengths is the ability he has to extract excellent young squash players year after year and give them opportunities in the sport. I haven't seen a coach or person in squash produce consistently excellent junior players the way that he has.

The reasons for his success are clear. It is not really for any squash knowledge or genius that these kids materialise year after year, though of course he has plenty of that. Where his genius lies is that he dragged his body out of his bed every Sunday morning for the last 30 years to Pontefract Squash Club and coached the two junior sessions every week for two hours. From these sessions his kids move in to his selected weekday sessions. This constancy and dependency is a form of genius, firstly in that he knew it was the right way, second that he bothered to make the effort every week.

It wasn't how Malcolm told them to swing the racket or hold the grip. Those were subsidiary ideas that were perhaps a small part of his sessions. It wasn't about any magical technical knowledge he would impart.

He engineered a support system of coaches, who also deserve acknowledgment here. I was, as a young teenager, one of the coaches who helped Malcolm but I came and went. I wasn't a genius because I couldn't stick it out for 20, 30, 40 years like him. I concentrated on my career in playing the game and also found girlfriends and Sunday mornings.

I believe Malcolm and his Sunday coaches still charge each child about £4 for the hour, though that's to be confirmed. Seemingly, near inflation resistant, It was only £1.50 when I used to go to the very same sessions in 1990.

He also created environments in groups where children had the chance to be social and crucially he got them playing. It wasn't structured routines and analysis but play, interaction and competition. Malcolm doesn't talk too much about technique to his young players. There's some direction but they find out and solve many of the problems themselves. They find a way and that's perhaps not the worst life lesson to learn.

Malcolm engineers his sessions so as to not make this childhood hobby of theirs become a chore.

So it's a recipe for making players: cheap, regular squash sessions with excellent coaches who turn up reliably, which then feed into Malcolm's midweek sessions with adults which also cost a pittance. That's why he has many kids enjoying the sport and playing for years.

I asked Malcolm what he thought about high quality squash ability and where it comes from. In

2014 at Pontefract he had a young player who he thought had international prospects. Sam Todd, aged 11, happened to be son of my manager Mick, Pontefract club owner and friend. Malcolm said at the time he was 'exceptional', 'incredibly gifted', 'the best prospect I have seen at such a young age since you, or Lee (Lee Beachill, Malcolm's Pontefract player who reached world number 1 in 2004).'

Malcolm and I had a really interesting discussion about young players starting early, and what those extra years at a very young age do:

Me: Do you really think Sam is talented, born with the gift for squash? Is that what all this is?

Malcolm: Yes I do. He is innately gifted with the racket. He has something very special that not every child has.

Me: What about his upbringing? He has been in squash courts in clubs, seen major events since he was out of nappies. His father owns a club. He ingested the game right from the off. Is that not his talent, or is that not possibly where it came from? He was at the Commonwealth Games when he was three. What if he hadn't had that environment? Would his talent have blossomed in the same way? Also, isn't it a bit of a coincidence that this child has been given all this innate richness of DNA for so specific a sport as squash, and that his father actually owns the squash club at which some of the world's best players play and in which one of the best coaches works?

Malcolm: I see what you are saying but no, I still think there is something that makes him innately gifted at squash, and able to do what other kids of the same age can't. I won't ever forget the first day I took David (Campion, my brother) on court when he was eight. It was a revelation. The kid had never hit the ball in his life and it was almost poetic.

So maybe these people do have something different, some innate gift, and who am I to argue with a coach of Malcolm's experience and background? Perhaps what Malcolm is talking about is minuscule. Perhaps this tiny DNA quirk affects a very small percentage of the whole. Also, as people in this book have pointed out, there are perhaps all sorts of different sub-talents which make a 'talented' athlete – talent to be able train hard, stay injury free, talent to do the work, psychological talent, talent to listen – so just because a young child like Sam has that early start with hitting squash balls and a great coaching system it isn't the whole answer to world standard achievement. But if Sam had walked on court at 11 years old for the very first time, it would be all too clear the vital importance his environment and early opportunities have had on him.

Whole books are dedicated to this subject so I won't labour here. It will always be very difficult to find out exactly how the early years affect what happens later, but nevertheless an interesting conversation.

JW: Somebody like Usain Bolt is a good example. We've seen the documentaries of him pounding out 200m sprint repetitions, on his knees. People don't always see that side of him. They just seem to assume it was his calling, that it just happens because he's born that way. Yet to a point, despite all his hard work, you feel there's something in his genes that makes him the MOST special.

JB: Yes, and this is exactly what people don't understand. You're looking at an extraordinary talent at a young age – when he was 14–15. There's no doubt it was talent, in the genes.

JW: People seem to bandy the word 'talent' about all over the place, and the more I hear the word talent applied to my achievements the less I feel my own success is anything to do with it. The talent I had as a child I think came from being at squash clubs every day, watching the game then playing a LOT from a very early age. Without really knowing it I put work in most days by getting on court with the other players at the club, repeatedly. People ask me for quick fixes, insightful answers about how to play squash. I just absorbed the game as a child. My talent would never have existed if I hadn't been on court all the time as a kid.

—

Now I train at the same club where I served the proverbial apprenticeship in Pontefract. My father Malcolm works to similar methods that delivered his two highest achievers: me – his son – and Lee Beachill. Of course, he produces many players who reach all standards in the game, but world-class players, he always concedes, come seldom. In his lifetime he has probably produced around ten really world-class players and perhaps 20 in total have worked under him at some stage in their career. Lee and I both hit world number one, and we were both in the top ten in the world at the same time. Malcolm knew that this would never happen again and that it was the most extreme rarity. To have produced two world number ones, right from the start, from the same club, is a near miraculous achievement for one coach. And when people flippantly ask him where the next James and Lee is among his ranks, he irritably enlightens them to the fact that there might not be another James or Lee in his time.

So why is it so rare? And how do you get so much happening out of a small mining town in West Yorkshire?

I suggested to Malcolm that he has probably had many, many players over the years with the innate talent to go all the way to the very top, to be world class, but that all the many, many factors that matter much more than the talent simply didn't come together. Most probably just wouldn't have wanted to do the work. He felt that the very top ones do have something innate, something that the most perfect coaching/training/ support environment can never create.

I argued that I don't think, in my own case, I would have realised the talent I had if I hadn't had the grounding and spent hours with rackets and balls, and endless time at the squash club. I was almost suggesting that the 'innate talent' might only have been borne out by the hours I spent playing as a young person.

It's tough to know. One day someone somewhere in a science laboratory will get to the bottom of this and produce very exact conclusions.

It's wonderful when squash fans come to me and say, 'That game was amazing,' or 'That shot you played was brilliant.' I would argue that the thing I've done more brilliantly than any shot or rally I've ever played was bothering to get up every morning, move my backside to the courts or gym, and to get through sessions when I least wanted to. The greatest talent I think I have is the talent to be able to absorb really hard work on a daily basis.

—

JB: It's hard work that makes you better. If you put hard work in daily, things begin to come together. In the depths of a tough match, a tough race, that work supports you. The hard work allows you to determine what to do in the heat of a battle.

JW: You had an immense drive to train, an ability to withstand intense physical pain repeatedly. Before some of the hardest sessions I do, I feel almost scared by the thought of it. I have to build up to it, brace myself and fight away the dread. Did you feel that?

JB: The interesting thing, James, is that it was easier in squash terms on the court, than on a bloody rowing machine, which I do now. I would never have guessed this was going to be an outlet for me years and years ago. And it's a very cold form of training. It's a really heavy disciplinary process. The mind mustn't be allowed to think about how many minutes have gone and how many there are to come. There were so many occasions when I would rather have done anything else but train hard. But the truth was and is that I knew I was going to feel a lot better when I had done it.

When you're particularly ancient like me, the first part is the most difficult, when the breathing is like the worst asthmatic in the world, and you're thinking, 'Jesus Christ!', just trying to stop the mind from thinking how long you're going to be doing it. The avenues open out after a while, during these horror sessions. But there are so many occasions where one goes to train thinking, 'My god, how am I gonna get through this?' That's the norm. It doesn't get any easier when you're older. I've got this bloody rowing machine here now, the sodding thing, and I haven't got an excuse. I can't use the rain as an excuse. I don't know what the general public really thinks about athletes, but I suspect most people have absolutely no idea of the sacrifice needed for people to win marathons or Olympic rowing medals. I'm sure they love being professional athletes but, oh, you can imagine the occasions when they would think, 'I just don't want to get out of bed today.'

JW: Was there emphasis on quantity over quality?

JB: The year I lost the British Open, the last two months I was on three sessions a day. What I failed to realise was that I needed longer periods of recovery. And because there was pressure about beating Hashim's record [Hashim Khan had won the most British Opens at the time], there was a lot of stuff in the papers. I churned out these sessions in the Midlands right up to it. In my mind I had a couple of rounds at the beginning of the British before the real tests. I hadn't realised how 'training tired' I was. I didn't know what it felt like to be fresh. This was a lack of confidence in a sense. I was older and my mind started to work in a different way. To give myself more confidence I trained harder and harder and harder and harder.

JW: A lot of squash players will do punishing two-hour sessions. Would you always aim to eclipse what the others did?

JB: After practice games against players who weren't as good as me, I would do extra ghosting [ghosting is a very specific squash training routine, first used by Jonah] to do more and more. Peter Marshall [former English world number two] was like that, an obsessive trainer, and he paid a dreadful price for it. He never recovered totally. [Peter, after years of brutal training, suffered with Chronic Fatigue Syndrome.] There needs to be an organised programme.

JW: The hardest sessions you did were with Bomber Harris, is that right?

JB: Yes, they came later. I hit a brick wall in terms of not wanting to go on court. At 34–35 I started to take a tennis racket down to the club and would play tennis with whoever. It showed that I had endured too much. With Bomber I was looking for some other support system. I had always driven myself and I wanted someone there who would push me and cajole me. That was really Bomber Harris at that stage. And those sessions had no sports science element whatsoever but were the hardest extended sessions that I ever did. I had more residual stiffness from those than I ever had from any other sessions.

JW: Were they circuit based?

JB: Yes. There was an awful lot of what would now be called plyometric work. We know the benefits of plyometric work today, but the athlete must apportion it very carefully. There has to be a lot of stretching and flexibility work with it. You don't do plyometric work for an hour and 20 minutes. And when a session lasts for two and a quarter hours, as many of those sessions did, it was probably dangerous. Health and safety wouldn't have liked it at all – jumping over benches and all sorts. Really and truly, there were abdominal sessions of up to an hour. And I survived. Apart from the soft tissue problems that could have arisen, it beggars belief, and the viral side that seems to hit people. But those sessions were off the scale. Four of them a week. I would warm up in the grounds for 45 minutes just to get rid of the lactic from the previous sessions. I was extraordinarily lucky not to run into difficulties but, on the other hand, it gave me the wherewithal to continue to be in the mix. I felt at 38 or 39 I was playing at a very high level.

JW: To the surprise of many, you became British Champion at 40 years old.

JB: Yes. Joey, my son, who played professionally, once said to me about five years ago, 'You are obsessive Dad. I want to have a life.' It was an argument or conversation that probably couldn't go any further. I was trying to say to him that this is an unbelievably hard business and it's harder now than it was five years ago. It was harder then than it was five years before. If you don't actually have a form of tunnel vision with regard to it, if you don't prioritise properly, then you won't make it. Of course, it's a very selfish thing.

JW: Do you think it's typical of a lot of champions in a lot of areas in other sports? Do you think you have to be a bit obsessive?

JB: Yeah, yeah. I wouldn't have said we're the best balanced people in the world. It goes against that Oxbridge thing about Corinthian performers who wouldn't be seen to be working hard. They would say not very well rounded.

JW: You railed against that. People laughed at you for training so hard at the time.

JB: Yes, they did. People took the piss. I hated it. They hadn't seen anything like it and it didn't sit comfortably with people who played the sport. It was a snotty thing; players put down their rackets in April and picked them up in September. I had long summers of training. It wasn't looked upon with any understanding. They had no comprehension of what I was trying to do, and when they saw someone rigorously running around a cricket field for 45 minutes, they wouldn't be looking at that, saying, 'That's terrific.' They would have considered his or her lack of ability. But that wasn't a concern for me. I knew exactly what I wanted to do, and my selfishness didn't affect anyone else. I wasn't with anyone at the time.

Selfishness has an adverse effect on others and is destructive. I had to learn when I was first with Madeleine, and I look back in horror now. I was so concerned with my day-to-day activities that anyone else's agenda was irrelevant. And I do think that has to be part and parcel of what's going on. It's too demanding.

You can't play cricket in the summer and football in the winter. You either have to be a footballer or a cricketer. You could do it more in those days; you can't now. Squash is known as one of the most demanding sports devised. It's a brilliant example of an Olympic sport because it's ultimately so testing in so many different ways. It's seriously uncontaminated, and because it's become so professional over the last decade especially, there's no way that the public shouldn't be much more aware of it. Squash athletes are super sportspeople.

JW: You played when you were younger, but the bug didn't quite grab you instantly. Could you have done what you did in another area, perhaps another sport?

JB: I was very lucky, James. It's very easy to ask, 'Don't you wish you had been a tennis player and made millions?' Not in the slightest. I think tennis is a fantastic game. I think football is a fantastic game, ruined by footballers. Rugby: fantastic sport. I love playing tennis in the summer and I love cricket, although I occasionally feel a tinge of disrespect when I see them smoking in pictures. I loved sports as a kid and …

JW: The squash thing registered later though.

JB: Yeah, my older brother was a lot better than me. It wasn't something that was influencing me at all. I loved team sports, which may seem strange in light of what happened. I loved tennis doubles, the camaraderie, except playing my brother, which was a bit of turmoil. But it would be trite to suggest that I would definitely have been able to do what I did in squash in another sport.

JW: What you achieved was made more unbelievable considering you came so late to the game. In many sports it's almost impossible to be world class if you start playing after a certain age. With physical sports like rowing and cycling it's different. Some Olympic rowers have changed midway through their careers to become fine cyclists. You could never do that with, say, squash and tennis. To become a world-class squash player you have to be invested in it in some way from very early. When you hear about kids nowadays playing from four years old, the hundreds of young Egyptians on the courts of Cairo, how do you think someone coming to the game late would fare now?

JB: The improvisation and skills some of the kids have are amazing. The older you get, the less chance you have of developing those skills in the same way, no doubt. Your game would surely be more limited and formal. You wouldn't have the capacity to improvise in the same way.

I've always said that there might be the possibility of a one-off, much less so of a two-off! In tennis, Michael Stich came to the game very late, whereas the others – Becker, Bjorg, all the winners – were very early starters. I know your dad said that nobody will ever come through nowadays without that pathway as a junior.

I would never say never but it's becoming increasingly unlikely because all around you've got these guys materialising from very young ages from young backgrounds. Without getting into the argument of too much too soon and all this, we know that if the parents are stupid and keener than the poor kid, then that's tantamount to early disaster anyway.

It's very important to get a good grounding though. You can hold somebody back, but that junior grounding needs to really be there, somehow. It doesn't mean you don't encounter problems in the seniors, but you're ready for it, you have experience to handle all that – the nerves, the intensity. If you've been accustomed to that since you were six, then you have a huge advantage. Starting late really hinders that, especially in very complex sports like squash and tennis.

You've been through all that. You had one of the most rewarding junior groundings of all. There are situations that you've been through as a youngster that stand you in great stead for all the difficult matches that you encounter in your professional career. You've seen it all. You've learned to handle these things.

Yes, you can perhaps do it in a sport like cycling or rowing; they are inherently physical and require far fewer complex skills. Even for those sports, it will have been necessary to have been involved in athletic endeavour of some sort early. The higher you go, the harder it gets to take the next step. You keep upgrading as you go, every little step. It's getting harder! It's getting harder! It's getting harder! You graft, graft, graft away. There's no guarantee but that's how it will happen. Players materialise when they go through this process. In squash, players have materialised in the top 20 whom I would never have said would have done so five years before.

Professionals need to put everything into it at key times in the development.

You progressed very fast indeed. You had that background and ability, but at one stage you realised that these guys weren't just going to roll over. They adapted to you and presented different challenges.

Jonah's views on the vital importance of experience

In 1998 I was 14 years old, a bit young to be anywhere near winning the World Junior Championships, which were to be held in Princeton, USA that summer. My parents decided to shell out the considerable amount of money required for me to play. We went, and I reached the final of the Classic Plate. I must have gained about a year of development on the back of that experience. It brought me on no end, an unquantifiable experience. Wide-eyed and squash mad, I soaked the whole thing up, and by the time it was my time to have a go three or four years later, I was ready. I had seen it and done it in Princeton, and later Milan. Who knows how much of an impact that experience had on my senior career even? We really saw it as a bit of a holiday at the time.

JW: Tell me about when you went to Australia for the first time, captain of the team, and you had never experienced jet lag before.

JB: We had to play with a different ball for a start. I found out about jet lag for the first time. I didn't know what it was. I immediately went for a run on Coogee Beach on arrival. I got carried away. I kept seeing 'squash court' sign here and 'squash court' sign there. I thought, 'Jesus, what have I come to? This is paradise.'

At the time there were something like 106 squash centres in Brisbane alone. The explosion of squash was unbelievable! They were everywhere. And you know, I'm jet-lagged out of my mind, I'm bloody running on the beach and I'm SO excited.

Well ... I was ABSOLUTELY fucked. I had to play. I played my first match against Ken Hiscoe. Jesus, I didn't know what was going on. My reflexes were non-existent. It was a calamity. I had no idea how to deal with it. I wasn't going to get any interest from my team-mates, who hadn't the slightest idea what was going on either. I think there was one match and that was awful. Then we went up to Queensland before the World Champs. I played a match there and this guy, Aub Amos, was sitting at the meal afterwards. There was a lot of betting going on, saying I was drifting after each match I played ... 4-1, 10-1, 20-1, 50-1 ... No mention of Hunt yet.

Anyway, Aub said, 'You're up the shit aren't you? You're all over the place.' I said, 'Yes. I can't hit the ball. I can't see it, can't move.' He had been through the ropes. Tough as an old boot, but kindly with it. He started to bring me round a bit. I came round, sadly much better when the bloody event was over. I was playing well by the end, but it was a tough experience. I learned a lot.

JW: Do you remember the highs and lows of training and playing? I've always found going from that heightened environment to the lonely environment very tricky.

JB: Well, I wasn't always a happy bunny. Not the best person to be around. When you're going from tournament to tournament to tournament, it's a job.

JW: Did you find it hard to come down from big occasions?

JB: Yes, it wasn't ever an easy process. Often these matches were late. Win or lose, it wasn't an easy process.

JW: Would you take your disappointments out on people?

JB: Madeleine had to put up with an awful lot. They always say you take it out on those closest to you, and I did with her.

JW: She was a runner, from a sporting background. She must have understood.

JB: Yes, I remember up in Scotland I had played and had a dreadful match and I didn't hang around. We just left. We had to catch a train down to Darlington. I just wanted to get out of that environment. The last thing I wanted to do was to talk to people about what had happened. I don't know how you cope with that. That was an occasion that I really was grateful to have her with me, and such occasions were plenty. Do you cope with the comedown?

JW: Not well at all. I tend to replay and reproach myself endlessly. You nearly didn't go to one British Open Final at Abbeydale did you? You didn't want to face the music. There was a fear.

JB: We were staying in Huddersfield. It was snowing. I got a cold. Felt horrible. Geoff Hunt lost to Gogi Alauddin, and I murdered Gogi in the final. But before, Madeleine had to put up with me whinging about this cold. She dosed me with

Vicks and eucalyptus. She had this stuff between the games. Whether I was dosed up to such an extent that it made me play brilliantly I don't know! These days I would probably fail a drugs test, but I was in the zone. I was so alert. Talk about being in the zone. I felt so confident. He didn't have a prayer. He didn't have a prayer. He was a difficult player to beat.

JW: So that was an example of one of those occasions when everything just happens, just comes together. I was going to ask about that.

JB: They gave the dinner at Abbeydale. This bloody cold was there. I was flat as a fart. But it was a fantastic feeling having won so well. Doing it effortlessly, without thinking.

JW: Conversely, were there times when you felt like you were swimming against the tide, and whatever you did you couldn't get it right?

JB: Yes, that first Australia trip was extraordinarily difficult in that respect. I don't think I had really been on a plane before. Well, I had been to Paris, but it's not Australia.

JW: What did you do before matches?

JB: I always warmed up privately, dependent on what areas I had. I always had half a dozen routines. I went outside to do strides, ghosting or hit balls. I used to hit balls.

JW: Was the day of the match difficult?

JB: Yeah. I've always envied people who don't have problems dealing with the before part. Whether they actually do or not is something else. A level of nervousness is healthy but it's not a good feeling. Once it gets to a certain point you feel as if you have a serious infection of some kind affecting your system. I don't know what you find but would you prefer a 3pm or a 9pm match?

JW: I prefer the early ones, I think. There's less time to think about getting nervous, to stew over it all. I've felt horrendous at times before matches. Sick to my stomach.

JB: And do you sleep well?

JW: It's not my greatest ability. Jet lag comes into it. When you go away the days are less tiring. You're thinking about squash. You rest more. Thoughts of the washing or the carpet fitter are no longer in the forefront of your mind. There's less baggage when you're away. So, I find I need less sleep. But with all the thoughts of matches I find it difficult.

JB: Do you think about the match the day before much?

JW: It's on the day for me where it becomes harder. I try to find as many things to distract me as possible. Walks. Music. Books.

JB: Do you get psychology help?

JW: Yes. I think the best psychologists keep it simple and talk it through with you.

JB: I could imagine your father not being that comfortable with it.

JW: I think you need to be open to accepting all information, and then take what's helpful. We're in search of anything we can get now. Anything helps. He's very opinionated but perhaps surprisingly open-minded with regard to the new sciences.

—

I would guess that very few world-class operators have it easy pre-match or performance. A recent documentary that followed Peter Kay, one of the UK's best-known comedians, behind the scenes before and during his massive 'Tour That Doesn't Tour', gave a very interesting insight into the amount of work that goes into preparing a 70-minute stand-up show for huge arenas. You would think with such a seemingly laid-back attitude as his that he might just turn up to the O2 Arena and do as he pleases. But it was clear that it was nothing like that. Instead, he revealed that he did 30 small warm-up shows, after which he could amend and adapt the lines, taking out gags that weren't working or getting responses. I thought match fitness was a sportsman's preoccupation, but after seeing this, clearly not.

And, like Jonah, he touched on the difficulties of dealing with nerves before a show. And it's good for those with aspirations, especially youngsters who struggle to deal with nerves, to remember that nervousness and doubt touch us all.

———

JB: I always say these golfers would never pay all this money for psychologists if they didn't think it was a great help. The classic right now is this bloke Steve Peters, and he has given Ronnie O'Sullivan steadfastness it seems. Someone like Chris Hoy you would imagine has tremendous strength of character, but he felt he needed that kind of support. It wouldn't be for no reason. In my time, you had to really sort yourself out. You had to figure out ways of thinking positively about the match you were engaged in.

That didn't prevent the nervousness, but it's a drug. You say you will never do it again. The worst aspects of it you sort of isolate and put under anaesthetic. Thinking that it wasn't like it was until it happens again.

Julian Barnes

JULIAN HAS written around 30 books: novels, short stories, essays, non-fiction and memoirs. In 2011 he won the most prestigious prize in world literature, the Man Booker Prize, for his novel *The Sense of an Ending*.

The first books I read of his were his most recent, the aforementioned and then *Levels of Life*. The latter was revelatory to me. My mother Lesley died in 2000, so this unbelievably unsentimental portrayal of his experiences of dealing with the death of his wife in 2008 brought many of my own experiences back to me in a startling way. It was so much more ingenious and complex than a simple memoir documenting grief.

During my late-summer visit to his North London home he warmly welcomed me and was gracious with his time, offering his thoughts so freely. Despite, I feel, not being entirely convinced about my thesis for the book, he attempted to help me with and occasionally refer to the comparisons between arts and sport.

I was given a quirky blend of unique tea, and Julian offered me biscuits, which was unprecedented amongst my interviewees. I was pleased with myself for noticing a subtlety to his tea, and after I had discerningly pointed out that 'this isn't builders' tea he happily confirmed that it was indeed his own special blend of different leaves.

At one stage in proceedings his bank telephoned, which naturally seemed odd in the context of my visit. I had read his brilliant books and just presumed people who produced such work lived free from banks.

As with Jonah's talk about the guttering, these seemed very apt occurrences, which prove that the people whom we regard as infallible heroes deal with the trivialities that life throws at us like every other human. It's good for us to know that, as we seek our own trails to fulfilment.

——

JW: How do you become a great writer?

JB: I don't think you can underestimate the luck element. With a sportsman, as with a writer, you tend to think you've done it all by yourself, except for those sportsmen who thank God personally when they win an event, which always seems to me very peculiar. You have to have a certain innate talent. An innate/early learned interest in and joy of language. If you're writing fiction, then you have to have an ear for how people talk, and that's not something that you can really learn. You can either hear how people talk or you can't. There's a luck to have that talent. Hard work, yes, and of course self-discipline because you don't go to an office. You stumble out of bed, you read the papers and you go back five feet from your bedroom. And self-discipline with a timetable to it.

One thing I realised about writing early on is that each book in your brain has a certain time during which it's alive and can be moved around. If you exceed a certain time, as I did with my first novel, which took me seven or eight years, then it begins to die on you. So, you have to know how to be disciplined over a specific period of time. Then you might write stuff that is completely fascinating to you, completely fascinating objectively, but if it's not fascinating to the people likely to pick it up and the people of your time, then it's no good.

Equally, there's an element of luck in the state of publishing when you come along. I happened to hit a certain sort of rise in the graph at the point. I probably hit it about three or four books in, when publishers started paying generous money for literary fiction, which they hadn't in the past. Literary fiction then became sexy. You can think of examples of bad luck with writers who published a book and then war broke out or something like that. The book dies. Or stock gets bombed and all copies disappear.

—

This is the one area in which sport and the arts can be wildly contrasting. In sport there really isn't much of an argument about who is better or what standard is best. Literature and music are subjective arenas within which to work and you can very easily go unnoticed having written the greatest piece of work on earth. Rock bands and writers and actors need to be noticed by agents and publishers before they can break through, however good their work is. I often watch a performance by an actor in the theatre and baulk at why they are so little known, but that's the nature of the industry. We've seen superb acting performances by little-known performers on stage and screen.

They scrabble away for work and attention but Brad Pitt gets the headlines. Fame is seemingly directly proportional to success within the arts, and in many ways the paths to success, or should I say recognition, are contrasting. In sport, you're either good or not, because you will win. Julian's books can't really beat others. People can only subjectively say they can.

JW: Were you drawn to reading and writing as a young child? Were your formative years key in that sense?

JB: Well, I read as a child. My parents were schoolteachers, books were respected in the house and we went to the public library. I certainly didn't have any notion of writing. I wasn't one of those annoying children who were scribbling under the bedclothes with a torch in the night. I think I wrote some small things in the school magazine when I was 15, 16, 17. I thought I would be a reader. It's not a natural thing to say, 'I'm going to be a writer.' It doesn't run in families on the whole. I won't say it's completely self-taught because you're taught by the people you read, and a lot of writing is learning to read properly. So, I didn't start any sort of writing until I was in my early twenties I suppose. I started doing bits of reviewing for the *Oxford Mail* and the *TLS*. I started writing a non-fiction book around the same time, which wasn't published, then I started writing my first novel, which was published when I was 34. So, I guess I started writing at about 26–27. I had no idea what I was doing really. I didn't think I had any authority to be a writer, and I didn't tell anyone really.

JW: So, when you look back, do you feel there were certain key times in your development as a writer? Perhaps your time at Oxford? Were there teachers or lecturers who were an influence?

JB: I made a complete mess of my university career. I went up to read French and Russian, then philosophy and psychology, and then back to French. I had a fairly inspiring English master at school. But I think from the first time I started to get literature I did think that this was what was telling me the truth about life. I thought I didn't trust the authorities: the preacher in the pulpit, the church, the newspapers. And I didn't really trust my parents as sources of authority. But I did absolutely trust literature because it tended, apart from anything else, to talk about things that weren't talked about at home, like sex and politics and love. The darker side of human life. So, I think it was literature itself that inspired me.

JW: Do you believe in genius? Gustave Flaubert is a favourite of yours, and he said, 'Prose is like hair, it shines with combing.' You've called him a genius, but doesn't this imply that he has worked hard and grafted to write the stuff he did? Do you have to dig deep at times to make it work? Presumably there will be times where it just flows easily ...

JB: Yes, and that can be the most deceptive time of all. It tends to flow on a first draft, and you think that this might be very close to final copy, which is complete delusion. It's sometimes a necessary illusion to think that. Most writing is rewriting, and you learn that. And sometimes it's things that the reader would assume were easy that turn out to be hard work and there are some things where the reader might think, 'I don't know how he did that,' and yet it will have just come to me like that. It's a strange process: a mixture of control and freedom and of giving yourself over to the process of self-abnegation. I don't mean the story runs away with you or the characters run away with you, but there's a sense in which one sentence leads to another and it brings with it something unplanned. And that's the freedom and the flow of it, which is contrasted with the control you must have in order to make it a finished artefact. Some people are better at it than others. They are geniuses because not only do they write perfectly, or as near perfectly as is possible, they also understand what human life is about more than the others. So, we read them for their insight, hundreds of years later.

JW: Squash players or athletes, I think, tend to be comfortable within routine. Not always, but often. Is writing a discipline that you feel is dependent on strict routines?

JB: One thing that you learn is when your brain is working best. The most important thing is knowing at what time of day your brain works best for original material, and in my case it's mornings, from about 10.30–1.00. That doesn't mean I haven't sometimes written a book all through the day. Oddly, that happened with a book called *Arthur & George*. I found I got to lunchtime and I just wanted to carry on, and I carried on through the afternoon, which is normally complete downtime for me.

JW: That's what it felt like reading it.

JB: Well, there was something in the book that said, 'Come on, come on, get on with it! Tell me more!' And even though it's my longest book, per page it took me the shortest time to write. That time in the early evenings, 4.30–5.00 until about 7.00 is quite a good time for me. You learn tricks such as to revise most of the morning's work in the evening, but not all, and to leave about half a page unrevised so that you come back the next morning and you reread your previous day's revisions and you have this half a page of untouched stuff, which you then start revising! That revising leads you on to the next page that you're going to write. So, I don't know whether there's an exact comparison to sporting training but there must be tricks of the mind to make you keep going in some way.

—

An athlete needs to be shrewd about how to compliment and balance work. Chiaroscuro here is good for the routine, as it is for the books or matches themselves. If I have two sessions of work in a day, I think a lot (more as I get older) about how they need to be apportioned, and within the week the sessions must be carefully balanced to retain freshness but to move things forward and gain the most out of each session. Julian feels that the evening is a good time to revise his morning's creativity. Similarly, I might do a very heavy fitness session in the afternoon, which would require huge amounts of intensity and application. Therefore, for me to get the most out of that session I wouldn't want to be doing heavy workloads in the morning or the night before. Balancing those sessions by doing something much lighter and less taxing would be clever. From what Julian is saying, it's not usual for him to back up two sessions of similar content to each other.

A physiologist once said something to me that made things very clear. He talked about the training schedule in terms of 'nothing', 'light', 'medium' and 'hard' sessions. He said how important it was to protect the hard sessions, let them breathe a bit. A hard session mentally and physically is draining, it leaves a footprint, so the sensible thing is to surround it with lighter or medium sessions, or rest.

In terms of training for sport, it can be quite tempting to keep going and going and going, pushing and pushing. But two very bad things happen here: firstly, the quality is compromised and the training output can't reach the intensity it needs to replicate a match, because the sessions are just repeatedly too hard, which then makes the training redundant; secondly, it tires you and makes you markedly less effective, prone to illness, and spiralling you towards a breaking point.

It's why kids doing exams perhaps could be encouraged to revise in small bouts and have frequent rests if they have to go through spells of increased study. The quality can't be maintained for hours on end, and the breaks are crucial. I've heard children, but more often parents, talking about the child giving up their leisure activities during an exam period, citing a lack of time, but surely it's at that point that rest and fun and leisure time is more important. That trashy film night or game of squash could really help the work sink in. Who can work for eight hours solid with real quality anyway?

If I had my time again, I would put more time and thought into the intricacies of shaping and balancing routines. I see young *players making dogs' dinners of it. I've had them turn up to play a practice match with me and I can see they are tired, whereas now I'm ready to go, not having trained for a day and a half. I'll be giving that session every last drop. For them that big session will be wasted because they are half dead, jaded from too much work. I can see it in their warm-ups. I've got plenty to be doing off court and I don't want to waste that session; I want to be able to give it every bit of quality I can. Why would these young players turn up for a valuable practice match tired and therefore not able to give it 100 per cent? But I did it myself. It's that eagerness that's on your shoulder in youth, not wanting to be unaccountable for a second of your day, feeling every session should be extreme.*

—

JW: Would you always revise immediately?

JB: Yes, I would always revise within a day or two, because the revising is part of getting into a state to continue and there might be something in the bit that you've written that was misjudged or misplaced, or would mislead you about what was happening next.

JW: You wrote your first novel, *Metroland*, at 34. You won the Booker Prize aged 62 with *The Sense of an Ending*. Do you think that you could have written that book at 34?

JB: [Laughs] I don't think *Metroland* was as good because I knew less about life then, so there was more truth in *The Sense of an Ending*. But I think this is one of the points at which we have to say early on that comparisons between sport and the arts break down. It's not as if I got to the age of 65 and I broke the world record! It's a bit more like doing figure skating I suppose, being marked by a panel of judges, but even so, it's not objective. Winning the Booker Prize is extremely good for morale and sales, but you would be a fool to think that that's your best book because of that judgement.

That's another part of the luck of it: who the judges happen to be in that particular year, and what books you happen to be up against. There was one year when I had a book that I knew was quite strong and they announced the judges. My wife used to come down to breakfast and read the papers before me, and she would sometimes annotate things for my attention. She had underlined all the names of these judges, each of whom I'd had some sort of run-in with over the years, and she just wrote: 'Forget it, kid.' I thought that was perfect.

JW: Do you write all the time? Do you give yourself rests and time off?

JB: As long as you're able to discipline yourself and your work then you can have time off. I'm in the first draft of a new novel at the moment, but then I might think tomorrow that the weather is holding, it's September, I'm going to get my walking boots and go off to the Chilterns for the day. And it's going well enough for me to do that and come back on Thursday and pick it up again. It's quite nice when it's an awful day and it's pissing down with rain and you go to the window of your study and you see all these poor sods going off to the office. And that marching to a different drum is sort of symbolised by liking working on Christmas morning. Because I love working anyway. It's not a hardship to go to work on Christmas Day. It's a nice start to Christmas Day, and then you've earned your pudding later!

JW: When you're writing a novel, are you conscious of the shifts in intensity and shade of the whole thing?

JB: Yes, you are. My books vary quite a bit in the writing. Generally I don't want to know the whole thing, but I have to know that there's a book there, and that in the course of the writing I'll discover more fully what the book is about. And it's, as I hinted earlier, an organic process. So, you don't block out a scenario, start at the beginning and then write until it gets to the end. P.G. Wodehouse used to write notes for his books, which were longer than the book itself. He was a tremendous professional in that respect. I don't think I could do it that way, and I think it would be less interesting, because it would be like painting by numbers. I find that sometimes the first page, or what I think is the first page when I write it, usually isn't, so I don't even think of starting at what might be the beginning. I expect the beginning of the book to sort of emerge in the process of writing.

The first page is all about making sure the handshake between the writer and the reader doesn't fail. You're establishing the terms of the book and the contract you're making with the reader. And how you're going to treat him or her.

JW: You're a Philip Larkin fan?

JB: I adore Larkin. He's the great English poet of the post-war years. Yes. And I always put little homages to him. I never met him, I once talked to him on the telephone.

—

Philip Larkin is a favourite writer of mine. Like many people, I found poetry elusive and difficult unless I studied it. From what I read, Larkin told it in real words and a more common language that I understood. It seemed as if he wasn't trying to be too clever or literary. I was obsessed with him, his life and views, and read everything. He lived in Hull for 30 years, which was just about perfect. The landscape of the city of Hull, where Larkin lived most of his life, was incredibly present in his poems, and that was even more fascinating to me as my home town Pontefract stands only an hour into the mainland of England, a short punch down the barren eastern half of the M62. It was a sort of gritty, stuck Yorkshire drabness, which is loveable and dreary and limiting and fascinating all at once.

I could really go on here but I'll leave the extended Larkin worship for another time. If you snuff your nose at poetry, give Larkin a go.

I couldn't, though, help feeling a twang of excitement as Julian talked about him. I was now talking to a literary hero talking about a dead literary hero, who said literary hero knew.

—

JW: Was he writing for a publication you were editing?

JB: Well, he would write for the *New Statesman*, and when I was working there under Martin Amis there would be one or two occasions where I would ring him up. He was meant to be a grumpy old sod but that was his public image; he was terribly nice to me. With that pretext I sent him my first novel, which he read and was very nice about. And that's another piece of luck. I happened to have to ring him up. He happened to be polite, and because I'm sure he's a polite man, he said something nice about my TV column. I cheekily then send him my first book and he's nice about me in a way that means more to me than any good review.

JW: Do you get inspired by literary figures around you like that? As a squash player I learn a lot from my rivals or from great players of the past. Do you read your rivals, contemporaries, other great novelists?

JB: Yes, I do read some contemporaries and I do have friends who are writers, and I do read them always. I think the competitiveness is various and isn't like the competitiveness of sport. I wasn't necessarily very good but I was very, very competitive and I hated losing. But there's no real equivalent in literature. You hate losing the Booker Prize but that's not quite the same, as we've established. There's a greater sense of competitiveness amongst male writers than female writers, and the competitiveness is with other men on the whole. I think that's a sort of horrible little extra dose of testosterone we've got, and that even though you know it's not a competition, part of you sometimes thinks it is. When you see someone who is a sort of rival get bad reviews, a nasty little part of you isn't dissatisfied.

JW: You like sport, don't you? Have you been watching the tennis?

JB: I adore Federer. He's just one of those sportsmen like Cruyff, who I once saw, and it's total control, total grace, his ability to play any shot. In his early days he used to get confused because too many options came up in that split second before he played the shot.

JW: I think with him, he brings the artistic element to sport. I suppose what I'm looking for a bit here, doing this project, is to explore how you can find aspects of light, shade and control in a great novel or great tennis, in many disciplines. He brings poetry to tennis and he makes it a thing of beauty, which is so hard to do in sport because of the physical pressure.

JB: Yes. And there isn't really an art form to compare it with; it's the control of the body you have in ballet, and boy they have to be tough. And there's a bit of inventiveness in the position that you're in on the court, which is a bit like artistic inventiveness possibly. There's the football player who can find the perfect pass, which no one seems to have found before.

JW: Are there times where you feel that you've produced something really very special? Do you know it?

JB: I was thinking about this the other day: that what you feel about the work has a graph that goes up and down according to some biorhythm, which doesn't match the graph of whether the work is good or not. You can actually do quite a good day's work and sometimes feel that it's been rubbish. Then you go back the next day and you see that it was actually really good. That's maybe a bit like training. You've done yourself some good but you're disappointed with what you've put in. I think the moments that are most satisfying are when you get into a rhythm of working and you're waking up in the middle of the night and you're thinking about the book. But you're not worrying about the book, you're naturally thinking about it, coming up with enough thoughts that you have to turn on the light and write them down.

And the other great moment is when things sometimes pull the book together. People who don't know about writing sometimes assume it's like taxidermy. You have a skeleton, and you assemble the skeleton, and you put the fur on it, and the flesh. It's not like that. It's a process in which the bones are formed while you're writing it and not beforehand, so there are times when you suddenly see in the course of a sentence something that will connect with that back there, and if you move this to there in the first part it will suddenly click into place. It's not like building a model of a locomotive or something like that because that's been done before. It's like building a new piece of machinery where you suddenly notice this sort of locking nut makes this piston work more effectively.

—

I really loved this comment on the intricacies. The best stories, symphonies or works of art have these 'locking nuts', which make 'this piston' work more effectively. This is Julian Barnes articulating a metaphor in his way. In the best art there are endless pay-offs, endless extra revelations and subtleties. You watch a Woody Allen movie or Oscar Wilde play, and you see these little connections or pay-offs between scenes, which are magical for the viewer.

76

I played a match recently where I had to battle hard to win the first game. I didn't at any stage feel comfortable but kept faith in the initial plays I was making, working my opponent, asking questions to which he was coming up with all the answers. My opponent won it and the second game was similarly tight. By the third game, as the physical implications for both started to kick in from the hard earlier work, I found that I was getting these accumulated pay-offs from earlier. The differences or weapons that I had used in the early stages of the match I could use differently in the latter stages, but with greater effect now. My opponent was finding it more and more difficult to respond. The plays I made later on were almost a direct result of or response to what I had done in the first two games. They were connected. In this respect, I found a match like this taking patterns like a story. And sometimes as a player, like as a novelist, you don't quite know how things connect, but they do. If this sounds preposterous and far-fetched to some, then that's to be interpreted, but the analogy to me is compelling and useful.

—

JW: Do you have people from whom you take advice, like we have coaches?

JB: I'm quite resistant and secretive now. I like to hold it within myself for as long as possible. I don't like to show it to anyone until I think it's complete. I have a friend who is my regular first reader and who has been for a long time. And then it goes to my agent and the publishers at about the same time. I know that good readers will see it, but most of that's part of the publishing process; you get notes from your British editor, your American editor, your Canadian editor all at roughly the same time. Some writers like to send their stuff round at an early stage. I think in a way I'm not confident enough to do that or am too anal-retentive. I don't want anyone to see it until it's almost unchangeable somehow, because that makes it all the more mine, whereas if I showed something at an early stage it might become theirs.

JW: But you're okay with listening to people?

JB: I think you have to listen. You should never stop because though some suggestions will seem preposterous, there are certain writers who reach a certain point where they think that no one can improve on what they do, or no one can help them improve on what they do. So they are like the tennis player who thinks they don't need a coach. Iris Murdoch and Kingsley Amis were two writers who refused to take any editorial suggestions at all. I have a friend called Carmen Callil who is one of the great publishers, who founded Virago, and at one time she inherited Iris Murdoch from the previous publisher at the firm. She dealt with Iris Murdoch's incredibly scrappy typing, with bacon rinds and toast crumbs inside the manuscript. As sometimes happens as people get older, they write in a looser style. The prose becomes looser and a bit repetitive. Carmen made a whole list of suggestions all the way through the book and she got a letter back saying, 'Thank you so much for all your suggestions, now please put it back exactly as it was.' And anyone who is an Iris Murdoch fan knows that in the later books the prose gets worse and worse.

JW: Was that related to the illness?

JB: No, it was before that. No, it's to do with the ego of the writer, as with an athlete, you have to have enough ego to do the stuff in the first place, then if your ego gets out of control you can't take any advice or criticism.

JW: Do you think critics and academics overthink what you're doing?

JB: Yes. I never read an academic article or book about me. Don't want to know. It's not that I think they are stupid.

I don't want to see how others look at my whole works. It doesn't help me to write the next book, to think of all the previous books as a body of work. I have to think that each new book is completely fresh and doesn't relate to the previous books. You mustn't go into a race and think, 'Well. I've run all these previous races.' Part of you must think that this is a completely new race, even if it's the same 1,500m and some of your opponents must be the same.

My attitude to critics and academics has done a complete 180-degree change. When I started, I just read everything, every word that was written about me, completely avidly. I had a scrap book, I stuck in every single review whether it was good or bad. And I would reread them. I think that's because you have some sort of desperate need for validation. Then after a while you begin to learn that you're never going to get 100 per cent good reviews or 100 per cent bad reviews, then you begin to notice that actually regardless of the quality of the book you tend to get a third good, a third bad and a third in between. You don't need to know what the characters are like because you know that, so you're really just reading the reviews for those words that say 'brilliant', 'original', 'witty'. I mean, I suppose there must be some sports writers who really do understand what it's like to be at the top of the game, and there must be quite a lot who don't know what they are talking about. Or those who turn it into a drama of a different sort to what it was. I'm currently obsessed by the Vuelta. It's the third big tour of the year and you hear these commentators saying things like, 'Yes, you can see the pain on his face! You can see he's cracked,' and stuff like this. And they never go back and say, 'I was sort of wrong about that actually!' Still, commentators are easy pickings, like shooting fish in a barrel.

JW: It's funny how they get to say their piece on things that they are not really qualified to talk about. They are commentating as if they know what it's like to be a world-class operator, like they know all the background to the athlete. Most of them have no clue what it's like, yet they often have the platform, through newspapers or television, to have their opinions heard above all others.

JB: It's like people who comment on royalty. They seem to understand the nature and character of all the members of the royal family and they have never even met them!

JW: Is it frustrating when people don't see the subtleties of what you're trying to do with the work?

JB: Oh yes, of course. How could it not be? I say to my agent, 'Send me the two best. Certainly the two most intelligent. I don't want the two that praise me most. I want the two that are the most interesting to read.

JW: Is there a certain book that you remember more than others? A time where things all came together as you wanted? Do you have a favourite work that you're proudest of?

JB: I'm very, very fond of *Flaubert's Parrot*. It was my third novel, and it was the first novel in which I really took on the question of the form of the novel. And ever since that book I've been very interested in form and structure, which it seems to me a lot of novelists are not. A lot of novelists have a story they write from the beginning to the end and then they stop. The different possible ways of laying out a story are of great interest to me, and I'm very fond of that because that was my first extreme experiment with form. Secondly, it was, to my astonishment, successful. It got shortlisted for the Booker Prize. But thirdly, it was the first book that sold abroad. And getting published abroad represented a surprising breakthrough for me. And they were very nice in France. I don't know if it's the best book, but it's the book that in a funny sort of way, even though I wrote it, I feel grateful to, for what it did for me. It's like having a Commonwealth medal on the wall and saying thank you to it. That make sense?

JW: Yes. Are there some rules in novel writing that you think every novelist should be at least aware of?

JB: I don't think that there are general rules that should apply to all novels. I think each novelist develops his or her own rules. I think the most important rules are not about how to tell a story, how to order everything or what form to use, but as I said earlier, exactly what the writer or narrator's attitude to and closeness with the reader are. For instance, through one of my characters, I can't remember which, I say that I think that there's a duty of clarity on the part of the writer. It's easy to baffle the reader and fool the reader to no purpose. That couldn't be easier. Being clear from the first point is an indication of how you value the reader and how you're going to treat the reader. Are you on the same level as the reader or are you above them speaking down to them? As some writers tend to be. I'm very much on the same level as the reader, and also on the same side as the reader.

Katherine Grainger

I'VE MENTIONED her already in this book and, really, Katherine stands as a ringleader for the notion that persistence and endeavour can literally find you the gold. She proves that, very often, whatever your version of success is, whatever that thing is that you want to achieve, if it ever comes then it mostly does so at a bit of a price. To win three silver Olympic medals is incredible, but it wasn't enough for her, and it wasn't enough, and never is, for the media. The usual old phrases were bandied about: 'bridesmaid', 'nearly woman', all pathetically predictable, unhelpful and unjust. It's a nice tag line, a nice compartment in which to fit an engineered version of events.

So, it was against all this that she stood as she prepared for the London Olympics in 2012, her fourth attempt to win a gold medal.

Apart from her charm, profound engagement and generosity as an interviewee, the awe with which we hold her achievements in sport are multiplied when you consider the discipline she undertook. With the perspective of a squash player, I can only admire and respect the capacity that rowers, runners, swimmers and cyclists have to repeat and repeat within their sports, making the same movements for hours on end, every day. For a squash player, each rally can be different, each training drill different too, and, therefore, although training is often brutal, the mind enjoys the subtle changes that the rower's mind doesn't.

The more repetitive something is (swimming length after length, rowing stroke after stroke), the more mental strength athletes tend to need to keep doing it. And what mental strength she must have had to keep getting in the boat every day and hurting herself. There's an overbearing inner need that great athletes seem to have to keep pushing themselves to these lengths.

I first met her at the Glasgow Commonwealth Games in 2014 when she was working for the BBC, and then again at a West End matinee of a Bryony Lavery play. I learned that she's completely multi-dimensional, with broad interests and views not always associated with professional athletes. She has a master's and PhD to her name, and loves theatre and classical music, as talked about in her interviews on *Private Passions* and *Desert Island Discs*. She's also chair of UK Sport.
—

JW: I've been listening to your *Desert Island Discs*. You know you're a real superstar if you're on there.

KG: I almost found it too sports focused! You're asked on because of that but you want more.

JW: What do you think, in a few sentences or more has made you achieve what you have? Fairly open question to begin with!

KG: Start with a tough one. It's a whole mixture of things. I didn't know what I wanted to be, was always competitive, but not always outwardly so. I've always had and continue to have amazing family support. I have a big sister a year older. When we were younger, I would join clubs at the same time she did, I would be spurred on by her. A year earlier than I might otherwise, which gives you an advantage. I think that helped me. It was a safe area, I think. She would be part of the conversation first and I was able to follow. She was the first person I could compete against, knowing that I was competing.

I enjoyed stuff at school. My parents were both teachers, and I was always aware of how important education could be. Sport was important but I never thought it would become a big thing.

Later, I was rowing at uni level and I really valued one or two coaches who recognised potential in me; therefore, I started having conversations to open up new areas. Without them I wouldn't have thought about going that way.

Looking back, coaches and teachers who gave me the ambition and knowledge opened the door a bit, and they were the first steps.

JW: Did you feel you were especially talented?

KG: You do get very talented people coming into rowing who can quickly pick up the techniques and actually often can succeed very quickly. The interesting bit is the people who have all that and then back it up with immense workload. I've seen people with immense talent who, because it came quickly, haven't been able to commit to that hard work. And they don't achieve what they could. It's that combination, that bit of talent mixed with all that hard work. Also, I've seen people with less talent who do all the work but who are missing a link in terms of what they can achieve at the top level. It's always a mix of both.

JW: Is there a pathway for young people getting into rowing?

KG: I started at uni, and at the time it wasn't an internationally recognised sport for a woman. So, the uni line was how girls would get into it. When I started, it was because of the community. It's a really tough sport at university so there's an incredible work ethic to the training, but it was sociable. That was attractive. Universities are still big feeders but there's more going on at school level. Talent ID has come in now, so people move from different sports into rowing. There's a very natural physical type in rowing – tall with long levers – so it's quite easy to find that.

JW: With ball sports, the highest-world-level professionals have nearly always started young. What happens in rowing? Is the early start a big deal?

KG: It's not a big thing. The skills of rowing can be taught and learned into teens and later on, but often these people will have shown athletic tendencies elsewhere. They will have a background of endurance or sport or fitness. It's certainly not a sport you have to have done at a young age. In a good way the athletes have had a background in other sports. I took up martial arts before I did rowing and I think that discipline over your body, the agility and flexibility and competitive aspect, can be trained in other areas. So, athletes can come in quite advanced in other ways, which can be of great benefit, before they master any rowing skill.

JW: I suppose if they are inclined to do rowing later as teenagers the likelihood is that they will have an aptitude or interest in the pain that comes with a tough sport, so will have done some of that work elsewhere?

KG: And they will get found out pretty quickly if they can't take it.

JW: I can imagine. Did your idea of success change as time went by? Is it all about medals? If the gold hadn't happened, would things have been different for you?

KG: It's not just age but maturity as an athlete too. Your expectations shift throughout your career. Sydney was a success. I was young and wanted to do myself justice. Our silver was the first medal for British women rowers in history, so that was a big deal. I was the youngest and most inexperienced person in that boat and I learned constantly from everyone. It was a good time. The medal colour was a bit irrelevant back then; we were thrilled to just be on the podium. The second silver, well you know it, how much you give of yourself, how much the training entails, how tough it is day in, day out. I was in a different boat with a different crew and it was a different part of my career, and that 2004 year was the toughest year I'd had.

Winning a silver was still remarkable but having gone four years on there was this sense of it still being the same result. Leading up to Beijing, success was defined by the gold medal, without a doubt. We had won three world titles going into that so we were used to delivering at the very highest level. Everyone was fit and healthy, we had got everything right and it was in front of a great crowd. We broke the Olympic record going in, then the Chinese broke it back. We led the course until the dying seconds, and it was an instantaneous feeling of failure. So much goes into that build-up from so many people and we felt we had got it wrong.

Going forward from there, as much as I tried to make it not about winning, everything anyone said, every story and headline was about winning in London. For Anna and me, it was our first Olympics together. We had been very successful in the three years running up and I knew the only way that campaign was a success was if it was gold.

I just had to stay in the moment the way athletes talk about, because once I started thinking about what the race meant or who was watching it, or the 12-year build-up to that point, it became too emotional and meant too much. It was about Anna and me being in a boat, making it work.

JW: And it's hard to explain why the momentous occasion becomes such a frightening and all-encompassing thing. If you don't win, life goes on and all the things that really matter are still there. Does it scare you do you think?

KG: I think by then we had won everything, and the Olympics was the only thing left. Fortunately or unfortunately, it's what will define you to a large extent publicly. At that point I was defined by not winning the Olympic Games.

Beijing really broke my heart. I survived it and came back and had a positive life. It wouldn't define me as a person; it might have done as an athlete, and I knew that, but I have enough interests and perspective on the world to not let it change me as a person. But for the athlete, I was still convinced we had what it took to win the Olympics. It was this absolute certainty that if we got it right, we could win the Olympic Games. Therefore, if we were doing our job well, we would deliver that gold medal. If I had never won the Olympics I would still be happy in my life, but the athlete part of my life would think something is missing.

JW: So how do you make it happen on that very day? Is it psychologically a process of making it just like any other day?

KG: You get people saying it's just like any other day, then others say it's the biggest day of your life, and you must treat it as such. I think either approach can be right. It's very individual. You want to think about what you need as a person to be performing at your best every day. For me personally, I knew it wasn't like any other day. I wasn't going to wake up on the final of the London Olympics and think it was any other day. But when you get out on the course, it was a 2,000m course that was so familiar. Both Anna and I had defined roles; we had so much trust in those roles. I knew what I needed to do for the six minutes. I knew it would feel different, sweaty palms and all. But what brilliant athletes do is they recognise what they can control, and they focus on that.

That day was always going to feel different, but it was never out of control. I didn't want to go down that road of it being the biggest day of my life that will define everything. That's too much for anyone to deal with. Underneath all that pressure sits something you know how to deal with, that underpinning thing. This is our event, we know how to do it and we've done it all before. So, I think you have to allow a little bit of that extra excitement to come in, but just enough to not affect what you do on the water.

JW: Have you accessed all the different support services that are offered to athletes now?

KG: Yes. When I started coming through there wasn't any support or funding. The medical support started to become a thing and we started to be able to access physios, strength and conditioning coaches, psychologists and all the other specialists, and that's evolving all the time. They have all played their part in my career. I certainly wouldn't have had a 20-year career without physiotherapists and medical support. Vicky, Anna and I, going into Rio, were very dependent on a group of people around us, helping us to work optimally. And as much as we have to adapt and evolve our work as athletes, so too do they in their fields. Ideas and science are always changing, and we athletes haven't the time or energy to put into researching these areas. To have people helping us in these respects has been a great boost. It's great to share it with them. We felt like we had very few chinks; we had done everything we could. We had marvellous coaching support and layer upon layer in other areas. We felt very complete.

JW: Do you feel like great athletes are just very good at responding to difficulty, rejection and defeat in general? And that might come in the form of a defeat, or that they can't master a technique in training, but they keep responding, keep trying. Sometimes for me, I've felt like I just can't see an end to a problem, like I don't know how to work it out, but if I battled away, things could start to get clearer. Has that process happened a lot, and are great athletes defined by how they respond to these difficulties?

KG: I get asked about what makes a world-class athlete and there are loads of different answers of course. Every person will give different answers. What it does often come down to is resilience. I don't know any phenomenal athlete who hasn't been tested along the way, who hasn't had setbacks, doubts and disappointments. Some are failures in performance, some in health and injury, some maybe relate to not being where you want to be in training, and it's constant. And the thing is, you never feel you've cracked it. There's always an area that needs to be improved, whether that comes from your opposition or yourself. And I think that's the thing about really good athletes: they always find a way to just keep sticking at it, and to make those setbacks not be the end of the road. They are just temporary setbacks. It's also important to recognise you never have all the answers. You might need the psychologist, the coach, your family, and to admit to yourself you're flawed or weaker in areas is hard. But it's a massive strength to do this.

It's through the disappointments that you really learn the most because you then force yourself to go deep enough, to really examine it to the depths. When you have success you think, 'Well that was great,' and you move on, whereas when you experience huge disappointment you wake up at three in the morning and start analysing it. In facing up to those moments, that's when you grow as an athlete. You break through old limits and make new ones.

JW: How do you feel when you're sitting there after a big event and the adrenaline is flushing through you? It's not a very level existence!

KG: Professional sport is often referred to as a rollercoaster because it's constant highs and lows. You don't sit high for too long. It's exhausting but it's also this adrenaline thing all we athletes live on. And that's hard when you get to the end. Normal life is a lot more steady, which in some ways is very healthy. But there are ways in which you miss part of the drama. You can imagine why athletes come to the end and can't replace it to the same extent. It's an amazing privilege while you can do it, even though it puts you through the wringer many times.

JW: Is balance in your life something you've thought about? Can you tell me about how you take inspiration from stuff away from the sport?

KG: At university I wasn't thinking about getting to Olympic level, but I was still putting an awful lot of time in. And I had a coach there who took me to British team level, and he was really big on encouraging me to balance university, rowing and family. He was happy for it not to be all equal all the time, but he would make me aware that you had to be aware of all three. He would always encourage me to redress the balance if I was putting too much into one or two of them. I loved my degree, I loved doing law and rowing; I had two areas I was healthily pursuing. I graduated and knew I wanted to make it on to the British team. I didn't want to stop my studies completely so I found a very part-time master's I could do.

I knew if I just got obsessed with one thing it could get difficult. To be forced to get back into the library, write an essay or study for exams, was a healthy thing. And likewise, if you were getting stuck on essays or study, then the gym or the rowing could help there. So, the commitment to both kept me honest in both.

Then the PhD was good too. I didn't want to do the PhD for an academic reason, I wasn't going to use it in that way, but I would use that focus to constantly give me that balance to my sport. And even when I finished that, I drew huge inspiration from the world outside sport. I was doing crime and criminal law and I thrived off all the interesting lessons and challenges within that. My mum was an English teacher; we've always been to the theatre and I've always loved reading.

My hardest year as an athlete was the year leading into Rio, and I drew a huge amount of comfort from the outside world, from reading stories about people through history, through other worlds in other spheres who had different challenges to face, dealt with situations and come through them, struggling and fighting. I love reading speeches and you start to realise that whatever you're facing, others have faced the same or worse, and found a way through. I find stories like this fascinating. There are so many things to find out from other people outside your own world, and in sport we can often get absolutely absorbed in our very small world. A lot of the answers you need do come from that world, but a lot do not, and I love going into these other worlds to access different ideas.

JW: I'm glad you've said the same. For example, I hope that people who don't like rowing can read your interview in this book and take something from it. I'm sure they can.

If you go to see a play or you listen to a symphony or whatever it might be, can you relate it in any way to what you've done in sport? Is there an element in your training or your races where you think about the contrasts of strategy, changing pace or rhythm for instance? It's quite hard to explain what I'm saying, but maybe I'm drawing from other spheres and areas for ideas about this. Is it an issue for you to think about in what you do?

KG: Rowing is a very addictive sport and the culture of it is part of that. But the biggest thing in rowing is rhythm and timing, that cohesion between yourself and other people and the water. And when that comes together, like all great sport, there will be a huge amount of effort going in, but it will look and appear effortless. That's because when the really great athletes and crews get it right, there's something that's so in tune that it elevates it to more than it just being about a group of people rowing as hard as they can.

When Anna and I raced in London that was the best racing we had ever done, and the boat was always the third person in that crew. We were trying to give that boat the justice, give it the most time. It almost demanded this incredible work going into it. It sounds a bit bizarre, but it took on its own way of racing, and as athletes you're trying to create that incredible rhythm. And we knew that when we hit that rhythm right, we would be faster than anyone else in the world. And it's the pacing.

You start as fast as you physically can, then come into a pace that will last through the biggest space of time in the middle section. Then you change the gears up again to the end and get the sprint finish. But throughout that whole thing the rhythm should stay the same, and all you change is the pace and intensity within it. But the rhythm and timing stay the same, and when you get it right, the whole thing becomes easier.

And it's right: sport is a fascinating mix of art and science because there's so much you can measure and judge. We have graphs and measurements and science going into what we do, but the rowers bring something else. Anna and I worked well as a combination too. Her knowledge of science and maths, her understanding of why all those elements had to fit together was brilliant, and then I brought in maybe more of an instinctual feel of how the boat should be running and the timing. Our coach always said that within ten strokes he knew whether we would win or not, if he could see us hitting that rhythm. So, the good thing about rowing is all this science and tech comes into it, which is so valuable, but you have to fit this in with the athlete's instinctive sense of movement and rhythm.

JW: When you had to do lots and lots of very, very tough sessions, how did you push yourself through? They are not exactly pleasant ways of spending your days, let's be honest.

KG: Well yes, I suppose that can depend on your mood and where you are. The same training session can feel an exciting challenge, or the worst dread on earth. The sport is cyclical too, so there will be different periods through the winter compared to the summer in terms of what training we're doing. The winter is just the money in the bank time where you put hours and hours in and it's very repetitive and relentless. It accumulates. As you get more tired you're still trying to hit the same marks. That gets mentally hard because you have to keep mentally telling yourself to get through it.

There's something about that relentlessness that not everybody can do, so by doing it you know you're doing something different. You also know the dread before, as awful as it is, is always bettered by the feeling of having done it. You just need to get through the next session. The summer will be coming, when there's less load but more intensity.

So winter is that deep-set exhaustion, summer is fear of the pain barriers! It's shorter, sharper and horrific pain levels, a slightly different dread. They are both linked to what I want to achieve. It keeps me going to know my opposition might be doing it, so I had better do it too, and more. It's that I just need to get through it, it's horrific, but in an hour or two or whenever, it will be over. And it's almost just wishing it away.

JW: That's true. I feel like that sometimes. Really quite sad.

KG: It is. It doesn't sound too motivational or inspirational, but the bottom line is that what those sessions are about is getting through them and saying to yourself, 'Soon it will be done.'

JW: I've often thought, as I'm driving to a hard session, why am I doing this? Why do I want to live my life in this way? It gets more profound. I've really questioned it at times, certainly as I got older. You're here once (maybe) so does it matter to be a champion so much that you don't enjoy it?

KG: Yes, and that's totally realistic. There's no fault in thinking, 'I can't wait until this is over and done and I'm back on my sofa tonight and it's all over.' It's a very human response. However, you find your way through that. The important thing is to get through it, because at that point, the easiest thing in the world would be to go home. Most of the population would be sane enough to do that and say no, but those of us who do go through it just have to.

JW: Yes, we go there because we have little choice. And then there are probably people out there who don't have to encounter physically tortuous sessions every day of their lives and they go along doing their more 'normal, less painful' work being not very happy either. So whichever way you look at it, most humans live life by the notion of the pleasure/pain principle to some degree.

KG: Well exactly! For all the highs we're chasing, the deal is that you row through those many, many lows but, my god, at least they make you feel alive, they really do. As awful as they are, they let you experience life in all its glory.

JW: Truly fascinating. Thanks for giving me your time.

KG: Have you talked to many people then? And do they all tell you about their demons.

JW: Yes. I've interviewed actors, writers, sportspeople, doctors, chefs. One thing that came up that I forgot to ask you about was whether you have this experience of trying and trying and trying to master something and you just can't get it to click. It's maybe a certain skill within your sport or discipline. An actor told me about how in the end he was trying to get a scene to work and it just didn't flow; it wasn't there, so he almost gave up. When he let it go, the subconscious took over and right then it all fell into place.

KG: Absolutely, I've had that, though it's sometimes hard to find that place of letting go, because you innately care so much that the pressure is there. But I had a similar thing with the 'catch' in rowing – it's where the blade hits the water. You're always trying to get a faster catch and we used to work on it a lot in Olympic boats. It was very much like what you're talking about with the rehearsal. We were trying and trying but actually what we needed to do was the opposite and almost stop thinking about it, let the muscles relax. It's sometimes about taking your mind away from it so you free the thing up to happen.

JW: But it's often so hard to capture that state of mind, like at London. You couldn't have done that and let go completely of all that baggage.

KG: It's not possible sometimes. Sometimes you can't let that go. As an athlete I didn't talk about it a lot, but then everyone else is, so we have to just let that be and take it on. It became a bit more powerful psychologically to just own it and say let's just do it. We remember looking at the lake in London for the first time and feeling it had to be ours. It was positive, we made it positive.

Alexander Hanson

ALEX IS perhaps one of the less well-known names in this book. As I alluded to in Julian's interview, top-drawer actors don't always receive top-drawer fame, nor I'm sure would many of them want it. He's a superlative actor who has played some huge theatre roles in the West End and on Broadway. If fame reflected talent, ability or achievement, then Alex would be household name material. Fame isn't representative of standard, and that's the one thing that people in the industries understand. It never struck me whilst talking with him that Alex cared about fame. He cares about his output, the work he does, how he can move people.

I saw him in *Stephen Ward*, a musical study of the osteopath who was made a scapegoat for the Profumo scandal in the 60s, and who subsequently committed suicide towards the end of his high-profile trial. This was a brilliant, brilliant piece of work, and Alex played Ward. It had such an impact on me that I saw it three times in its four months in London. What's intriguing is that I was seemingly one of few to connect with the show on such a level. It closed after four months and obviously wasn't quite capturing the imagination of the public, or at least people weren't going to see it. When you consider that Andrew Lloyd Webber's show *Phantom of the Opera* has been selling tickets for every night since 1986, the Ward musical in this day and age is often termed a failure by critics. It wasn't a failure to me. And that's where the subjective 'success' of the arts is interesting. It's why I've tried to use the word 'inspiration' over 'success' in this book. Success is down to numbers, targets, parameters, facts and figures. Inspiration can come from anywhere you wish to look, and can be more important, interesting and affecting.

—

JW: How has it been after *Stephen Ward*?

AH: You loved it didn't you?

JW: Yes, it was outstanding.

AH: Are you a musicals fan?

JW: I love straight theatre and musicals. I've enjoyed a lot of Andrew Lloyd Webber's stuff, an unfashionable thing to say. I come down to London a lot and love theatre. I've seen you a few times.

AH: In other stuff?

JW: I saw *Sound of Music*, and *An Ideal Husband*.

AH: Did you see that? With my wife!

JW: That's right. I took my dad, and we were rolling about in the aisles for two hours during the latter.

AH: Really!

JW: We walked away after *Stephen Ward* and couldn't believe that the show was closing. We were rapt, it was mesmeric. It must have been hugely disappointing for you, knowing it was so strong.

AH: I'm probably pretty biased. I'm in it and not looking at it. I try to imagine to myself because I don't go to a lot of musicals. I don't really like them.

JW: You were trained as a traditional actor.

AH: Yes. And musicals pay good money, I love doing them and love the challenge of it. But I thought the subject matter of Ward was really interesting. The part was fantastic, and it was very flattering being approached by Andrew, who said, 'I want you to do this,' right at the very beginning, before it was finished. He asked me to sit in a room with Christopher Hampton [book writer] and Don Black [lyricist] and kick it around a bit. I've never been in that situation before. I loved the period of the piece and I thought it was kind of *Mad Men*. I loved the story and I thought we had something to say.

A lot of people have asked, like you, why it was closing! It wasn't a turkey, it was a good show. It was perhaps flawed, I think, and I've never been in a show that has divided opinion to that degree. A lot of people asked why he chose this as a subject. Because it's brave and exciting and scandalous. That was one point of view. Some said there wasn't a tune in it! There are plenty of tunes in it. I was reading an article the other day about the state of the West End and how so many original shows are shutting. *From Here to Eternity*, which I didn't see, was apparently a cracking show. There was a time when shows, even if they were flawed, would get an audience. What's really packing audiences in are jukebox musicals, shows where people know the music. And you want to say to people, 'If you listen to *Stephen Ward* a few times on a CD before you come, you would get more from it.' But as a first go, it's always the case that the music doesn't hit instantly. The *Stephen Ward* music needs to sink in.

JW: Of course it does. I was listening to it in New York before I saw it, and it was seeping in deep. The first number, 'Human Sacrifice', is remarkable. It must have been wonderful to sing that.

AH: Oh, it was fantastic. Fantastic number, really good.

JW: And the whole 'Chamber of Horrors' bit was so clever and compelling.

AH: Yes. It was a stroke wasn't it. Really cool that. It set you up wonderfully. It was a really powerful beginning.

JW: So, when you walk away from a project like that, even though many seem to want to term it a failure, what do you make of it all? Are you proud of what you achieved? It must be difficult when it's talked about as a failure.

AH: I'm very proud of what we did.

JW: At the end of *Stephen Ward* you sang 'Too Close to the Flame', an incredibly powerful depiction of Ward's suicide. You down pills and are in tears. The emotion involved is quite staggering and you're having to do that eight times a week. It's not like you're doing a film where you can have a few takes and then it's done. How do you get up for that? And how do you come down from what must be quite a high/low every night?

AH: Yes. It helps that you're on stage most of the time because you build up a head of steam. I'm trying to equate it to what you do. What's the biggest tournament? Commonwealth Games, World Championships? I look at it with rugby players. When you're in the Heineken Cup or you're playing against the All Blacks, then you go back the next week to Exeter. How do you get yourself up? I've been in the game a long time. There have been plenty of times in the past when I haven't got myself up for it and have felt a lukewarm response. It comes to me analysing, as I'm sure you do. What went wrong in that game? How would I approach that differently? I think when you care about what you do and you want to be up there and there's a certain level that's expected of you, you just have to do it. And you do get that feeling 'I can't be arsed tonight'. But I counter that by saying, 'No! How long is this? Ten minutes? That's all it is.'

And you do develop a technical way of doing it as well. You can't just rely on that, but it can give you a springboard. An audience will do a lot of the work for you.

I was reading about Chiwetel Ejiofor, a wonderful actor. I haven't seen *12 Years a Slave*, but from what I've read it was intense. They asked him how he would decompress after the filming finished. He said that his sister worked in New York, so he got himself a flat in Brooklyn, quite a luxury, but just to go there and let the character leave him a little bit. I was interested by this and I thought about Stephen Ward. You finish and then you don't actually know who you are! You've invested so much in the person and you develop this way of being, and then after a few weeks you realise: 'Hang on, that's Stephen, it's not me!' And I really felt that after playing that part.

JW: You must have absorbed the whole Ward story. The material is dark, heavy.

AH: It's a heavy story. You have an image. I had a picture of him in my head. I had done a lot of research about Stephen Ward. I read a lot about him. What was interesting was that I'm not sure how much I would have liked him. But it was important that I wanted to be the person that I was playing.

JW: What about when you have back-to-back performances? A matinee, say, and an evening performance. Are there certain processes you go through to help yourself? Are there rituals? Do you completely rest? How do you occupy yourself?

AH: I think you get into a routine that works for you. During this show, because it was quite a big sing, you get tired. I'm not as young as I used to be. After a matinee there may be some guests in, and I would see them and have a bite to eat. Then I would have one of those power naps. A ten-minute job.

JW: Do you get a bed?

AH: A sofa. I put the TV on low, lights down, and if I drop off, great. If I didn't, then I have a coffee and get some fresh air in Covent Garden.

JW: Quite normal …

AH: And then every now and again something would knock you off that routine. You would have to do something else like an interview and you lose your routine. Actually, it's rather good when you're knocked off it because suddenly it pushes you into a different place. I think as human beings we're creatures of habit and every now and then being pushed out of your comfort zone is good. Particularly during a long run. You need something just to mix it, to vary it. I don't know if that applies to you in what you do. Presumably you're doing the same thing over and over …

JW: There's an element of repetition to what we do: we're hitting a ball against a wall every day. But I should think there's a little more variation for us: we travel to different places more frequently, practise with different people every day, so it's not that we're doing the exact same thing every single day, in the very same place! We also have to back up one match with another soon after, like you, which is mentally trying. But you're singing those same tunes, repeating and repeating, with the same people, day after day, for months on end! People go for their first time, and they don't always comprehend that you're having to get yourself up for it each time.

AH: That's a key thing to remember. It's the first time the people are seeing it and they have paid a lot of money. It's important that you believe in what you're doing. The message I received from you and your dad when you came during the last week, it meant a huge amount. I know how I feel when I go to see something that has an impact on me. It loosened me for days, and then you want to repeat that. You want it again. That's what makes good or great art. Something that affects and lives with you for a while and may even change the way you go about things. But back to the squash: you have a different strategy every time?

JW: For each player, yes. You, the actor, can't have a different strategy each time. You need to perform your part to a certain standard each time, and a lot is expected of you. For an athlete, less is expected and, basically, I'm not letting whole audiences down if I don't perform my part, so to speak. It's just a sporting contest. I'm trying to play and win for me. You, on the other hand, are performing for them. You can't have a breakdown on stage.

AH: You can't?

JW: No, you can't. I can! Because it's down to me. For example, there have been times where I can't take another game. I can't go out there and give the standard, due to mental tiredness or whatever. I've just gone. So, I go and be miserable and eat cake for a few days and read books. You can't do that. You have a six-month contract to perform eight shows a week. If you don't keep reaching the standard, presumably you're sacked? You can't go and sulk and eat cake presumably, however tired you are.

AH: Well, I'll certainly sulk and get cross.

JW: Would that be after a bad performance?

AH: It can be. Actually, most of that anger will happen when you go up for a job, and you don't get it [after an audition].

It's the humiliation of being rejected, which is part of our job. Ninety per cent of the time you don't get it, so we have to cope with dejection and failure. I actually thrive on that, though, and use it as fuel. The pattern will be that I'll go up for three or four auditions and I won't get them. I'll get increasingly annoyed, and it's that very reaction that will push me to another level, and I'm sure you recognise that.

JW: When you're in a bubble like with *Stephen Ward*, do you get feedback? Are things being worked on and analysed to make it better? We would get feedback from coaches about matches. Does that happen in theatre?

AH: We have a resident director who will watch. He also has to rehearse the understudies because there's a whole raft of understudies who are there, particularly in musicals. Very rarely would we do *Stephen Ward* with the full original cast because someone will be ill or on holiday. But yes, the original director would come in now and again and there would be a resident director who would give feedback. I think when it comes to the main act and actors you pretty much police yourself. It's perhaps more crucial for the youngsters who have just come out of drama school and are still learning a lot. We're all learning but there are levels of experience. Presumably you have a team around you. Trainers, coach …

JW: Exactly. Do you have access to advisory services? Do you speak to coaches, psychologists, nutritionists, as athletes would do? I would have thought keeping healthy and strong is quite important, so eating well would be important for you?

AH: I think more and more. It's like anything. Sport in the 60s – the athletes would have a beer straight after, and you think, 'My god, how did they do that?' There was an extraordinary game when the All Blacks played France in the semi-final of the World Cup. The All Blacks had Jonah Lomu, and they were trouncing France. They came out of the dressing room and in the second half France did that Gallic magic that they can do and beat the All Blacks. And you're thinking, 'What happened?' And I was reading something that said most of them had lit up fags at half-time!

JW: There's something to be said for that!

AH: I suppose my point is that I don't think you could do that now! And yet, you've got to have a sense of relaxation and a sense of devil may care, which can help. Michael Gambon said that it's just not as fun as it used to be. That's his take. He's old school. People pissing around. It's different now. For me, I'm very conscious about food. If you're a character actor, you can put on weight and it doesn't matter. I'm a leading man, and I've got to keep myself in decent shape. With straight theatre you can go out all night and the cigarette voice actually can add to it. You can't do that with singing, the voice won't take it. So, you've got to get your sleep, eat well, keep healthy, especially when it comes to singing.

Going back to the feedback issue, the person I trust most is my wife [actress Samantha Bond: *Downton Abbey*, James Bond]. She's a fantastic judge and a fantastic actress, and she gives the best notes in the world, so if I'm feeling really a bit lost, she will come in and just sort of help me to reboot. I'm sure you have somebody like that, who can say something. And it can be a tiny little thing. But yes, I think there's a lot more goes into it now. Also, I'm very conscious that you've got to live your life as well, and for some of those Hollywood stars it really is so bloody scientific.

JW: Can you explain a little about how you came to be where you are now as an actor? Is it just hard work? Is it luck along the way? Have you been given an innate gift to act?

AH: The singing's always been there. That needed developing but I've really only consciously started developing over the last few years. I'm a straight actor who can sing a bit, and I think that's important. You learn more about the craft of acting doing straight theatre rather than musicals. So much is done for you in musicals in terms of the mood, the music, the rhythm. I always find it very important, after doing a musical, to get away and go back to straight theatre. I was probably a decent actor, but it's the old Gary Player adage isn't it? The more I practice the luckier I get. I think it's that as well. And luck plays a part, no question. Things need to fall into place.

JW: You went to Guildhall School of Drama. Was that as a young man?

AH: I was there in 1983. I was about 21–22.

JW: Leading up to drama school in your early twenties, were your childhood and teenage years all about acting?

AH: Yes, I had been exposed to it, but it was a bit left field. It really wasn't in my family's culture. I sang in the choir but certainly wasn't thinking about being an actor. I was going to go into the family business, which is restaurants, gambling, amusement arcades and betting shops. At school I had done a few plays; I was always involved but it wasn't something I was going to do. I left school and went to work at the Ritz in Paris. It was with a view to learning a bit about catering, but I soon realised I didn't want to do that. I love Paris, but working in the hotel from the bottom up, it's worse than going back to school.

Anyway, a whole catalogue of things followed, I ended up living in a squat in Soho. I just thought that I would apply to drama school, knowing nothing about drama school. I applied, thinking that becoming an actor might be a good way to meet girls. The only two I had heard of were RADA and Central and I applied to these places, from back in Nottingham where my family were, and I got recalls. I had no experience really, so I threw myself into amateur theatre in Nottingham and got into Guildhall the next year.

JW: Just on the back of that? There was no previous drama study?

AH: No.

JW: You had to go for an audition and an interview?

AH: At Guildhall, yes. You know, my kids are now at drama school. My son's at RADA. It's harder to get into RADA than it is to get into Oxbridge. There are so many people applying for such a small number of places. So, I got the recall and that was it.

JW: Can you give us an insight into the rehearsal period for a big show?

AH: Rehearsals can range anything from three or four weeks to seven weeks. If you're at the National Theatre, it's often seven to eight weeks. For *Stephen Ward* we were five weeks, and then you go into technical rehearsals where you leave the rehearsal room, go into the theatre, then you're working with the set and lighting. That's a painfully slow process. Then you go into dress rehearsals.

JW: Are the rehearsal days strict on routine?

AH: Yeah, you've got your core for the next day, and very often the core will change according to what's needed. A scene may need more work. But yes, we work within a structure. That structure is about saving time. Time is money and you have to get the most out of it. Once the structure is there you allow things within that rehearsal framework to develop. So, I spend quite a long time creating a structure. That's the way

I work. It takes a long time for things to click, well into the performance. You don't just do the rehearsals and then be brilliant immediately. It takes time. In fact, the moment it changes is often when I get a sense of frustration and boredom about what I'm doing. There's this complete self-loathing that sometimes strikes! 'Oh, fuck it, I'm crap and I don't care.' And then suddenly something exciting will happen. And I tell you, so much of that's about experience from the many years of work. It's about doing it and doing it and doing it and understanding yourself and who you are.

You talked about breakdowns and stuff like that. Understanding what these things mean, it's not necessarily a bad thing. I get to the point where I think I fucking hate what I do, I hate it. And I now understand that I need to change things up. I've really found listening to Stuart Lancaster, who has completely transformed the England rugby team, inspirational. I get a lot of inspiration from sport. I used to box for Nottingham. Liverpool have hired a psychologist called Steve Peters, who was with British cycling, and it's about those percentages. Like when we were talking earlier about diet. But the difference perhaps is that in our game I'm wary of saying I want to be better than somebody else. In your game you need to beat others. If I can bring the best out of myself, that's what matters. And a lot of that's about enjoyment. It's called a play. You're playing. It's finding a balance. It's hard work, but when you're up there in front of an audience you can have great fun with a big part. If I'm in front of 2,000 people it's kind of hairy, but a lot of it is experience and building technique. And there have been so many shows I've done where I just didn't get there. The great thing about it is that we can start again. You recalibrate the way you rehearse, the way you approach it.

JW: It's really interesting that you draw comparisons with sport.

AH: Steve Peters talks about self-doubt. As actors, as artists, we're full of it, and I think that's important because you're being a human. As an actor you resell confidence. But you need the self-doubt in there as a human being to understand the people you're going to play. There are so many times I've walked into a room and I've already talked myself out of a job. I'm sure it's the same with a game as well. You think, 'I can never beat this guy,' and you talk yourself out of it! Now that chat, Steve Peters is saying, is unhelpful. Something with a monkey?

JW: *The Chimp Paradox* is the book.

AH: I'm going to read that book …

JW: He's made a killing out of aligning a chimp with what we all know as self-doubt; it's a good analogy that has helped people understand. We all feel that little voice on our back, feeding all the negative thoughts that don't help when we're trying to perform well. It's about getting rid of the negativity or perhaps welcoming it, not being afraid of it, because, as you say, we all get it. The trick is to then override it.

AH: I think the bigger the chimp, if you can deal with it, the better you become. I don't know – I'm talking off the top of my head. I'm probably talking bullshit, but my chimp is so fucking big at times.

JW: Good to hear, mine too. It doesn't look like it on stage by the way.

AH: In order to overcome the doubt, you have to be the person you play even more. If it's just me out there, the chimp's hard to allay. I have a picture of someone in my mind. Even if you're playing Fred West, at some point you've got to want to be that person. Having said that, there was a good article about Dominic West who played him recently, saying there are certain times when you have to play it technically, you can't get involved. I'm paraphrasing. I tend to get a bit methody with what I do. You don't want to get methody with Fred West.

JW: When you act the method way, does that really mean in between takes you're talking and acting like your character?

AH: In films more I think, not so much in theatre. But I think rehearsals can be a real struggle, because you're jumping from me, an easy-going guy, to becoming this whole other person, and I just think I can't do it, I can't fucking do it.

JW: So, on first night for instance, are those doubts surfacing?

AH: No, not so much then. If I'm not good enough, I'm not good enough, but I say to myself now that I'm going to strut my stuff. Yes, the nerves are there, but there's this thing about puffing out the chest and telling myself not to be frightened any more. I'm just going to go and do it.

———

I often get young players in particular asking me about how they deal with nerves. Dealing with the pressure of a situation is one of the defining factors related to success. In all walks of life, success often comes down to how each person deals with that. To be a champion we have to deal with a pressurised situation at a very particular time (the contest), to go far in music or drama we must perform specifically in the audition or show. I know nothing about the stock market but to be successful in any venture related to it you can't just be savvy, you must be savvy at the exact right time. To pass an exam we must show our knowledge within a two- or three-hour timeframe. There's no room in anything to say, 'Sorry. I would have been better yesterday.'

Life contains a whole roster of experiences for us that demand performance, that need to be executed within a cruelly specific window. We can't just wake up one morning and decide we feel good and that it's best to compete in that Olympic final today.

Of course, it's somewhat about how much you practise and how good you are, but more tellingly it's about bringing a performance to the surface at a given time. It's all well and good that Jessica Ennis-Hill is as good as she is, but if she doesn't perform on those days in July and August, then none of the brilliance is realised. For her that pressure is outrageous. The chance comes round only once every four years, and what happens affects her whole life ahead, in terms of how she's perceived, what she earns and her future success. This of course creates pressure, especially when you know how capable you are.

To the kids, I often say, there's no right or wrong. There's no secret way. But what I try to convey is that it's quite sensible to almost embrace the doubt first of all. Doubt will be there, and doubt is normal. We definitely shouldn't be led to thinking that because we doubt then we will fail. We all feel it, however successful or brilliant we are. One message that's coming out of this book is that however exceptional anyone ever gets, the doubt is one thing they can't avoid.

The key thing to try to implement is that for every negative thought, either replace it with something positive or somehow spin the negative, or use it to move yourself towards a forward direction. 'Okay, so this is a weakness today. But it was stronger today than it was in my last match. I've trained hard, I'm really strong at the moment, so it's slowly improving.'

———

JW: You talked about experience. You've been on Broadway, in the West End, played to sold-out arenas the country wide – how much does all that background give you?

AH: Experience is huge, it's vital. I have to give myself a pep talk because it seems to count for nothing. When I was a young actor, I used to hear older actors saying, 'The older you get, the harder it gets.' I thought, bullshit. And now I understand. You raise your own bar each time. Or hopefully you do. And all you remember of the last thing you did was how fluent you were on stage. But that was at the end of your run. And then you're at the beginning of another. And you think, 'Why can't I do it? Last time I acted I was good!' And of course, you're at a different part of your process. You're starting again.

JW: In squash this is the whole matchplay issue. For example, if we stop in May and go back into competition in August, I can't play. I'll have trained hard and will be as fit as I can possibly be, but for those first matches I feel awful. You must really improve through the course of a run.

AH: You do. It's so gradual. It just infuses into you. I said it before, with *Stephen Ward*, I'm shedding it now, but I didn't realise how much he was there. But yes, it's exactly what you say about that matchday thing. You're so fluent, you've been playing so much and you know how to play, and then you have a break and you start again and you don't know how to do it. And yet, after a while, you do know how to do it! And you're slightly better.

JW: Then I suppose that's why they have preview periods in theatre [preview shows before first night – precursor shows to the actual run].

AH: Yes, the preview periods are important to iron out the creases. Especially with musicals, which have longer preview periods because they tend to be much more technical. There are orchestras, more lighting, choreography. And also, you need an audience to give you feedback.

Do you think there are a lot of sportsmen or women who are interested in theatre? I'm finding it a bit unusual how passionate you are.

111

JW: I'm always interested to see how great performers work. The arts really interest me because people think that the artist just gets sudden streaks of inspiration when they are lying in bed. I can see from talking to you that you have to put in an awful lot of hard work to achieve what you do. I'm not sure whether sportsmen and women are massively into theatre necessarily, but I think quite a lot might be if they were exposed to it. Theatre is quite exclusive, and that says it all. Why shouldn't athletes like theatre? They like film, and many of them like live entertainment, the live experience. This is what really appeals to me about theatre. You get to sit in a room, and you get to watch a conflict or drama unfold in many dimensions. Theatre is hugely popular, but I would love to see theatre a little less exclusive to a certain type of person who has a certain standing in society.

AH: Federer is somebody I love, a great hero of mine. When I was out in New York doing *A Little Night Music* [alongside Catherine Zeta-Jones and Angela Lansbury], I was put in touch with the Broadway masseur, a very camp gentleman. He massages Federer when he comes to the US Open. Federer said something really interesting. He had been to see one of the shows, a musical with a lot of dancers. I think it was a show about Sinatra. Really tough dance routines. And Federer couldn't believe that they had to do this every night, eight shows a week, which I thought was really interesting, but of course it's different. Every discipline is different.

JW: Well, it's about having that appreciation isn't it. I went to see a ballet and I haven't seen many, but wow, the appreciation we have for that and for what you folks do is immense, or it should be.

How do you deal with the highs and lows, the comedowns? There must be a few of those ...

AH: Yes. Playing the starring role, being lauded and then suddenly nothing. My family helps to bring me down, but then again if you're in a lonely hotel room, that's tough.

JW: Yes. Presumably after *Stephen Ward* you would go home each night.

AH: Yes, yes, it's different when you're on tour. Other interests, too, are helpful. I met Danny Cipriani. He's a friend of a friend of mine. I was doing *The Sound of Music* at the time and my friend asked for tickets. He came in with this guy and I asked him what he did, and he says, 'I play rugby.' I looked at him and practically genuflected. 'You're Danny Cipriani.' I didn't recognise him because he always wears his skull cap and he obviously wasn't then. He asked me for a singing coach contact. He wanted to do something different, and he said they are encouraged to have other interests. So, I put him in touch. I get that. I think with what we do, where you're trying to be so good at what you do, you get obsessive, and it's difficult to come off that.

I don't sleep very well at times. The other thing I find incredibly important, that off season you have that rest, that six weeks downtime, it's amazing how much seeps in through the subconscious, and how much work that does. I feel that if I can't learn my lines I'll keep looking at them until midnight. Is there any wonder you can't sleep? No, because the mind is running wild; you need to switch off and the subconscious does such a job on that. It's only now that I'm beginning to really understand how much work it does for you.

Years ago, I was in a film, *Robin Hood*, a weird and wonderful film. There were some nightmare sequences and we had to do a complicated sword-fighting scene with a wonderful fight director called Bill Hobbs. You learn the routine and it's athletic. After ten minutes we would take time out of it. We all wanted to carry on, but the guy knew exactly what he was doing. We all had to go off and have a cup of tea. I realised it was the very break that did the work! Even to this day I never quite trust that. I want to keep working and keep working! The subconscious is so powerful.

Prime it and send it on its way. What I actually feel as an actor is that, during rehearsals, I've never understood how actors can go out and do something of an evening, go and socialise. From the theatre I go back, eat my tea, and then another hour of work, then watch the news and go to bed. But it can actually be counterproductive.

I was doing a show years ago at the National, terrible thing. It was an updated version of *The Beggars' Opera*. I was playing Macheath and I didn't have a bloody clue. We were getting closer and closer to the performance, and then one night I was in front of the TV – Jools Holland or something was on. And REM, Michael Stipe. And that was all I needed. I saw it. I saw exactly how I was going to play the guy. And I can't remember whether I saw it visually, it might have been a song I heard that showed me who he was. At that point I was crying out for some kind of stimulus, an idea, and I just think if I'd have relaxed more through the process, it would have come easier. It almost came to me when I lost heart and let go. Can you relate to that?

JW: Absolutely. I can relate totally. Sometimes when I'm training longer, more hours, forcing it, it can get more tricky. The mind is more blurred. I keep trying and trying and dig myself into a rut. You let go a little bit, and it's not easy to do that, because you want something so much. But you let go, and then things can suddenly fall into place.

AH: There's no doubt, it does so much work, so much work. I suppose that's what makes great coaches as well. Once you recognise it, you know how to.

JW: Yes, the coach can say to the player, 'Look, you are doing too much here. Ease back. Today we are going to do a fun, light session.'

Having faith in the process and the work: taking the foot off the gas

One of the most fascinating ideas that has come from this whole book was the point that Alex made about the subconscious.

In August 2011 I set off to Australia to start a new season of squash. I was in phenomenal shape, and the training that summer had been uninterrupted. It really flowed and I was imperiously fit. No blips, just great work, day after day, week after week. I was short of a few matches to bring it together, but nothing more. I lost to Greg Gaultier in the quarters of the first tournament, the Australian Open, and felt awful. I flew back to Germany for the World Team Championships in Paderborn, where I lost the deciding rubber of the final match so that England lost the world team title to Egypt. I was devastated and mystified. It was one of the hardest losses I ever had.

Back in Manchester in September I tried to put things right but lost in the second round of a World Series event to Adrian Grant, against whom I had a winning record. I was now in a mess. In the shape of my life but unable to play.

I remember vividly the disappointment that week. I had a day or two off and remember getting back on court fairly immediately, more because I didn't know what else to do. I remember the chats with Malcolm. I went on for a practice with his groups, and my confidence was shattered. I felt like I couldn't hit the ball, and it was worse because

I had worked so hard. At this stage I would have laughed if someone had told me that at Christmas I would be the world number one. The signs simply weren't there.

On the day of the semis of the Manchester event I drove there to have a session with my brother, as he was working at the tournament as a national coach. I told him I wanted to do a heavy session, to really get to the bottom of the well, physically and mentally. It would make me feel better, but I also thought that sort of training might help what was happening on court and would strengthen me up. Those tough sessions are always good strengtheners, and despite being fit, maybe I needed a little bit more of this specific squash-based work.

The session was one of the toughest I can remember. We repeated set after set, and it seemed interminable. I collapsed at the end, but because it was done away from the crowds on cold squash club courts, nobody watching, in the suburbs of Manchester in the wake of a bad loss, it was 20 times harder. I had trained all summer to win events like this one in Manchester, not to be sitting them out doing brutal sessions. I questioned why I kept persisting when it was all coming to nothing.

Somehow, amongst all that failure in the early autumn of 2011, I stuck with it. David and Malcolm, and my trainer Mark, who had put so much good work into me that summer, never once became negative, and I simply stuck by the process and battled on.

I flew to Philadelphia and had a better result, reaching the semi-finals. I lost but played well this time. That night was happier, and at dinner I hinted to David that we should get back on court, follow it up with a session the following day. This can be a bit dangerous after a tough tournament; there's a comedown to deal with, but had I won the match I would have had to play the final, so I thought why not train, as I would have played. I was buoyed by having played well, so didn't see the point in resting when we were both in Philadelphia, not flying back immediately.

We were on court again, on the back courts away from the fanfare. As the finalists prepared to play in front of the crowds and the music in the stadium upstairs, we slogged it out on the courts downstairs at Drexel University. It was hard again, mentally and physically. Everyone had left the club, the other players had gone home, it was anti-climactic, but we did the session. We could have easily gone shopping in Rittenhouse Square.

I had another couple of decent results, a final in Doha and a disappointing loss in the semis of the Worlds. I was battling for the wins I had and couldn't find any fluency. I felt I was stronger and better than the results were showing, considering the output I was unleashing on the training court.

After the loss in Rotterdam at the Worlds I made room for booze. I was so disappointed and felt like I could do little else but let go of the intensity, and what's more, I needed to sleep, rather than spend all night doing endless reruns of the loss.

The following week I worked on ridding the hangover. Vanessa and I looked after her nephews, who were full of colds and coughs, so we were busy. I knew I would never be able to avoid the germs, so I just sort of accepted it, and didn't fight it with hand sanitisers. I only managed to put one session on court in and some physio. I had little option. I let go of the training, came off the gas a bit, and took the mental intensity completely out of it. It just happened that way. And part of me said, 'Fuck this. I'm working so hard and nothing's happening. I don't care if I get ill and miss training.'

I went to Hong Kong the week after and won the event, and just hadn't seen it coming. The week after that we were Kuwait bound, where I repeated the result. Two major World Series wins in three weeks. I came back to England and kept being told that I was getting close to becoming world number one. I flew to India and won again, beating Gaultier in four games, one of them a 57-minute brute. Three World Series wins on the bounce, highly unusual for anyone, let alone me.

And there it was: world number one in January 2012.

It demonstrated the process. It demonstrated the difficulties that have to be encountered. It demonstrated that all that training was worth it, and it was working, but there were some shaky bits along the way. It also demonstrated that I didn't quite have the balance right, and that it wasn't all about hard training all the time. It demonstrated hugely that the hard work doesn't always bring the rewards immediately.

More than anything, it taught me that the down period after the Worlds was almost as crucial as the hard training; that period before Hong Kong where I let go and had time with Vanessa and her nephews, letting the subconscious work on things, exactly as Alex had talked about. This was as important in a way as the tough sessions in Manchester and Philadelphia.

I needed to find a way to be relaxed as well. I look back and realise that to almost stop caring for a while helped.

People have their different ways of balancing this. Some people perform well when they are always intense. I certainly can't be like that, though I do find it difficult to switch away from it.

People who are world class at something usually need to find a way of making time for relaxation. Some play computer games or watch television, some find balance with their friends or family, some play golf, some perhaps don't need to think about it.

> I wasn't consciously thinking before Hong Kong that I would switch down the intensity. I didn't plan it, and it was even better because it wasn't forced.
>
> One thing is for sure, a balance helps. Rest time, leisure time, time for other things, is almost as important as the training itself. The unconscious mind can make magic happen.

JW: Can you tell me a bit about *The Sound of Music.*

AH: What got me through was experience. In the summer I had been working down in Chichester doing a series of Noel Coward short plays. We were rehearsing several pieces within the five-week process. It was really, really tough, and we pulled it off, and it was good. I looked at it and couldn't see how we would do it, but we did it.

Anyway, suddenly I get this call about *Sound of Music.* Andrew Lloyd Webber had just done the TV show finding the Maria, which Connie Fisher had won.

JW: You weren't auditioned?

AH: It wasn't working out with the guy who was doing it, who is a terrific actor, but it wasn't working. They called me on the Sunday morning. We did the deal that day, met the director that day, and went in on the Monday. Previews were up and running. And the press night was ten days away on the Wednesday following. I asked them when they wanted me on stage. They said, this Wednesday. I thought, 'Oh Christ.' I remember they picked me up from home in an Addison Lee car and took me to The Really Useful Group HQ, and I immediately learned the waltz with Connie. And I've got two left feet. So, I'm doing this, and someone rushes in and says, 'We need Alex at the Palladium.' This is at lunchtime. They needed to do some filming for the publicity. 'Come with us,' they say.

'Any chance of a bit of lunch?'

'What do you want?'

They went to Pret for me and I was whisked off. I got there and they said, 'We want you to sing "Edelweiss" in front of the cameras.'

'But I don't know "Edelweiss".'

'Everybody knows "Edelweiss".'

'But I don't know the words.'

'You'll be alright.'

So, I wrote the words down on my hand. They took me to the dressing room, and I put on this lederhosen stuff, which belonged to the understudy, who was my shape. We got on to the stage, and I met these seven kids for the first time, and we were up and running. This is Monday lunchtime. We did that and then we were back off to rehearsals.

That night I went to see the show, with the understudy performing. He had never done a run of it. I thought the show was dreadful. That was my fear. I had just signed a contract for ten months and I'm looking at this thinking, 'I can't do this for ten months.'

It was in previews, and musicals take a long time to come into their own, so it was supposed to be rusty. But all I could see was all the bad stuff. I was crying during the interval. I rang my wife saying, 'What have I done? What have I done? What have I let myself in for?'

There's the panic of knowing I've got to go on stage in two days and it's crap. So, I'm doing this thing, learning these lines and learning these songs, and I told them there's no way I would go on stage on Wednesday. But they wanted to run with their new leading man. And it's kind of one of those 'no pressure' situations, but it's there. I told them I needed one morning with the script, alone. Von Trapp didn't have a huge amount of dialogue. I needed from 9am–12 noon, and at 12 on the dot that guy was knocking on the door, whistling. I didn't know all the moves, but I kind of knew the dialogue. The show on the Monday was so bad I thought it wasn't so much pressure. Preview audiences love to think the actor's only doing this scene for the first time and it could be a car crash, or that the stage might fall down! That's why they go!

I had no expectation of myself. That first night was a really interesting night, I had no nerves. Nothing. And I've gone on stage, pushed on. I would come off in between scenes and the stagehands would grab me because I had no idea where I was going next. Once I was on, I was okay, because I knew the scenes, but I didn't know how to get there, or where I went on. All I could do was keep the lines in my head. They would drag me round, down stage and then I would know where I was. It was absolutely fine.

The audience went berserk; they thought they had seen something absolutely extraordinary, and in a sense they had. I think one of the reasons I was able to do it was because of experience and because of the job I had done in the summer, which had been a far harder piece. And then once you've done it you know you've done it and then it's repetition, repetition. Then that gave me a few shows before the press night, on the following Wednesday.

JW: Did it then come together?

AH: It took much longer to get to where I wanted to be. Essentially, I was rehearsing in front of 2,000 people every night. I had three days to learn stuff, but I wasn't rehearsing, and I interpreted it for myself. It took me a long time but after a few months I was proud of it. I look back at what I was doing initially and I'm so embarrassed. It was very black and white, there was no shading in there. It was very loud, awful! But it was good enough and the audience were going to see Connie Fisher, of course.

JW: What do you feel about the celebrities getting the parts in the West End, when they are in the part through fame rather than ability? They are not fully fledged actors with big backgrounds.

AH: It only bothers me when I don't get a part because they have chosen somebody famous! Because they are famous, they can put bums on seats. When I was on Broadway doing *A Little Night Music* everybody was saying I might get a Tony Award nomination. Of course, when the nominations came out I wasn't there, and what they do on Broadway is they get film stars to sell tickets. These awards are about reaching more people, capturing new audiences, getting them into the theatre. That year Denzel Washington was doing *Fences*, Catherine Zeta-Jones and Scarlett Johansson were around.

It's about bums on seats. But having said this, there are many famous people who are brilliant. Helen Mirren, for instance, is somebody who can really do it and is incredibly famous. There are plenty out there who just don't have a clue on stage and it's a false economy. They can get these famous people to do a play, and because they haven't got the wherewithal to do it, word gets out and the audiences don't come. It's difficult because many do it well.

JW: Do you feel like you want more fame?

AH: In our game it's about selling seats, and if I were a bit more famous it would be quite helpful. And financially it might help! I don't care, it's not why I do it, but if I become famous, which is possible, then I'll be ready for it. But I remember thinking from a very young age I was very frightened of being famous because it might involve chat shows and they would ask questions. I wouldn't know what to say and I would make a complete dick of myself.

And when you're famous, you can't be unfamous. You can become a failure, not unfamous. I think I can go anywhere and that's important. No one knows who I am, yet there are times when your identity is bound by what you do, and you want the respect and recognition.

When I was working on *Jesus Christ Superstar,* with the superstars [Chris Moyles, Ben Foster, Melanie C and Tim Minchin], my agent had rung me and said, 'Tell me if you've had enough but they have asked me if you're interested?' I was interested because I've never played arenas and I probably never will do again. I wanted to do *Jesus Christ Superstar* at least once before I die, and this would probably be my last chance. And also, those guys are all from different disciplines, which are related, and also Tim Minchin is just an amazing talent. I sort of just wanted to hang out with him. I loved them, they were a great group of talented people, and wouldn't begrudge any of that.

JW: Are these great composers or writers, like Lloyd Webber and Stephen Sondheim, demanding? Like demanding coaches!?

AH: He's not a relaxed person, Andrew. He's a creative type. Not easy socially. A charming man but can be great company. If you're a banker and you're in the city, it's important you don't reveal feelings all the time. I guess that's why people go to the theatre, because they are often locked in jobs where everything is repressed, and they go to see something that taps into their lives. Why do we read books? To realise we're not alone. You go to these things to recognise that you're not weird. It's a fascinating thing to be a part of that with great writers like these.

They come up with great art, and it just tears your heart out. They can have quite gruff exteriors, but it's protecting something so vulnerable. You have to have a childlike quality for what we do, because you're dealing with weakness and failure. That's what they are doing. You have to understand all these things, so all of that has to be available to you, and you need to protect it too.

Persistence

Every interviewee in this book has had to be able set aside disappointments, ask why something is happening, analyse and question themselves, and to persist and try again. They are not afraid to change or keep working the issue out, however badly things are going, however many losses or rejections they suffer. It struck me that Alex had had his fair share.

I understand much more now that losing was part of the process. I realised it was important to try to remain positive in some way and to remember the small steps forward I wanted to make when the disappointments came. However difficult it is, I feel now it's best to respond to what has happened with an element of forward motion or positive intention. It's healthy to be very disappointed, but it's unhealthy to have it be a lengthy disturbance or strain.

All the characters in this book have different ideas and philosophies about how they've done what they've done, but one thing they've all suffered is disappointment or defeat. An actor, as I found out through Alex, feels that same disappointment an athlete does losing when they fail an audition. They may not 'lose' as such, but they too have performances or auditions that turn out to be failures and they have to react to it.

Comedians seem to have plenty to say on this subject. Listen to their interviews and there are stories from their apprenticeship years performing in dark Edinburgh Fringe underground clubs, where they were heckled by a crowd of 12. If any experience would test patience for stand up comedy then that would be it. They endured them, accepted them, learnt from them and didn't lose faith.

I'm more writing this book to discuss, explore and show rather than advise and tell but having undergone that disappointment more times than many (in a sporting context of course) the one thing I would say is this: there will be negative moments/ outcomes, but try as soon as possible after the event to look realistically at the negative aspects and work to address them. Always take one positive from the outcome, and there will be at least one, and take yourself forward with that. That now becomes a positive response. If it's then possible to go ahead, work hard to correct or improve the issues for the next time and continue to re-evaluate, then you can't do anything else anyway.

I've got better as I've got older. There is no point in stropping about for three days after some sort of failure. It's wasteful and just self-pitying. If I played badly but prepared as well as I could, then I work out why and go and try and correct it. If my drop shots were crap when running on to the ball then I will acknowledge that fact and turn it in to a specific positive: 'I can get this better if I work at it, and so I'm going to concentrate hard on getting practice sessions in where I work on this with my coach.' For me, instead of driving to Scarborough, I now try and feed myself comments like this when appraising my what I've done on court. It makes me feel better. Plus, there are worse things in life than losing a squash match. There's no harm whatsoever in reiterating that every now and then.

Jonny Wilkinson

THIS LEGEND of British sport needs none of my ramblings, but still, I will. If you were alive and certainly in England in the early noughties, his name and contribution to sport on a global scale will have been difficult to miss, as he helped England to win the 2003 Rugby World Cup.

Teams are rarely successful because of one man, and Jonny would be the first to say this, but it was his face to whom the press and public attached themselves. They probably felt they had good reason; the number of points he scored with his left boot during the campaign was astonishing. The consistency and sheer brilliance of his goal kicking threatened almost to take the emphasis off what was a sensational rugby team.

And what a fascinating and humble fellow to chew the fat with for an hour and a half. We all know hard work is required in some form to achieve the success, but Jonny Wilkinson had a reputation for working so hard and it may have come at a price nobody could ever understand.

He arrives to where we arrange to meet in a three-quarter-length Parker, woolly-hatted and unshaven like I've never seen him. It's chilly outside but I assume this change in appearance is part of a disguise, as moving around without attention can't possibly be a given for him.

He doesn't hold back at all when we speak and thinks deeply about his answers. He certainly wasn't going to simply talk for 20 minutes and be gone. In fact, he engaged thoroughly with me; a dream interview then, which I appreciated.

He is, as we speak, at the end of his career and reflecting on how he handled it. The endless hours of practice certainly worked for him in some respects – achievements, trophies, adulation – but he has questions that he still seems to want to explore:

Did his work ethic to an extent cause some of his many injuries? Did the fierce training regimen burn away his vitality, his love for rugby?

People talk about putting time in, doing the 10,000 hours, and speaking to Jonny makes me at least question the whole theory again. I feel myself that I've practised so much squash that, at 33, I've hit a ceiling that I'm trying to stay under. I don't watch as much, I do many more other things, and I need to be around squash less, so that I get less tired of it and am able to give it more energy in matches and training.

I've specialised and repeated for so long now that I have much more of a limit than I did, but I've learned that this helps, allowing me only to practise far more specifically and intensely and far more productively for much shorter periods. This in turn gives me time elsewhere on other things and to hold mental and physical energy back.

Jonny speaks honestly about this in our interview and acknowledges that the mammoth practice sessions got out of hand at various points in his career.

—

James: Are you enjoying retirement?

Jonny: Immediately afterwards there was a big relief, and it finished in a successful way, but then I start watching everyone else doing it and want to play. My mind's telling me that I want to find a new path, but the body's facing the other way!

James: Can you encapsulate what made you reach the highest standard you did in rugby?

Jonny: A combination of things. There was a coincidental coming together of an incredible support base, constantly supportive friends and family. There was a natural gift towards the game itself, and an obsessive work ethic. My own journey began with my parents and my brother, then Steve Black, Dave Alred, Rob Andrew. Without Steve Bates at school I wouldn't be at Newcastle. My wife has given me so much support, which I needed to continue. Then I think of all the teams who had to be who they are to make me successful. I needed all that support from all these people. Of course, I had to do the work, and when I say I was obsessive, I mean dangerously obsessive. I simply couldn't afford to fail.

James: By the end of your book, *Tackling Life*, your outlook changed, and you seemed to say that it's not all about winning and losing. Were you able to find a balance and do you wish it had come earlier to you?

Jonny: In a way, sometimes I wish it hadn't happened at all. If you look at my path from 1997 to 2003 it was an upward curve where I was getting used to just playing and getting better. I was seeing the evidence every weekend – it was almost like I owned a formula to success. As a youngster I had written my goals down and had found this way of achieving them, but then I encountered the injuries and I missed four out of five years. That was the period where things changed. And when you ask if I wished it would have come earlier, well no, because it wouldn't have fit with who I was.

If you read the book that I wrote earlier on in my career, it's a very, very dogmatic outlook I have. That driven, egotistical outlook worked for that person. If I had tried to put a more spiritual open-minded learning approach that I discovered later on to that person, it wouldn't have worked at all.

During the middle was the transitional phase. It wasn't just a matter of sitting there with the notepad and going through it. I was having to question whether I wanted to carry on playing rugby and examine the way I viewed myself, and through that came the learning.

So, there were two very distinct parts of my career. The middle bit was the confusing time, mostly made up of sitting down injured and losing respect for myself. I became confused about who I was and what I was doing. Without that middle bit, though, I wouldn't have got to the end bit. Had I been like I was in the first part of my career all the way through and then tried to deal with retirement, I think I would be a mess. As it is now, I'm keen to find out what's new, and to learn.

James: The injury list is amazing. At the time I wasn't really aware of how injured you were, and how frequently. Was the worst and most frustrating thing that you weren't able to train to full capacity?

Jonny: I was thinking about this recently. After my neck injury it all went downhill. I had an operation, and they were telling me to stay in bed for a while. Complete rest.

The next day I was on my bike with the neck brace on. It's easy now to question what the hell I was doing but I could actually train, so there was no way I could let time slip away.

What makes me like this? Well it was a synchronicity of events. We were all winning together, and it was an amazing life – we had won the World Cup. Then with the injury thing it's the flip side of the coin, the negative aspects of it all. I was in a very interesting position as a 24-year-old, reaching my ultimate goal and wondering what was next.

I was confused about it, but at that stage my saving grace was that I could just get back out there and do what I do and plan to win these next things. So, I felt like I had the answers, and I could do things straight away when I got the injury, by doing every exercise I could do apart from the injured part. That was how I controlled the situation. All my values were about being the best and feeling I can accomplish things, and doing this training made me the strong man in my head. A lot of that ten months was in reality about confusion and worry: worry about what everyone else was doing, not having faith that I could keep up, so I overtrained. Even though I didn't play in that period, I trained nine to five for nine months ...

James: You did all the stuff you could do ...

Jonny: Yep, but then broke down. And then the issue came as an identity crisis because you create a set of values based on these dogmatic training principles. That's all great until you take the rugby away, and you're not winning. If I wasn't playing rugby and was doing nothing, I just felt weak and worthless.

Playing without the spotlight and without being able to challenge to be the best, I literally became empty inside. I wanted to get back on the field and be back to my best from minute one, otherwise I was failing. Then that extra pressure meant that I was trying to hang on instead of being free to attack and express myself. In my head it became more pressure, more stress, more training, and when it didn't work out, more negativity. Each injury brought more depression. That was where the whole new angle of looking at things had to come in, otherwise it was curtains.

James: So now, would you think along the lines of less work, more rest?

Jonny: Taking time out, and I mean really taking it out and re-evaluating in a positive sense rather than a negative one, is what was needed. After the first injury I should have felt like I had that time and space to rebuild and to not be perfect. To not feel the rest would do me harm. I needed the patience and the confidence to say, 'Right, let's relax here.' Even now though, as much as I can concede that rest is great, I'm probably as bad as I've ever been. There's part of you that just can't let it go.

Then at the end of it all you think maybe I had to be like that to be successful. As much as it made me a nightmare off the field, and to a degree on the field, it was also on the field that it made me strong when I played rugby. Or maybe the strongest people are those who can identify the changes and break from the negative cycles; when you can do that, you experiment and explore other areas, and deepen understanding.

I overdid things and found it hard to break out of it. My natural inclination is to keep pushing myself harder and harder, even when I had changed, and the spiritual reform had happened ...

James: It kept creeping back in ...

Jonny: Yeah, absolutely. Especially at the end when you're thinking this could be the last game you ever play.

James: You said at the time of the second World Cup that you had become lighter psychologically, but before the semi-final and final you experienced those horrible nerves, that sick feeling in the hotel room.

Jonny: Yes. I was back in prison. I was building it up, waiting for the evening games. In that World Cup there were a lot of games played in the evening, so we were sat around all day. We couldn't go out because we needed to save the legs and switch the mind off, but then ended up thinking all the more. I don't miss that stuff at all. I would like to have explored better ways to deal with that intensity pre-match.

James: It's not that easy just to say 'relax'! And that sort of thing is so much easier to say after the event. When you're in the midst of it, it's very difficult to think clearly. It's tough to simply say 'snap out of it'.

With rugby, have world-class players usually had early exposure to the sport? In some disciplines it's necessary for kids to start young to become world class.

Jonny: It's a funny one with rugby. I played alongside Paul Grayson, who was a footballer until he was 17 and he decided to go with rugby. That was certainly something you could do more of in the amateur era. The age is coming down, but my brother still kicked off his professional career in his twenties. The skills are not quite as complex as in racket sports like tennis and squash, or say golf, so there's a bit more room to start later. But still, there's no substitute for people who are consistently playing well and trying to get better earlier.

I was involved from a very young age and I learned a deep understanding of how the game worked. I had a more intense grounding in the game than most.

Not everyone starts in the same way or has an identical environment or level of opportunity. That's why studies on talent development will always be quite inconclusive. The variables will never be identical in squash. You had a different background and upbringing to another player, which means it may have been harder or easier for you, or that you may have had a head start in some particular area, according to all the many differentials. Such a complex topic.

James: Do you feel that imitation of great players like Gavin Hastings was key to your development as a child?

Jonny: The role top athletes play can never be underestimated. I used to watch rugby and then go off and kick rugby balls around the garden, pretending I was Gavin Hastings, and that's what kids do. I've been sent lots of pictures and letters from supporters, and so many of them are young kids doing these funny stances when they are doing a kick. It's been a lovely thing.

James: Yes, I vividly remember watching Wimbledon, and afterwards I just went and hit balls for hours pretending I was Sampras or Edberg. Despite not knowing at the time, it makes you wonder how much that sort of thing develops you later.

Jonny: The youngster gets an impression of what that player is like in person. Whatever they see on that screen is all they get to form the impression. So, I try to remember this, I try to remember how much players influenced me when I was little. And when these kids are trying to kick like you, are they going to have to ignore the fact that you're a prat? When I saw Gavin Hastings, I didn't hear of him doing stupid things. He never really fought on the field, never got yellow carded. I wanted to be like that.

James: You were fairly undemonstrative on the field, so was that exterior you portrayed important?

Jonny: I was very quiet and shy as a young person, and because of the nature of the sport, I had to bring an extroverted side out. As a fly-half you have to speak, sometimes shout, let the team know information. So, it's not good enough as a fly-half to say well I'm just shy and quiet but I'm giving my best.

I did go through a period when I was 21 where I became nasty on the field. I got carried away with the pressure and responded in a very egotistical way. I learned very quickly that this was putting extra pressure on me, and other players lost respect for me. When you feel that way about someone it's a lot easier to get motivated and you've simply added a new fuel to the fire. When people ask who I hate playing against, well, it's the guys who are incredibly talented and who are nice blokes as well. You've got nothing to latch on to. No fuel.

I tried to play rugby the right way, to help my team win within the rules and leave it at that. But I look back at some of the things I said and did and think 'Jesus'.

James: What about the highs and lows that came with your life in rugby. Not only are you going from competing in 90,000-seater stadia to being alone in a hotel room dealing with nerves within the space of a few hours, but you also had such intense media attention to deal with.

Jonny: I don't know whether I dealt with it well. When I look back, the stuff on the field was the simple stuff. My whole career was played out as a battle of dealing with stress on and off the field. When I was dealing with it well, those were the successful periods of my career and life.

On one side of the coin is the public perception and media comment, and on the other I just wanted to be the best I could be, and to concentrate on getting better. If you can steer your journey towards the latter, then you're winning, but there's so much that's dragging you over into the other side. The challenging bit was tempering the emotional effect of all the outside stuff. The environment and support we had in 2003 from the England staff was incredible because it meant that we didn't have to work as hard ourselves to find that balance. We had every base covered there, we had the optimum set-up, so that we kept on the right road.

James: Was that the best the support systems have ever been, in 2003?

Jonny: More than anything there was this feeling that the support system was just so tight that if we slipped up in any way, we wouldn't take a big fall. Any mishap, any mistake was covered.

The whole enterprise was about making the players feel secure, regardless of whether they were going to play every game or not.

Making them feel that they didn't need to watch their backs or worry about having a good or bad game. Some coaching teams today lack faith in a player if they hit a run of bad performances, and this forces a player to look down, not ahead. That pressure wasn't there.

There's always a reason to think of the negatives as an athlete until you realise that in terms of where you want to go it's all unhelpful. I survived all that exterior stuff I suppose in the end, even with all the negativity.

Reflecting back though, in the second half of my career I could have been better. I was concentrating too hard on trying not to fail, rather than to be as good as I could be.

James: Was the work you were doing not as solid?

Jonny: The training work was good, but the performances weren't, because I was shooting for eight and maybe getting a six and just surviving. I didn't know I was doing that at the time, but fear of failure is protecting yourself. Maybe you take away risk, but you put a ceiling on where you can go. At my best times I was aiming for a ten, not eight.

Because I worked so hard, because I had that work ethic for the training, I could easily think I was giving it my all when I wasn't. I was the guy that always went the extra yard and worked harder than anyone. Ironically though, I was holding back mentally without knowing, but I was afraid of losing and failing, and was protecting myself.

In 2003 we looked ahead. The blokes could just focus on aiming for ten.

And, for the record, winning things isn't the same as getting the best out of yourself.

James: Where does the quality of training over the quantity come in? Is it a matter of how many hours you do, or is it the quality of the hours?

Jonny: I've got on the wrong side of this balance for a long time. Everything comes down, in the end, to game-realistic training, and less is more. But the less is only more when it's incredibly focused mentally, game-realistic. You want to get yourself where you need to be as quickly as possible. If you can do it in the first practice kick, then you know you're on the mark. So, it's about getting to the place you need to be quickly, then being able to maintain that ability for a while, and then getting out.

Finding that place often takes incredible mental effort and visualisation, and that's why game-intensity training is hard to do.

If you're trying to learn the skill at the beginning, there's a period where lots of time is needed to be invested. I can't come to you if you haven't ever kicked a ball and instruct you to just go out there and do a great kick. You don't know what it feels like, so in order to do that you have to train that side of it extensively. Then as you get that and have it imprinted, there come the times where you need to develop the skill.

So there has to be inordinate repetitions in there, especially initially, and that gives you an ability to feel, which allows you to later take the stress off the repetitions, do more of the work mentally, get there quicker, do shorter work. In order to work on new things to get better again, or to improve a technical aspect, the repetitions may have to be higher again. It's almost like a cycle of acquiring the groundwork and volume, then encouraging the game-realistic pressure side. Once that's done, then start a new move or skill with repetitions again, and so on.

The quality of practice

The number of squash players I've seen with extreme ability and yet who didn't have the motivation or want to further themselves through hard work is worth noting. You hear it said: 'He or she would have been top class if ...'

And the question is 'if what?'

To whomever created us, let's give thanks for making it like this. It really wouldn't be fair if those who grafted in life didn't get rewarded somehow. The other thing to add to this is that there are those people who are talented and able, who do all the graft in the world, and STILL can't reach the heights they want!

Getting up each day would be a fairly pointless exercise if everything in life came down completely to the innate implications set out at birth. The reason the best are the best and the very able are just 'talented' is because the best always know about having to get off their arse and work repeatedly and, more tellingly, work at the right intensity.

So these people figure that it's not just about doing any old work, but about doing the right work. And this is what Jonny is getting at when he's talking about game-intensity training. People have called it 'deep' or 'deliberate' practice.

There have been extremely able squash players who practise quite hard. They certainly put the hours in, but remain ever so slightly within a range that comforts them, thinking that's enough. This player can hold a very decent standard, perhaps a very good standard, even a national standard, but they can't regularly push themselves to the depths in training, they soon realise the heat of the situation, and at a certain level they plateau. The fact is that lots of people could have been a lot of things, but they maybe didn't want to or couldn't go to the depths of intensity in their learning process.

The strong motivation required to do the deep practice, the nasty practice, the practice that's horrible and intense and demanding and painful, isn't always there.

It's a degree of repetition but with the added concentration. It's what those who are world class always have the strength and willingness, often delusion, to do. And this is no criticism on those who don't. I've questioned my life in squash often. I only have a limited amount of time, probably just one life. How long do I really want to keep doing the same thing that I've done year after year, which is unkind on the body, and strenuous on the mind? Why strive to be so good at just one thing? Why so specific? Maybe these world-class people are not stronger, or more admirable. Maybe they are too single-minded, narrow-minded, too one-dimensional! There's lots to life – nice options, lovely ways to spend afternoons, in parks or cafes, eating cakes. Wouldn't it be preferable to stroll through life a bit, doing a job that allows you to be in a comfort zone?

After all this discussion, the point is that people who achieve high, high standards get into the habit of practising, training or learning intensely, with total commitment. It's not half-hearted, it's devotion in fact. And it's usually extremely uncomfortable.

In acting, Alex doesn't just learn lines and hope for the best, he analyses the script in detail, works out motivations, discusses the play in depth with a director. Jess doesn't just sit on a bike for an hour listening to her favourite tracks and pissing about, she will be discussing every aspect of her hurdle and long-jump technique with coaches, or in the gym pushing her body to the limits it must reach in an Olympic final. Julian doesn't just write a draft and send it to the publisher. He examines and contemplates every word, has it edited and re-edited and drafts the thing multiple times.

Jonny: What I would do early on in my career is get there early before games and kick and kick on a Friday and Saturday morning. I would kick, say, 100 balls and get 90 out of 100. That ten I missed would be enough to create the doubt.

But when you come at it from a quality angle, you might hit ten instead and make nine, and then the one missed isn't so much a problem in your head! But I would hit so many, aiming for such perfection, that I would tire myself mentally and always fail in my own mind.

So, what probably should have happened was that on Monday and Tuesday I wouldn't be kicking at the goal posts and working with such a 'pass and fail' element to it. I would start with something that is related to a certain aspect I want to achieve. So, if I'm kicking at the goal posts on Monday I would be dealing with cross tick cross tick, and why? So, I might work on the strike, then on Tuesday the line, then body shuns through the ball or whatever. By the time I get to Thursday I can start to hit at the posts, but rather than maybe think about hitting volumes of balls, I build it up and break it down technically. Then by Friday I might have more chance of looking at the ten out of ten.

I can go into the game on Saturday fresher. Before, I would go through my same intense routine of kicking goal after goal, and I was probably ready to play on Monday or Tuesday! By Saturday I was just worn out with the intensity. It's not sustainable.

If you do it the way I suggested, by Saturday you have pure evidence. I know what I've worked on through the week: I've got great feel, great strike, great results, am hitting great lines, and I've ticked the boxes and am fresh to go out and play. I was playing a game every day with the old method.

James: How did you approach the really horrible, tough sessions? The ones that hurt.

Jonny: I was lucky with Blackie because we never knew what we were going to do with him. So, we simply went out hard, no matter. He would set us off running, and those who went hard he might tell to stop. The ones who didn't might be kept going. You would be on the bench press and he could say do two reps or 12. You would never know, and I think this was actually a great way to do it, because it translated on the field. I wasn't thinking about shall I run for that, have I got energy for this, shall I track back? It was just go for it, get that ball, no questions asked. We just went out hard and he wanted all we had. It made us tough.

I had to win any fitness test. My competitive side came out in these situations. I would go to bed early and not sleep, thinking about these fitness tests, treating them like games. I would go to Blackie and say, 'Look, I know it's not ideal but I want to train for the next fitness test.'

There were things I did during my career that were ridiculous, not helping in any way, but that was how I was designed, so I was doing stupid amounts of tests. I couldn't see them as just fitness tests. It was a do or die thing and I had to succeed. I still train now and get incredibly nervous before those sessions. I know they are going to be tough and I friggin' hate them, but at the same time the feeling you get afterwards is unbeatable.

James: There's nothing like it. Horrific beforehand, blissful after. So, you approached them by not questioning or thinking about them.

Jonny: Yes. It's not good knowing about the session then having it hanging over you.

James: How much analysis of every detail must be done? Do you watch matches back and dissect every detail of it, and can there be too much?

Jonny: It was in many ways already happening from within me. I almost didn't need to watch videos. I would hate it. I would know. Mistakes in games would just hurt that much that I never wanted to feel like that again. I could sulk for three days afterwards because I hadn't made a decent pass where I needed to.

What would frustrate me after matches wouldn't be the things I did wrong, but the things I didn't always have the courage to do. I would go out and practise all these amazing things in training but then not go with them in the match. I would be furious with myself about this and thought this was one of my biggest failings. In that masculine, macho sense I thought I didn't have the balls to go out there and test it. The only way to get better was to force yourself to believe it, that these things could be converted on to the field on the big occasion.

You have to ask yourself if you want to go out there and be the best you can be, and keep searching to better yourself, or whether you just want to hold on to what you know, to what you're comfortable with.

—

'Fortune favours the brave' is a familiar sort of cliché, but as I got older, I came to love it and appreciate it as quite a clever motto. One of the worst things that can happen when you're striving so hard is to plan to do lots of excellent things in whatever you do, in your practice and preparation, only to then not implement them when it matters. The worst thing is to stay safe. In sport especially it's so, so easy to defend, to not take the game to an opponent, to take the percentage option. Of course, at times we're all on the back foot and of course we need to defend or consolidate, but sometimes we really need to go with it, especially if we've practised it.

Having said that, it's mightily, mightily hard to do. I came off court countless times after matches berating myself and wondering why I didn't just free myself up and go for those plays that I constantly practised. In the heat of a battle it's difficult. It would be the same for actors in an audition or for an after-dinner speaker. In each case it would be easy to not say or do the things you wanted to, or had practised. Going with instinct, being yourself, is a fantastic state to explore, and I'm so impressed when athletes have the guts to go for a risky shot in a big moment on a big occasion.

Latterly, I tried to not be hard on myself if I made errors going for a risky shot or play. If I had practised it, then I had to try it, and should never be regretful for trying it.

What a great lesson to at least try to heed, though, for anyone in any walk of life. To not get too safe, too comfortable, or risk-averse. Keep being different, practise differences, constantly vary the landscape and be brave.

———

James: Can you tell me a bit more about how you incorporated visualisation?

Jonny: There were times where I would have a CD on the morning or the night before the game, from Dave. I would have the crowd buzzing, the sounds of the tackle, and I would lie on the bed and immerse myself in it, visualising scenarios. When I was injured, I would go down to the swimming pool and draw ticker tapes on the pool. It was all visualisation. We would pass and step in the pool.

To not involve the mind in forms of practice is like negating the activity, it's a waste. For example, Blackie would set us these bike sessions, and the idea was never simply to go faster or slower. But as we put the resistance up, we would be imagining making a break, or going into a contact, going into someone's legs. And we would all be there, eyes closed on the bikes, just doing it. In terms of skills, what it means is that because I've visualised these scenarios, the template is there for when it happens in a game. It's no surprise, I've seen it and dealt with it before, and we all know that practising a scenario makes us better.

If I pass a ball, I know already how it's going to feel. You start to bring your visualisations into the match situation. And when it starts to align, that's when you confuse what's visualisation and what's training.

I used it during my time with injuries too. If you can't train, well you can lie on the bed and visualise. Five minutes a day can be powerful.

It has to help. If you do an aimless bike session, for instance, not even relating it to rugby, what have you done? Nothing to do with a rugby match at all. Without somehow putting that activity and relating it to the one you want to get better at, your improvement will be limited. The mind works incredibly hard during competition, so it makes sense to tap into that side of things. Why would an athlete simply practise the movements without using the emotional and mental side of it?

The actual practice itself can be more exacting too, so the visualisation sessions can give you a form of training that tires the body less, which can be really helpful at times.

If Jason Robinson does a speed session, I doubt he's going to be thinking about what he's going to eat for lunch. He will be imagining himself while he's training even, in these scenarios, with a player hunting him down, and so on.

James: The tapes you had before matches, what would they have on them? How detailed technically?

Jonny: Very technical. So, the voice would say, 'Okay, make a left shoulder tackle, accelerate into the tackle. Low shoulder, big leg drive.' But also you would hear on the tape Ben Cohen [team-mate of Jonny's] shouting something, or the crowd coming in. Dave was a genius with all this. He understood brilliantly the mind, body and skill acquisition, and that's what it was. The first tackle I made on the field that day wasn't the first tackle I had made that day, if you like.

And it's worth noting, when you do mental visualisation it's very rare that you imagine things going badly.

James: Does it always have to be a positive visual?

Jonny: Why not? You can actually make it practically perfect. So, I would advise practising something perfectly in your mind first, then doing it for real, whilst trying not to worry about anything technical.

You could do one without the ball and the action, and one with the action, and try to match them up, then you can start to match them together.

James: Thanks for the advice!

Jonny: Ha! You're welcome!

Alison Rose

THERE ARE few people who have given so much to me personally for so little in return as Alison. There are possibly three or four people without whom my squash career simply would never have existed the way it does, and Alison is one. I consider myself fortunate beyond belief to have met her and she has been my physio and friend for 13 years. She helped me through two surgeries and a lifetime of body maintenance, as I worked it hard every day on court. Squash takes a huge toll out of any body, and her countless hours of effort have kept me sound. She would spend dedicated time repairing me, aligning me, recalibrating me, only for me to jump on more flights to play three weeks of matches and arrive back crooked and burnt out. She would simply start the process again, or perhaps we should say continue it.

I certainly wouldn't have enjoyed the last few years of my career if it wasn't for her. She nursed me back from hip surgery, prior to which one doctor had declared I would be hard-pressed to play again. She actually gave me the chance to experience playing at the highest level again, in wonderful venues around the world. I got to play another Commonwealth Games, reach a semi-final of a World Championships, the finals of the World

Series at Dubai Opera House, and win two more British titles. She's the most modest person, considering her frankly astounding understanding and knowledge of physiotherapy and intuition about how the human body functions; she's a strong character and leader who always instils me, one of her patients, with such confidence.

Olympic champions Jess Ennis-Hill and Kelly Holmes moved the earth to have her in their corners and she's worked with successful British diving and triathlon teams extensively, amongst many other world-level athletes, but she talks as animatedly about helping her 80-year-old neighbour in Otley back on his feet.

It would be remiss of me not to mention her team in Leeds, including Graeme Everard, Jenny Birch and Ian Mitchell, who I've relied on so often for help. Her clinic in Leeds is an operation that just oozes excellence and high standards. People, including many athletes who know of its reputation, travel from all over the place to get a session there. How grateful I am to have lived only 20 minutes away for much of my career.

—

JW: You were saying earlier to me that you were interviewing today for new staff to join your clinic. Could you perhaps start by saying how rigorous this process is and what you're looking for?

AR: We set them some questions, look at backgrounds. We consider their ethos of treatment, how they go about looking at various injuries. Their experience is also important, who they have worked with. I'm very interested to speak to them about how they might manage certain issues. For example, if we're talking about an injury to an athlete, then I want to look at how that gets managed through the coach.

We want someone who can fit into this environment and communicate freely with other staff and patients. I've no time for egos. It's absolutely vital, too, that they are able to acknowledge if they can't solve something and ask for help.

In specific physio terms I'm looking for people who don't just look at the sore area; I want to see if they can take the whole body and look at the reasons why injuries might be happening. So, it's a rigorous and considered process.

JW: You've made a reputation for yourself. Many people would acknowledge that you're a world-class physio. Did you or do you have ambitions for this?

AR: I wouldn't see myself in the same way you described at all! If I'm successful, then that comes from what my patients tell me. But, basically, I want to do a good job. I love the body, how it works, how it all fits together. I'm intrigued and want to keep learning.

But whether it's the man off the street, who is trying to put one foot in front of another, or a world-class athlete in an Olympic stadium, in the end I just want to help people get on their feet and be able to use their bodies the way they want.

If you're that person who has too much pain in the mornings to be able to have a nice time with your kids or to go to work, then that's a miserable and often unnecessary state of affairs for them to have to deal with. If I can get someone pain free and able to move well, I get great satisfaction out of helping them to discover it.

I find it a bit bemusing when people talk about me as successful or having standing in sporting circles. Working with world athletes perhaps gives you that reputation, especially if they happen to talk about your work. I'm just there and have a job to do. What's good about our high-profile athletes endorsing it readily is that it might get the wider public to invest in physiotherapy and understand it as a preventive thing. There are ways of achieving good body health, and that doesn't have to mean living on painkillers. We've had loads of people coming forward when our high-profile athletes talk or write about it.

I do appreciate people within the profession, though, and really recognise some as being at the top of their game in our industry. I want to learn from them. I've worked with excellent, world-class people, so yes, I'm always aspiring to improve what I do.

JW: I understand. Being world class at what you do, I'm not implying you just work with superstar athletes. Your being so good is what makes the person off the street recover from their hip replacement. Are you still learning? You do courses, don't you?

AR: I love going on courses. I'm not someone who enjoys reading scientific papers particularly. I love the courses though, learning new techniques. Although, if I've got a problem and I want to research, I will. But the more experience you've got, the more you can work things out. Getting someone better is like putting together the pieces of a jigsaw puzzle, and background and experience helps.

The last course I did was fantastic, run by a guy who was absolutely top notch. I took so many things from that and applied it to what I was doing. You have to be so open to these things.

JW: You're very good at delegating or asking other physios for input to a problem. Why is that important?

AR: Big egos are pointless. We all need help. We can't solve everything, so you have to lean on others, seek other opinions. We all rely on inspiration; I can't figure out everything and no one ever will, however good they are. They have to see that in themselves and not be too proud to ask for opinions from others who might work better with a certain problem.

I've just asked a doctor colleague to come to the clinic today because, quite frankly, I'm working with a patient and I've hit a dead end with it. I'm struggling to see the wood for the trees. I have to be able to admit that though. Hopefully, his perspective can help me a little. And like all squash players, I would think, physios have certain areas they are stronger in. Some handle problems with ankles better than problems with backs or nerves, for instance. One of my physios might have a special knowledge or experience relating to a particular problem, so why wouldn't I then ask their opinion on it?

—

Ali has touched on something here that's pertinent to any person wanting to reach a standard, to achieve high, or to improve. The point is to keep the horizons wide, to open the arms to ideas but then to be discerning and clever about which to embrace. We all need a second, third or fourth pair of eyes. If anyone ever believes they are the only source of information, the only opinion and that their method is the only way, then I'm not buying it. I struggle with the whole phenomenon of autocratic leaders. I'm not sure it's possible for them to actually exist successfully if their autocracy is total. Maybe they have done, but being autocratic implies a closedness, and it has to be questioned to be the best way.

People in the UK might think about football managers Brian Clough and Alex Ferguson as being big characters and autocratic leaders. Everyone knew who was in charge but were they totally unequivocal in their opinions and regimes? I can't believe they were. Just look at the range of players they managed and developed, all with different styles and ways of expressing themselves. Their disciplines and high standards may have been extreme and eccentric, but they did create an environment from which players could flourish and find their own styles. From the outside it looked like there were rules and systems, but certainly no pressure to have to simply do it one way.

Those who know my father Malcolm would perceive him to be totally autocratic, allowing no answer back from any quarter. In reality he's a sensitive romantic softie, and whilst his methods of discipline and structures were legendary and perhaps sometimes a little feared, one of his abilities as a coach has been his willingness to actually be adaptable and open to any changes I've needed to make as a professional squash player. His style of coaching is quite open too, meaning that he doesn't impose strict techniques on his players, which helps you understand why they all end up different.

In the past I've had freedom to work with other coaches, tried to embrace all aspects of the game, and taken on different ideas and thoughts under his watch. He has readily embraced and taken on these new ideas, rather than ever feel them as a threat, and not only has this helped us both to improve at what we do, it has, more importantly, helped to keep our relationship a happy and healthy one. He's a father as well as a coach, and too heavy a hand from him wouldn't have been conducive to a long-term squash career.

As we get better as businesspeople, athletes, physios, teachers, politicians, it would be easy to think we know best, and that nobody could possibly help us to push further. It's at this point we tread dangerous ground.

———

JW: Yes, you sometimes refer me to the osteopath when you've had enough of me. I've noticed that. Are there lots of levels of physiotherapist, like there are levels of athlete?

AR: Physios do the same basic degree course to begin with but there are universities that run better courses and have better lecturers. But after that it depends on you as a person, how you use the skills, the people you work with. We can all be called physios, but it's the ones who push themselves that gain a reputation through what they do. Everyone passes a driving test but there are different levels of driver.

JW: Is there an innate ability in physio or are you learning it?

AR: There's natural ability. There are physios who can feel things, the geniuses have got that ability to feel things, that sixth-sense thing. Some I find have an ability to really listen to the story of the patient at the beginning. They probe, they ask the right questions, and then they have an intuition about the answers they are given. They might be able to figure out that a fall three years ago had done some underlying damage. There can be things that happened to patients ten, 20 years ago that all add up to what you feel in the present moment with a patient. I've taught people things and spoken to them and I know they just can't feel what they are trying to treat. This can be improved through time and effort, but some people clearly have a natural ability for it. I think learning about the visceral and cranial stuff has helped me to get better at this.

JW: Sorry, can you tell me a bit more about what you mean by visceral and cranial? It's not on the physio degree courses is it?

AR: No, the visceral work I've been exploring is an osteopathic technique. Jean-Pierre Barral, an intuitive genius, created these techniques. I've been learning it for ten years now and it's about the organs, how they function and move within the body. Organs can go into spasm and not move very well, then, put simply, that can add stress on other areas of the body. Cranial treatments are osteopathic. Bones in your head are like tongue-and-groove joints: there's a bit of movement there that can enable the fluids in your brain to be healthier, so to speak. If you've have a head injury or dental work, there can be issues that can then offset the nervous system and create problems.

JW: You've been a high-level marathon runner as well. What do you think of the word 'talent'? Has innate talent been a big part of what you've seen, both as a physio and an athlete?

AR: To get to the highest level in anything I think you need a degree of talent at whatever that particular thing is. But this is a complex issue; for a squash player there are a whole bunch of things that fit under that, it's clearly not just one simple skill. For a start, I would actually add that there's probably a degree of talent needed for not getting injured.

But we all know you can have all the talent, and without the will to work hard it will get you nowhere, which is why so many talented people can't make it. There are definitely people who have less talent but who work and work and work and can make it to a very high level. There are people like Kelly Holmes, who has the work ethic and natural ability together. She perhaps didn't have the ability for staying injury free. Lucky enough for both of us, we worked together for the last two years of her career to keep her healthy for the 2004 Olympics. Once she did have that free run, all that talent and hard work could come together, and she could fly the way everyone knew she could.

You look at these brilliant athletes, like Jess, and you quickly fall into thinking it must be easy for them, but Jess worked incredibly hard, through injuries, and especially coming back from the pregnancy. The phenomenal work ethic was there, masses of talent, she had a great brain and was a great competitor. She's also good at – and this could also be a talent – having balance in her life. She knew how to rest well. Then she chose her team wisely – biomechanists, coaches, strength coaches – she had the foresight and talent to listen to the right people. So, there are lots of talents that she probably had, and they came together to make her the world's best.

JW: That's actually a talent in itself isn't it, knowing when to wind down, having a life!

AR: I've seen so many people never come down from their training. They overtrain and it's all far too intense. They don't recognise that they need to implement certain things into their routines and that includes balance outside the court or training. It's easy for athletes to do the training we love, that makes us think we will improve ourselves or feel like we've worked hard, but that isn't always the best. You have to be very clever about doing the different things, the stuff you're weaker on, the stuff you don't easily feel is improving you but actually is.

JW: Such a great point. We convince ourselves we've worked hard, and we settle for that, not knowing it could be totally ineffectual with regard to what we're actually trying to improve. Many people will remember Kelly not quite being at the very top before the Athens Olympics, and she was injured a lot. So how did you work that out with her?

AR: She was always brilliant enough but was lacking a smooth run. She never got the results she deserved because of the disruptions. At the Atlanta Games she was primed but then got off the plane and discovered a stress fracture. She still came fourth, by a small margin. That's incredible. She knew the risks too, and was told not to run, but she did. In Sydney she had been injured and got a bronze. We found a way of managing everything in those two years, everything improved, she was able to train freely, her injury resilience got better, she knew how to maintain her body health. Confidence grew and she knew she wasn't just going to fall apart.

She came to live near the university where I was in Leeds and we were working together often then. She knew Athens was going to be her last Olympics. She would get the smallest niggle and turn up on the doorstep. We wouldn't stop until it was fixed.

JW: How did you meet?

AR: I had met her a few times, and she was in Sheffield at the EIS where I worked, seeing the doctor. Around then I went over to South Africa to work with her and we kept going.

JW: She clearly felt comfortable.

AR: It just clicked. Bryan English, the doctor we worked with, was fantastic and intuitive. He was diagnosing things brilliantly. She changed coaches and the attention to detail she gave the whole thing was first-rate.

JW: Can you give a little bit of insight into the depths you go to with patients during rehabilitation of big injuries. You don't just send people off for major surgery and tell them to rest, do you?

AR: Rehab after surgery is a massive deal, and the whole process is important. It's crucial for the person treating to be aware of the whole issue, the history of the patient, the whole body. There's no point in me simply giving a patient a whole load of eccentric calf raises to do for an Achilles problem if the problem originates from the hip or upper back. It's a global approach that's required. Then you have to carefully plan and incorporate what cross-training to introduce and when. It's crucial the physio can identify the underlying causes rather than just simply alleviate pain short term.

JW: A word perhaps about the work you're doing with cancer …

AR: It began when I was working with a lady who, as she was in the last six months of her life, had systemic abdominal problems, nausea and bloating in her abdomen; lots of pain.

She wasn't able to breathe or eat easily. At this point the nutrition and general health is compromised and things just spiral. I had heard about a doctor using Kinesio tape, a tape sportspeople use to attempt to change some of those symptoms. I said to the lady that it might be worth a try. She had some of the most amazing results and her quality of life was vastly improved over the last six months of her life. We're aiming for funding to research it now. It's drug free, non-invasive, and it could be something that just helps the body to function that bit better, which can be significant for someone who is badly ill. It's obviously a great thing if it can help in a small way to increase that time a person has left with friends and family. So, it's an exciting project.

We don't get people with cancer considering going to a physio, and it's really good to be pushing this forward now as an option to really help.

JW: It's been great hearing an insight into your world. It's good for people to understand how much goes into what you do.

AR: It's one of those funny professions where if you're injury free all the time because the coach and physio do a great job, then you can find it hard to measure the importance of physio. What we're in essence trying to do is put ourselves out of a job, in a funny way.

JW: But those people who you help ought to keep you in a job by investing in physio on a long-term basis as something that can sustain body health. Athletes like me know about how vital your work is. If I'm getting through tournaments consistently, then that means your work is spot on. I presume getting this over to non-athletes is the challenge.

AR: Yes, but even some top athletes still don't fully embrace it. It's a performance-orientated physio package we put together and many fully buy into it, but there are athletes who might not see the benefit of spending an hour or putting money into it. You can understand that to a point, but people need to see it as essential. When your car needs fixing, it gets fixed because it's a priority. Eating good food is a priority, regardless of expense. It's a long-term thing we're talking about, but hard to measure.

The reason Jess won those gold medals after the injury, and then the Worlds after having had a baby, was because of attention to detail from her and her coach. Hard, hard work. Training in a boot, unable to walk, working on the javelin throw with her arm when she was only capable of sitting on something. That attention to detail, tedious as it was, was there.

JW: Her recovery to become world champion after having a baby was amazing. Almost the best achievement of all!

AR: It was a new experience. Toni, her coach, had to be very skillful in managing her reintroduction, as did she. None of us knew much about bringing a new mother back to competing at Olympic level again, and it's quite rare! Toni had everything analysed, yet it was territory he probably didn't know much about at first. From my point of view, it was essential to bring Jess carefully back in, making sure every area was strong enough so she could move on to the next levels of training.

Alistair Brownlee

ALISTAIR IS the Olympic and multiple World Championship-winning triathlete, who lives and trains in Yorkshire. He's often mentioned in relation to his younger brother Jonny, also a World Triathlon Champion, and together they have become superstars of the sport. They have pushed each other to the limits over the years, and probably know more than anyone the intricacies of the North Yorkshire cycle networks. You can catch them skirting the Yorkshire countryside on runs or bike rides, or filling up on teacakes at the county's best cafes, notably often with the training partners they have known and worked with since they were kids.

They are certainly modern athletes, who have remained unusually down to earth with regards to their attitudes towards training. I know of very few great athletes who are in the unique position of still working at the original clubs and with the original groups they always did. Often, and quite necessarily, world-class athletes move on to bigger things, fancy central training centres with all the latest technologies and advancements.

Of all the people I interviewed, I feel Alistair is the one who keeps things as simple as possible, sometimes eschewing, without ever dismissing, new-fangled techniques. His work is done up hills, in pools, gyms, not in science laboratories. It's what people refer to as old school. Not rocket science perhaps, but like all hard training: ridiculously difficult.

What's certain is his work ethic and lifelong commitment to improvement as an endurance athlete.

He was genuinely interested in the comparisons in different fields too, and the subject of what makes a world-class performer or artist.

—

JW: Can you explain what makes you so successful as a triathlete?

AB: Erm ... I don't know really! I think a large part of it is genetics. I think this is especially important in an endurance sport. That ability to have a big aerobic engine. More and more for triathlon you need a massive capability for aerobic fitness. I believe starting young is an advantage; I've got my parents to thank for that! Swimming is a sport in which you have to start early to get the technique, and I was fortunate to start that young. I started running young, and serious endurance training came in at 14 or 15. It's a time when you can change a lot of things about how your body works. But all this was fortuitous. My parents were into it, and having a brother to race and compete against has been important. And more than anything you probably need an instilled love of it! I wake up every day thinking how fortunate I am to do something I enjoy. It's my hobby and my social life but it's how I make a living as well. I just derive a deep enjoyment from being outdoors and active.

JW: If one of those pivotal, coincidental factors hadn't materialised. do you think things could have been different? In your book you talked about a cycle ride that you did every day during your school years. You wrote that you felt it was lucky that there was a safe canal path route to take, which gave you hundreds and thousands of hours of cycling to and from school – experience that you could have missed if that one cycle path hadn't existed! Your mum wouldn't have let you ride had it been less safe, or if the only route had been on main roads.

AB: I've thought about writing a book about this! I could probably find 20 or 30 complete coincidences that ended up having a big effect. That example, riding to school, is a good one. We happened to go to a school that my parents liked the look of, but it just happened to be ten or 12 miles away, most of which was on the canal towpath. It sounds dodgy but it was the perfect traffic-free environment for 15-year-olds to cycle along, and I could do it every morning. Just think how many hours cycling I built up there.

Then the school happened to have a history in running. There was a running teacher, and they had produced a fair few good athletes over the years. They took kids out running every lunchtime to do time trials, and without that I definitely wouldn't have taken up running in the way I did.

Where we lived was another big factor. It was not only important that we could go out into the countryside, which had all the routes, but there was also this culture of sport. I know literally hundreds of cyclists and runners that we see almost every week who we can go out and train with. One Tuesday night when I was 13 or 14, my dad took me down the track. I started doing a lot of running but I wasn't fast. Someone said I needed some track work, so we went to the track and bumped into Malcolm Brown, who then became involved in my career in a major way. Since then he's been programme director for British Triathlon. He helped me out countless times, including funding training centres and all sorts. I could go on and on. You just think, 'What if?'

JW: Were you born a good triathlete or was it all those coincidences and all the work coalescing?

AB: I think talent's really interesting isn't it? In triathlon, if you break it down there's that definite physiological talent that most people think of: your talent to run for a long time or run fast. That's definitely very important, I think. So there's physiological talent, and aerobic talent is your baseline. But the bigger part of it is how well you respond to aerobic training, and that's the genetic thing that you get from your parents. I feel like that's massive. I feel like I'm a talented responder to training. When I train, I respond very, very quickly compared to other people.

I think there also has to be a mental aspect, a mental talent to it if you like. Not only to be motivated and tough enough to train day in, day out, but in my case it's enjoying being outdoors so that I can train for long enough. That's a talent in itself. Coping with pressure around the races could be described as talent. And also, that talent to actually be motivated then allows you to train. But they are all definitely interlinked. You have to go out and do the training. I'm sure there are hundreds of people my age out there, probably even in Leeds, who have got the physiological ability I had, but then it's all the other things: that I took up swimming at a young age and had the technical ability to do it; that I took up running at a young age; and by the time you stick in all the other factors you narrow it down, and that's where an Olympic champion maybe comes from.

JW: Do you think you could have been good at another sport if all those factors had been in place?

AB: I think any sport that was endurance-based I would have had a good go at. If I had concentrated on one of running or cycling at an early age I could have done well, but nowhere near the level I've reached in triathlon. Cycling, where there's a need for a big endurance engine, I might have done well at. Anything that involves hand-eye coordination, skill or sprinting I could forget. I'm sure that's where the genetics play a part because I was never going to run a fast 100m or play squash particularly well!

JW: How important are junior systems in triathlon? I started playing squash young and I passed through a system. Is there a system for a junior to pass through in triathlon, set competitions for example?

AB: Yes. Triathlon is a bit convoluted because traditionally kids come into it through swimming or running backgrounds and they can't rely on a 'triathlon' club. You have to be doing massive volumes of swimming from being about 8–14. You have to be doing a fair amount of running and a fair amount of cycling. You can't get that in one club – it would be nigh-on impossible asking a junior club to put on 15 sessions a week. There might be one out there, who knows? You want to be involved in a swimming club, which isn't always easy because swimming coaches don't necessarily want to be coaching triathletes. You have to be involved in an athletics club, which is a bit easier but still unusual. They don't always get involved with triathletes. There's a series of races that you can do from being about six, then you can qualify to race at the inter-county championships. So there's a pathway but I wouldn't say it's clear-cut. From these inter-counties and such you can move into the world-class programme.

But just going back to what you were saying about people asking how you do it, I think it's really interesting. Programmes are all well and good, but I sometimes say you 'can't see the wood for the trees'. It gets too complicated. In the same way for you, squash was about getting on the court, and your mind and body working through every possible shot and situation, which shot to hit at the right time. Time doing it. Triathlon is about swimming, cycling and running. People can ask what their running technique should be, what drills to do and what to practise, but because programmes and camps have the resources to pay someone to coach this little bit and that bit, doesn't mean that you should live by it. I think it can all get a bit complicated and convoluted at times, when, really, it's a simple sport where you need to go out and do a lot of training.

JW: What about the 10,000 hours business? Where does quality come into it? Is it just all about hours as a kid?

AB: You know, I'm not sure about quality as a kid. I read it, and why the 10,000 hours study is a bit wrong is that they did it on a violin school. They ended up with three or four groups. I think it was three, one that was local level, one that was national and one that were the top dogs. The 10,000 hours came from an average, but in that group one guy had done 3,000 hours and one had done 40,000 hours to get to that level! So, 10,000 was just the average once they had added them all together and divided by the number. Some people in the bottom group had done 20,000 hours, but they were nowhere near the guy in the top group who had done 3,000.

There's definitely a strong practice element in anything, like you were talking about in squash, for example. It's training your body to be as efficient as possible, and through repeating you build the skill. Triathlon is an efficiency sport: you get through the swim as easy as you can, you get through the bike, then you get through the most important part, the run, as best you can. You do that by making your body very efficient, and the earlier you start training that, in any way, the better.

JW: How do you approach the toughest sessions? Or is all that just mentally easy for you?

AB: I don't feel like it's an issue, it's part of the week. I'm just doing it. It's what I've done for the last ten years. You're probably the same, you work a lot off routine, and I wake up and know what I have to be doing that day. I try not to make too much of any one session. Yes, some sessions are going to be heavy, like my Tuesday night track session, but I don't worry about it. It's what it is, and I enjoy the feeling of having done it afterwards.

JW: From what I've read, you seem very relaxed in your approach. Many top athletes have obsessive compulsive traits or superstitions. Do you feel like it's helped being quite laid-back?

AB: I think so. For many fairly good athletes there's a bit of obsessive compulsive there. Whether that's because it's your personality or it's just the love of exercise or addiction to exercise … I do have a bit of that, but compared to Jonny it's nothing. We're at opposite ends of the spectrum. He's very OCD.

JW: The mental intensity of competitive racing takes its toll, so if you can be relaxed away from it you must be saving valuable mental energy.

AB: I always think that races are the easy bit. You spend months and months training for them and then you have a race, and you get five days of easy training. You can go somewhere and enjoy it and do the race. I think it's important that you can control the race and the outcome. It's interesting comparing triathlon and squash because I feel the nerves before the start line, but then once we're off, that goes. With squash, I would think, because of the gaps in between rallies, you have that time to get anxious. Maybe the nerves hit you again in between?

JW: Possibly. You always have periods in between points where the mind can start to play its tricks and you have to consider strategy under considerable physical duress. But it's similar, in that when the first rally starts there's a certain settling. How do you cope with the nerves and pre-race anticipation?

AB: I'm not bad. I have been nervous. I was definitely more nervous when I was younger. But it's better.

JW: How fine are the lines at the very top level? Running into the Olympics, people in the media and public just heard and saw you were the best, so they just think that in all likelihood you will win because of that. In reality it just isn't that simple is it? You can't just turn up and win.

AB: Yes, the lines are so fine. And since the Olympics there has come along this whole new demographic of people who watch triathlon who don't understand quite how fine it is. It's ridiculously fine. One of the best examples was a few years back in London where I was racing. I don't know what happened, but I had the smallest stomach problem, even if it was a stomach problem! That meant that I didn't absorb any water or gels in the time that I was racing and that had catastrophic effects for me. I had a temperature of 42 and was dying. If I was just a little bit better, I would have won that race. I was in a good position with 300 metres to go. Just a little bug and I ended up tenth and nearly dying!

JW: That was tough to watch. You've kept some of the training sessions you do the same for years, and you still go riding with the same groups you've always done. It brings the social aspect in and ensures you keep enjoying it. You make sure that you train in the countryside, which you enjoy. Does training in this way help you?

AB: It's very, very important. I think we've noticed it recently. It's the set-up that we started creating ten years ago just after I met Malcolm, and Jack, our running coach, when we were going on local tracks and area camps. A few years later Leeds became our High Performance Centre, and it has carried on from there. It was always funded by the university, so it's been a long time creating the environment and the sessions, and it's adapted and changed from being 15-year-olds to adult athletes. Outside that there are guys that we ride with who are top-level pro cyclists and I've known them since I was 12 or 13 years old. We go out for rides, stop at cafes, make it as enjoyable as possible. And there are people I've run with since I was ten years old. Sport is good like that isn't it? It brings people together and should be sociable. The more I think about it the more I would like to go slowly back towards that, a more traditional approach – swimming with swimming clubs, running with athletics clubs – certainly as we get a bit older, to keep the difference and freshness. It's the people, I think. A lot of the time when I've had a disappointment, like London 2013 when I kind of expected it, I'm just so glad it's over. Whereas the people that we're training with in that environment, they are just there for the love of it and that's motivating.

JW: It's something I really related to, reading your book. Because top-level sport is so intense, you do have to put incredibly hard sessions in that reach that intensity. But one thing my dad (and coach) is always trying to do is rein that tension in, so that some of the sessions we do are less taxing, where I'm not madly focused on specific shots, they are just done for the fun of it. It's good for self-preservation!

When you have a big disappointment you're not manic are you? You handle it quite well …

AB: A lot of the time when I've had a disappointment, like London this year when I kind of expected it, by the time I had done that race I was just so glad it was over. The few weeks leading in, of worrying and stress were probably the worst I've ever had because I knew I was in trouble.

JW: Anyone in big-time sport has to cope with highs and lows of competition and performance, of dealing with audiences and expectations. It's always the area in which an athlete's lot is wildly different to those people in 'normal' jobs. There are more extremes I feel. For instance, lots of normal jobs don't cause you to lie in bed replaying certain aspects of your work that day, making you unable to sleep. The output of adrenaline, the heart-rate increase, is drawn upon more regularly for a 'performer', especially one in the public eye. You talked about London 2012 being a big comedown. How do you deal with that?

AB: You build and build and build up to something like the Olympics, then you cross the line, and everything changes. Everything that you've been aiming for specifically for two or three years, it's suddenly gone, you've done it and there's a big hole to fill. I've always felt that sort of emptiness when I achieve something. It's a strange feeling.

The lows for me are injuries. Not just because I want to get out and train and get better, but like we talked about before, it takes everything away. It robs you of who you are: injuries take away your hobby, your passion, your job and your social life all in one.

JW: You hit the button when you were injured and couldn't train, when you said, 'Sport was so ingrained in me that when I couldn't train I lost perspective on life.' You actually do! If I'm ill and can't train, I get grumpy and lose a sense of contentment. The days don't work properly. They stumble and splutter and stall.

Have you embraced the new science that comes with professional sport nowadays?

AB: Well I've tried to test things and see if they work but with clear mantras. The first is: 'You've got to be able to see the wood for the trees.' Triathlon is an endurance sport, and you have to train for it. It's quite easy to get distracted. If it makes me go any faster, then it's worth trying. If it doesn't, then it's definitely not. I've experimented with all things. I've explored sports science in my early days and did testing regimes. We had these test results and I was always asking the day after, 'Does it change the training I'm doing? Am I doing anything differently?' I wasn't, so to me it wasn't worth doing. Attention to nutrition has been one thing that has made a big difference for me. I had a few stress fractures when I was younger, which I don't seem to have any more. Taking calcium after exercise has been very important because your uptake is a lot better. Performance nutrition is even more important. Water intake, calorie intake and how you take those in during races is something I'm definitely learning more about as I race more in the heat, especially if I eventually want to do longer racing.

JW: Longer than triathlon?

AB: Yes, Ironman perhaps. In a few years, maybe yet …

JW: Hellfire!

AB: Just to add, a lot of science that goes into bikes and the production has been helpful and interesting. We've worked on positioning on the bike and the bikes we use. We looked into all sorts before the Olympics and it's been an ongoing thing. Psychology I stay clear of. I've never seen a psychologist and raced faster. I suppose I have the 'if it ain't broke, don't fix it' idea about that. It's a very personal belief.

JW: The more I look at high-class performers in any field, I see changes of rhythms and pace. The best composers produce symphonies with light and dark, the greatest screenwriters know just when to follow a comical lighter scene with a darker dramatic one, and I know in squash that I can't just hit the same paced ball one after the other continuously. I take it this exists in a triathlon?

AB: During the run, the ability to change pace is very important. We spend a lot of time training for that in the different sessions we do at different paces. It can be how you break an opponent and quite often how you win a race. It's not just as simple as running as fast as you can.

JW: Are your weeks structured, and do you stick to a timetable, or is there room to adapt?

AB: When I'm in full training, the weeks are laid out and planned, and it's difficult to change things around. I'm not one who gets really worried if I'm supposed to ride my bike for two and a half hours, but I end up only doing two. Sessions can be tweaked here or there but the general sessions – swimming, riding and gym – will all be in place and planned. Everything else isn't especially fixed but they really have to be done at certain times, so we can fit them all in. So it's quite calculated and planned.

JW: Is there a session you like the least?

AB: Swimming's the one I struggle with the most because it's boring, it's inside. You're swimming up and down. We do it in the morning and I don't like getting up early!

JW: Are you good at letting go of the sport outside of training? How important is this side of your life? Do you give yourself a chance to eat and drink your favourite foods and treats, if you have them?

AB: Yeah, I think it's very important to enjoy your time away if you can, and I don't worry about diet massively.

JW: You probably don't need to worry about restricting calories, I guess, with all the burning you're doing.

AB: Do you have to watch what you eat?

JW: I'm more prone to putting on weight, so I have to be careful if I'm in a rest period. I'm a fluctuater.

AB: I can put on weight! I don't worry. I'm an on/off person, and when I'm off, I'm really off. That's my mentality. When I have downtime I enjoy a drink or two.

JW: Yes, I've had some disgusting off seasons. The coaching staff at England Squash saw me with my top off one summer and they started asking questions. I must have been about four or five kilos overweight that summer after having had my two weeks rest plus another two weeks of illness. After the first two weeks, I needed to stop eating, but because I was ill I didn't. It was a disgrace, an elongated and brilliant rest. Interestingly, I became world number one for the first time eight months later, the following season. I always think about that. Who knows what good having that graze did me!

Quoting from your book again: I remember where you wrote that when you were injured and couldn't train, that not training was messing with your pipes! People who don't exercise won't know the buzz you get from doing it. When you can't do it, you really miss it!

AB: I understand why a lot of ex-athletes become alcoholics and substance abusers.

JW: Thanks for talking with me. It's been really interesting.

AB: It's interesting meeting people from other sports. The same principles run through it all. I did *Superstars* last year and that was fascinating. Mo Farah was there, a runner, swimmers, and as an endurance athlete I can relate to what they do. And rowers, they are an interesting bunch. There was also a shooter and a high jumper. It's interesting because some of those are so completely different that they are similar. The shooter said he needed a six-week block of training and that it lifted him. He said he needed to do that block.

JW: Some people can't imagine certain sportsmen or women adhering to strict training regimen. Some people sometimes ask me, 'Do you ever go in the gym?'

AB: Yes! When you know nothing about a discipline, you just think they turn up and do it whenever they want. But all athletes seem to have a propensity for dedicated work. And the six-week block, I do the same. I saw the parallels.

Environment at a young age

When I find myself in a favourite city for a world squash event, or walking in front of 800 people in a major final, or even if I'm miserable and feeling sorry for myself because I have to stand in another passport control queue, I imagine how fortunate I've been to find variation, travel and novelty whilst playing my favourite game, for cash.

Yes, the travel gets tiring; yes, the training gets painfully hard; yes, being injured is crushing; but it's a charmed life. I can choose to get out of bed when I want to, there's freedom and riches to be enjoyed as an athlete, and competition to me is a form of natural high, which I'm grateful to have in my life. A form of competition is challenging and taps into that combative instinct some of us harbour, and this gives me direction and purpose to every day. I dread the day that competition isn't part of the routine.

None of this would have been possible without fortune. To be the squash player I am today, who enjoys this life, I had to have a seriously specific and conducive environment to ease me along. I had no idea what was happening when I was young, I just went about it. But when I look back and think what I had available to me I can't state how important it was: a world-class coaching set-up and facility, a social hub where I saw pals and professional players, and which also happened to be my dad's workplace. Pontefract was an inviting and inclusive squash club that allowed kids on court at all times of day. No stuffiness, no elitism, no daft rules, and as was the case with Alistair, it was near where we lived.

I would come home from school and go straight to the club because it was the most comfortable, exciting and stimulating option available to me. I didn't think I was training, as Alistair probably didn't when he rode to school and back every morning and evening. The winter weather in England is dank, so there were fewer kids playing out back home in the winter anyway, and Dad worked at the club, so it made sense to just go there.

I remember watching the last half an hour of the professionals' training session (as the kids sometimes do now) whilst hoovering a Sherbet Dip, then I would change and join in Malcolm's group sessions for an hour or so. The hours of learning I got through during those young years no doubt gave me that life later down the line, but I never would have known at the time that that lifestyle would give me my career.

It doesn't have to be quite this ideal, but many things have to fall into place. The other masterstroke about this whole system I lived through is that the kids who are part of it are not thinking this all might be affecting what happens in a major professional tournament final in 15 years' time. And neither should they unless they contain that ambition for themselves.

Pontefract is still my home club, and despite living a bit further away now, I always try to get there two or three times a week to join in with Malcolm's sessions, the sessions I always did as a kid.

I find mixing in with different people and doing different things within the sessions gives me variation and a sense of enjoyment, and I feel lucky to walk into a place to work where I feel such a warmth.

The point here, as Alistair alluded to, is that not all training has to be all-out clinical, severely calculated and completed at great intensities. It can be so invigorating and helpful for me to go to practise with the groups at Pontefract and just get on with that session. Alistair probably doesn't always need to be training with other world-class triathletes, and in fact I very rarely step on court with anyone who has a world ranking when I'm at home training, because it doesn't matter. We're training so often, so hard at times, that it's vital to make training motivating, variable and fun to an extent, and I feel I get a lot of worth from hitting with different standards of player. There's a sort of freedom about going back to my club and training with the players there, and it was the routine I grew up with. I just feel, especially now looking back at it all, that I couldn't walk into an intense atmosphere where the training just nails you into the ground every day. There has to be lightness, because otherwise it's burn-out time.

I go to training and coaching camps where people ask me for the big answers to the big questions on technique and tactics, and I often tell people that I spent hours and hours on court hitting the bloody ball down at the club, working the geometry of the squash court out for myself. For some reason that made me good. And yes, training has become scientific; yes, as athletes strive to improve there's a certain level of analysis that needs to be explored, but to quote Alistair's favourite phrase: 'You can't always see the woods for the trees.'

So, if you want to be good at something like squash, in essence, find some mates, get on court and practise, and have a nice pint in the bar after. Or if you want to be a good triathlete, find some other mates, run with them, cycle with them, swim with them. And stop for a toasted teacake halfway.

Ali Jawad

ALI WAS born without legs in Lebanon, where doctors suggested he be killed off for his disability. He moved with his parents to London at six months old and found weightlifting at 16 when he walked into a gym to throw weights around casually.

Purportedly, heads were turning in the gym at the weights he didn't know he was lifting. Since then he has won World and European championship gold medals, an Olympic silver, and two Commonwealth bronzes, all whilst coping with a debilitating illness, Crohn's, which causes constant difficulty and requires incessant dietary vigilance. He later endured periods of crippling doubt and disappointment, which soon morphed into depression.

As an athlete who exists in the category of the hopelessly undervalued by the sporting public at large, his achievements go relatively unnoticed. His constant pursuit of betterment, to push the boundaries of human possibility with regard to strength in the face of considerable duress is, though, undeniably admirable.

'Everybody's got hurdles,' he says. 'Everybody's got difficulties. I've a little bit more, but it's just a little bit more. It's not a big deal.'

JW: Could you describe what becoming a world champion entails?

AJ: I've got Crohn's disease and doctors have advised me at times to retire. I've needed the team I've had to stay behind me. I guess a big part of my being an athlete has been patience. There have been so many setbacks to deal with. That ability to be patient when it's all going wrong might be one of the main reasons that I managed to achieve what I've done.

JW: Have you always had strong influences around you? Coaches, mentors?

AJ: I've been lucky to have influences everywhere teaching me different ways of thinking and solving problems. I wouldn't have learned as much as I have without them. And I feel like all that will stand me in good stead for normal life too, not just what I've learned from them in sport.

JW: By any athlete's standards you seem to have had your fair share of lows, albeit with some highs thrown in. You've had to deal with Crohn's, you had periods of serious depression. How have you dealt with the difficulties?

AJ: When I was diagnosed with Crohn's I was quite set that it wouldn't define me. I really didn't want it to be the reason why I retired. I appreciated the fact that I would have to have spells out, six months, 18 months, but I didn't want it to end me. I don't know, having that mentality seemed to help me get through those flare-ups. And 2012 was a difficult time, the diagnosis, then the controversial decisions in London, and that all made things worse. But I had to deal with it and fight back. This whole notion of not wanting to let it call the shots helped me to get through somehow.

JW: Can you remember specific days, or was there a period of time where you felt at your most desperate?

AJ: Early 2012 to early 2013. I had been diagnosed with Crohn's in 2009. I managed to make it to London, barely, but it had been such hard work to get there. I don't think I was necessarily expected to medal but to then be right there, only to have a refereeing decision go against me, just made it very hard to take. That all pushed me over the edge.

JW: How did you deal with it? Did you speak to family? Who did you turn to?

AJ: After the event I switched the phone off for four days, which worried my parents. I didn't want to speak to anybody. It wasn't until December time that I kind of opened up about it.

JW: Can you explain how powerlifting works in terms of how athletes develop? With ball sports there are so many deeply ingrained skills required that take years and years to embed. Professional squash players at the top of their sport will have been playing since very young. Is it the same in such a predominantly strength-based sport? How early did you start?

AJ: When I was growing up, I was told it was a grown man's sport. To get very, very strong it takes years and then natural growth. When you're younger your body hasn't developed for that to happen. But, having said that, we're seeing now that young kids can do really valuable safe technical training, which can really give them a start. Because they are underdeveloped, heavy weights early might not be the answer, but safe strength training early could be.

Some people get injuries later on because technically they haven't got that background. I'm lucky that I started fairly early and I worked on technique, which holds me up now, I think. So, I think it really is important that you start as early as possible, with careful physical effort if you want to build that foundation. Our sport is hard, so when you get to that level at the very top, that foundation work you did long ago counts for so much.

JW: You've described before the first time you went into the gym to lift weights and people were really surprised what you could do.

AJ: I had just turned 16. I had never lifted a weight in my life.

JW: Is innate talent involved with what you do?

AJ: In our sport you have to have something innate physiologically. So, for instance, anyone with long levers will struggle. Having genetic ability does help, as it did for me that day when I went into the gym to lift for the first time. I obviously had a capability for lifting weight because at that point I had never done it and people were surprised at what I was lifting.

But after that, well, you have to pursue it. I was lucky enough to be found. But being in a gym wasn't something I had imagined pursuing until I had actually done it.

JW: And can you maybe describe some of that effort that you put into training? Are there times when it gets too much, and you can't face the next session?

AJ: I'm used to working, when I was younger especially, and it was very much old-school training and less scientific, basically lift until you can't lift any more. That hurts your nervous system. Now it's a scientific approach. But the effort I had to put in when I was younger, week in, week out, felt much harder because I just felt tired all the time. The standard I was attaining to was so out there that I actually thought I had to do that sort of work. Our sport isn't great for doping so I would kill myself to keep up. And I'm not sure that was the best way. There's a smart way of training.

JW: Has doing a degree informed the way you work as an athlete?

AJ: To be honest it could be the other way around. Having the experience of actually training was even better for the degree than the degree was for the sport in some ways.

JW: I know what you mean. I've spent so much time with the physio over the years that I almost feel like I've done half the degree course.

AJ: It's all well and good reading all the science behind it but you have to do it! It was good to be doing both, and Leeds Beckett helped me. I would have time away and I was supported.

JW: How important is your outside life in all of this? Do you think about how you balance other areas into what you do as a world-class athlete?

AJ: It's a good question and it got raised this year, how I've approached my career in the last ten years. I feel like I've had to turn down a lot of opportunities because of what I do. Because I was chasing that gold medal, I sacrificed a lot of outside opportunities. Since Rio, the last 18 months I've had more of an opportunity to think about it myself as a person, not an athlete. If the person is happy, the athlete is happy. I spent all year out last year and it gave me space to focus on other things. I've been sitting on the UKAD athletes' committee and that's given me something to think about in terms of a life post sport.

JW: Do you know how and where the flare-ups with Crohn's come from?

AJ: I feel like I know when something could happen and am more able to stop it. For me the obvious indicator is if I'm happy in my life or not. If I'm happy and not stressed, things are okay. It's whether I can maintain that happiness. That's where the balance comes in.

Diet and lifestyle can really help with the Crohn's, but normally because I live an athlete's lifestyle that can be taken care of naturally. I've tried to work on finding happiness and reducing stress this year to help with the illness.

JW: Are there any aspects of life that inspire you especially? Family members perhaps, other athletes?

AJ: My big inspiration has been our Performance Director, Tom Whittaker. He coached me from … well, he saved my career in 2011 when I was on the verge of retiring. He's lived the whole thing with me, is one of the most hard-working and inspirational people I know. He provides me with a team that motivates and inspires me.

Stefan Edberg

REMEMBER THOSE people who featured so prominently in that childhood imagination you once had? Those whom you watched, learned from and idolised in a way you never quite do again as an adult. Back then those juvenile eyes filtered our heroes to the brain in a way that gave them colour, made them vivid, more untouchable, more god-like, more brilliant. We have inspiration and heroes as adults, but we always remember how they are just like us, with human needs and desires. They all eat and drink and sweat and urinate, or argue with other halves and have strange habits. It's not something that's factored into the train of thought of a child. It's a shame that we lose this innocence, this ability to be captivated in an intense, aching sort of way. There were many athletes, musicians and actors that I was in awe of and learned so much from, and when I see a timid youngster approach me at a squash event I try to remember what it felt like. To me I'm nobody, or at the most just like everyone else. To them, being a professional squash player, I might actually be or mean something to somebody, however strange that seems.

Stefan Edberg was one of those people for me. I'll never forget the summers I spent in the early 90s at our home in Ackworth in West Yorkshire. It was there I became obsessed with sport: Christie and Gunnell in the 1992 Olympics, *Match of the Day*, and where I first got to watch McEnroe, Edberg, Lendl, Becker, Sampras, Graf, Navratilova, Martinez, Sanchez-Vicario, Seles, Capriati, Novotna.

As the sweat constantly clung to my young brow on those hot afternoons, I spent swathes of time switching between watching the action on the BBC from Wimbledon to actually 'being' them in my back garden. It was an intense stand-off between which of the two I preferred doing more, the doing or the watching, but I look back now and see that the one just kept nourishing the other. I would watch these players, and literally I would need to play tennis, or I would wet myself. There was no way out of this; I had to get the racket in my hand.

Outside in our fairly cramped garden I used what was available to me in creating my own Wimbledon, my own theatre. I sliced and top-spun the shots, played rallies I had watched on television and remember being in a state of unimaginable bliss. And I actually liked Edberg the best. I loved his skill, his quiet, understated image. I remember vividly being so obsessed with Wimbledon one summer that I would race to the squash courts and copy Edberg's movements, especially the way he received serve. I must have been laughed at, but that wasn't of any consequence.

I remember training one afternoon in Halifax, and feeling thoroughly knackered and miserable, sorry for myself because of the intensity of the training I was doing. There were a couple of kids next door playing, not knowing I was on the court next to them. They said to each other about playing, and then one said to the other, 'You be so and so, and I'll be Willstrop.' This was really quite a moment because it took me back to that childhood energy and potential I once had myself, and because it was the greatest compliment. It was almost more exciting than winning, to have captured the imagination of one child. He could have chosen any squash player, or he could have been out playing football instead, being Beckham. It instantly reminded me of the privileged position I'm in, and to stop fucking feeling sorry for myself.

Fast forward a decade or two and Stefan is now a keen and very capable squash player. He's involved with the companies running the Swedish Open squash event. Just as he had started his tenure coaching Roger Federer, he gave up his time to talk to me in London.

As you can imagine then, this interview took on considerable significance for me, thinking back to those afternoons in Ackworth, playing squash-tennis. I've perhaps shed some of that awe I once felt about those heroes in the early 90s, and that frenzied idolising has inevitably been dimmed by the onset of time, but it's the people we value in our younger years perhaps who keep the strongest hold. So quite a big morning for me, nonetheless.

A bit nervous, I opened with a belter of a question, echoing Peter Kay's famous taxi question.

—

JW: A busy day ahead?

[There's no need to worry then, Parkinson.]

SE: Yes, one practice, then Roger has some other commitments.

JW: Are you enjoying the work with him?

[Crikey, have to do better than this …]

SE: Yes. He's a nice person and that helps. Not something I thought I would do but there you are.

JW: I wondered how much of your success as a tennis player has been down to talent, luck, environment or hard work? What made you become a six-time Grand Slam champion?

SE: I was lucky enough to grow up in a place where there were good people around me and kids to train with, about the same age and a little bit older. I had a great coach when I was young. The environment has a lot to do with success. The courts, the facilities must be available, and they were for me. You need to harbour a passion for the game and, in order to succeed, you need to play a lot of matches in tennis. I think I played hundreds of matches from being 11 years of age and I feel that's how you learn the game.

JW: In squash, the junior system is set up so that kids will have tournaments most weekends, so by the time they are adults they have done an awful lot of playing. It sounds like it's the same in tennis.

SE: It was very similar in Sweden. In wintertime it was a bit harder to practise, but usually over the weekends you would have tournaments and league matches, and we probably had one of the youngest teams in Västervik, where I grew up. We played the first team in the club and the average age was 13; we were playing all these guys that were 20 and 21. That was great experience.

JW: And Tony Pickard was your coach from a young age?

SE: No, I had some coaches back in Sweden; two coaches who supported me until I was 16. Then I went to Stockholm to see Percy Rosberg, who worked with Bjorn Borg. He helped me with some finer details. I met Tony when I was 17.

JW: How important in tennis is it for kids to start very young? Are those formative years crucial? And do you think there's a certain age where it becomes too difficult to make it as a top-class player?

SE: Things have changed a bit since I was playing; a lot of the players could win their first Grand Slam at 17 or 18. I was 19 when I won my first. At the time, the bridge from going from junior to senior was still a challenge, but I think in today's game it's tougher. The aim is to play and work hard for longer and to improve the physicality. Players don't really break through until 20 or 21 now. But there's no doubt, to reach the top, kids need to gain serious exposure to the game at a young age.

JW: How much did you sacrifice? What did your training days entail?

SE: Well, I would say there was sacrifice, yes; maybe missing out on a few things that your friends do. You have to stay home when they go out sometimes, but I didn't really look at it that way because there were so many other sides to it that I could enjoy. There was a lot of hard work at the time, and I think I really started practising very, very hard when I was 16, after leaving school. It went from being say ten hours a week to 20 hours a week. I had all day then, though. I could practise twice a day and do the physical training on top. Luckily enough, my body held up through all that. It was a big step, to go from ten to 20. Your body could break down, but I think through playing all those matches when I was younger, I was strong. I do think an element of this was probably from the fact that I was just born strong. That was a natural thing I believe.

JW: When you were in your hardest training spells, how would you balance the training? Would there be more racket work than physical work?

SE: Well, I would say as a tennis player, when you're young you probably want to be playing or training for three or four hours a day, at different intensities. Half the time you can work on things, half the time you need to play games because, to an extent, learning comes from playing. At the same time, you can't stay at home too long. You have got to be out there competing. Playing matches is key. That's where I believe you become a better player, because when you go out and practise your mindset is different. You might think, 'I'm gonna work out for one hour or two hours. I'm gonna do this and that …' Your mind gets a little too set. In the matches you're out there for three and a half hours and you have to push yourself longer than you expected. Those are the matches that make you stronger and better. The matches are a very different kind of training. Winning a hard tennis match is probably the equivalent to 20 hours of practice because it's different muscles, higher intensities, and different tensions and forces are taking hold.

And I found that the more matches I could play, the less I had to practise. It's a simple concept. I would actually rather play matches than go to practice! A lot of players, I feel, might waste a lot of time on the practice court, then they can't bring it out when they play matches. It's a delicate thing.

—

It's interesting to hear these comments. I'm learning a lot about what Stefan is talking about at this late stage of my career. He seems to be emphasising the 'doing' over the 'theorising' or 'over-practising', and he's endorsing replicating your training in the way you want to end up doing it – in other words, ultra-specifically. It's a simple concept as he says, and as athletes we sometimes lose sight of it: in my case I want to get better within that intense match situation, so why not play matches more, or at least as much as I do static solo practices that don't resemble the intensity of a match?

So nowadays, if I have the opportunity to play a match within my working week I will do, and I'll have more rest, rather than doing five hours' practice or pounding away on a bike. The bike certainly has its place, as does the solo practice, but the match is highly specific, the nearest you can get to the real thing. It allows me to think about winning points, finishing rallies, the patterns of play, moving on to balls and executing shots under pressure, and crucially there's an opponent. Many practice situations don't always bring into play these elements, and it certainly can't simulate the intensity of a match.

The more I play professional squash, the more I understand the importance of matchplay, best of all in a competitive situation, with referees and an audience.

So does this filter through into other areas, other sports? Well, certainly it seems it's a valuable facet in racket sports. It would appear that athletes from sports like cricket, football and rugby are also served well by practice matchplay, as they all partake in pre-season tours. Of course, the fact about these sports is that the athletes involved are almost continuously competing, unlike say boxing and some athletic disciplines, where meets or bouts only come along once every few months.

In professional theatre there are previews, which might be a week or a few weeks long. Sometimes in the case of a million-dollar Broadway musical it can be months. These previews serve the same purpose as matchplay in tennis. They are giving actors and crew a chance to work things out in that intense situation, with the audience, under the lights. I know a little about this from my own recent forays into acting. I recently played a big role in a First World War drama in Leeds, and I remember our first night. I must have gone through three shirts, lost so much sweat, and was actually aching and cramping at the end! We got through it but were a bit of a mess, missing lines, fluffing scenes. But five nights later how different things were. It was slicker, easier and fewer shirts were used. But it was the actual doing of it, with costumes, props, furniture, the lot, that helped bring us on. It really taught me that for some things there's no substitute for just doing whatever it is you want to improve, in the most specific way possible.

I went on a short writing course once, and one of the best things I remember from the day was when one of the speakers, almost decrying his own position, told us not to get too worried and bogged down on the theory and technique of writing. He said, 'Don't think too much about what you're doing, but DO it! If you want to write a crime novel, read lots of crime novels and write lots of crime novels.'

Any apprenticeship in the big wide world backs these points up. A physiotherapist really gets better through a good placement at a reputable clinic, and a great film director often learns from shadowing other directors in his or her early years. How many parents find the second child so much easier because they have done it all before. They are not better because they read books about raising kids, or even because they practised. They are better because they are so well versed in the doing of it.

I applied it to squash, and this echoes Stefan's sentiments. People think of me as an expert in squash. Well, maybe, but no theory I can give, no in-depth coaching session I can give, can make a player better. It can help, but in the end the best advice I feel I can often give is to tell people who ask complex questions not to keep looking and searching for the magic piece of theory, but to do two things: watch the game being played, then play it. Do quite a lot of training and practice too, get a coach to help by all means, but you want to play well, so make sure you play.

—

JW: Does quality far outweigh quantity when it comes to the tennis player's routine?

SE: I believe so. And it depends on how you practise. You can have somebody standing in one corner running you around, and after 45 minutes of high intensity you won't be able to move for the day.

Players have to work a lot of hours, very true, but what some forget about is rest. The body needs to rest in order to make the progress. I actually think a lot of people practise and train too much. They don't really take a day off or a few hours off to get the energy back, especially when they are younger. I'm seeing that in Sweden. Rest is becoming something people are forgetting about. In order to get stronger, the body needs to work hard, then rest, and then go again and rest again. If we work hard all the time, body and mind will break down and we leave energy on the training pitch when we need it most in matches.

JW: It's such a delicate balance isn't it? Not always that easy to get right.

SE: It's the hardest part about training. The balance where you practise enough but not too little or much. From experience you learn about how the body works, and also a major role of the coach can be to try to monitor or influence this. A coach who knows the athlete and who can say 'no, it's time to stop', or 'okay, we need to do some work here', can be a huge asset. The coach can often see things in a way the athlete can't.

JW: Is it in this way that you feel you're helping Roger now?

SE: With Roger it's a different story. I would say I'm more a mentor than a coach. He's coming towards the end of his career. I know the game and it's maybe just about finer details now, being there for him and having perhaps an extra few things that he can think about.

JW: You were talking about switching off and downtime. I always feel the life of an athlete is about highs and lows, light and dark. So many contrasts and extremes. There isn't much level in there. When you were playing, how would you deal with this? Did you have specific ways of switching off and was it easy?

SE: No, not easy. The travel isn't easy, especially in the beginning when you're young and used to being at home.

I quite liked to be away. To begin with it was one of the driving forces: that you could travel through tennis, with friends and no parents! But I think you need to find time in between where you can do something that you enjoy, whether it's watching movies or seeing friends or something else. When I was travelling it could get boring because there was so much less available to you for your leisure time. If you wanted to make a phone call from Japan it would cost a fortune, and there were no newspapers, no internet, so we spent our time differently, talking or playing cards. Communicating and being away today is so much easier. Lots more ways to spend that valuable off time, and it strikes me that the players now are able to spend their downtime in any number of ways, which could really help to relax you and to perform well.

JW: And when you have a big match, and there were some huge ones in front of huge crowds, how was it after, win or lose? It can sometimes be quite strange. You go to a hotel on your own. Did you struggle to sleep?

SE: I was just happy when I had done the preparation and I had that belief in myself. It's a combination of many things really. Dealing with winning and losing in tennis is something that you learn about. It starts when you're young. You're not going to win everything in tennis. You have losses. If you look at the top, top players, they will lose seven, eight, nine matches a year. That's the best of them. Most of the time I was able to handle the losses well. But there were some hard ones. In 1989 it was the year when I made seven, eight, nine finals and won only one of them, and that's when it got frustrating. Losing the Wimbledon and French Open finals in 1989, two Grand Slams in a row I remember was one of the roughest times. In tennis, as in squash, there's a significant difference between winner and loser. If you go to Wimbledon and look at the boards it doesn't tell you who is second, just first.

JW: Disappointment is a massive part of the deal when it comes to being successful. Whoever you are: Usain Bolt, Roger Federer, everyone has to lose …

SE: Everyone has to lose, at least in tennis. You find yourself dealing with losses in different ways. Sometimes there's disappointment because you just didn't play well enough. There are matches where you might play good tennis and yet were unlucky; that was easier to deal with because at least you gave a performance. The ones where you had expectations and yet played poorly were the tough ones to deal with.

JW: And injuries. I remember one against Lendl in a big final. That must have been disappointing. Everyone suffers when that happens! The player more than anyone.

SE: Hugely disappointing. I pulled a stomach muscle and it got worse and worse. I knew time was limited and I didn't want to damage it by playing on. I was lucky on the whole, I didn't have any major injuries apart from some tendinitis in the knee, pulled stomach muscles and a few back problems. The longest I was out of the game was with an injury that laid me up for two months, and that felt like an age!

I was on the bike twice a day, cycling, boring for a tennis player, but two months is nothing when there's a whole career to go at. But I'm very sensitive with my body, so it was a benefit for me if I started feeling something. I quickly sensed the problem and I tried to deal with it as soon as possible. If the doc said I should take a week off, I might take a week and a half off. I think most players would choose to try to come back earlier, but I would always give it a little extra time. Maybe that was something that helped me to stay sound. Dealing with injuries was key, and again having the right people around you to tell you to rest and to say, 'There's no way you are going back on the practice court!' Players often start panicking, thinking they might lose ground, but it's not always so bad.

JW: The players today have a lot of people around them. There weren't the physios, the trainers, the racket stringers, 20 or 30 years ago. The knowledge wasn't there like it is now. Did you have good support, at events or at home?

SE: Yes, but I didn't want a lot of people around me anyway, and if I was playing today I wouldn't want to have too many people around me. Most players have and had a coach. I had a period towards the end of my career where I had no coach and travelled alone, which I think worked. But I should have had a physio with me, someone who would take care of the body. The physios at the event are very good but they are limited to what they can do with the time they have. That's a really important aspect, where you have somebody really looking after your body, doing stretching and treatments. With the increased knowledge in this area nowadays, you can probably play longer and keep in shape for longer, so this is something I would have factored in. There's a lot more knowledge about nutrition now too. It would have been good to tap into that knowledge, but we didn't have it back then.

JW: Were you very careful with diet?

SE: Not so much. Alcohol is not my strength! I was happy to stay away from that! I was good, pretty sensible with what I ate. I didn't have a diet that I followed. It was moderation with everything. That could work pretty well today. Looking back, I was probably eating too little; I didn't like to have much sitting on my stomach before playing. Maybe I could have done things differently in that respect.

JW: A lot of athletes have obsessive tendencies. Rafael Nadal has obsessive rituals and routines to channel his performance. Were you obsessive, or did you have superstitions?

SE: There were some superstitions. I think many people have them, one way or another, whether it be something in your routine that has to be the same, eating habits, or maybe finding a lucky place in the locker room. All the same, it can be excessive and can get to you, and if you can't satisfy your rituals then you run into problems, and I didn't want to depend on stuff. They don't want to be taking over your life.

JW: I appreciate the way you presented yourself on court: your calm and unruffled demeanour. Having that calm exterior isn't always a very fashionable thing in sport. I've tried to build what I do around that way of playing: the way Roger, yourself, Sampras and Borg played. Was that just how you were, or were you taught to have that attitude, and do you think it helped you to be successful?

SE: Well, I was taught like that in Sweden. Having Borg as the Iceman himself was bound to have an impact. Swedes are often pretty calm and cool, and that's maybe generally how we approach sport. It did come naturally to me though, and it always took a number of things for me to get really upset. Despite the calm though, I know within myself there is/was a fire in there. Instead of throwing the racket on court I might scream out behind closed doors, alone.

That was me, and there was no point in me trying to change that. Being yourself has to be the better bet. At the beginning of my career I was hard on myself, and if things didn't go well I would drop my head. But that's not the image I wanted to project as a sportsperson. In the beginning though, being calm made people think you were pretty flat, but I found that if you stay the same over time, people start to appreciate it. Then it becomes a trademark. But like you say, it's not so fashionable; in today's sport, people don't want someone to be normal, they want someone to be extremely good or passionate or showing extreme emotions. People like this, I can understand that, but it's no good trying to be like that if that's not you. There's no point in pretending, just to put on a show.

JW: Your opponents never know what you're thinking. It makes a lot of sense really to give little away.

SE: Yes, if you can have a poker face it can be of benefit to you, as long as you can handle it.

JW: As a young person did you watch a lot of high-class sport, or tennis? Was that a way for you to learn, to find inspiration?

SE: To tell you the truth, if I could have, I would have watched more tennis but the only thing you could watch in my day was the Davis Cup, which was once or twice a year. There was maybe Wimbledon and the Stockholm Open semis and finals, and that was it! There were only two channels growing up, and watching tennis was a real luxury, so undoubtedly it was an inspiration.

But we hung out and played a lot of tennis, and I think we were quite creative when we were younger. We would have small tournaments, find somebody to play matches against, and we would play best of fives. We were spending a lot of time on the court. When I grew up, I think television only started at 6 o'clock in the evening! So, nobody was really watching before then. It was far different growing up then, compared to today. Kids have much more available to them and can certainly watch much more sport through television than we could then.

JW: Even since my childhood, things have changed out of sight. I remember having three or four video tapes of squash tournaments that were the most precious thing I owned. I would have been inconsolable had those broken or been lost. Now it's all so very available.

From where you are now, do you encourage young people to watch the best players play, to learn from them? And do you watch a lot now that you're working with Roger?

SE: Yes, well, I watch a lot more now since I've been working with Roger. I was watching a lot of the big matches before but only if I had the time. I wasn't planning my life around watching tennis. But now, today, yes, I think we can learn an awful lot by watching. Nowadays I think kids want to spend time with their gadgets so it's more about getting them away from the gadgets too!

JW: Do you remember during your career, or during heavy training, if there were times when you felt that you just needed to stop, at the point where you couldn't play any more tennis? To get to your level you expend a lot of energy and effort. Did it ever become too much, so that you felt you might have to step away?

SE: Honestly, I found it more difficult when I was younger. There were maybe a couple of times where I felt like quitting tennis because of a bad period where nothing would go right. As a professional, being away, going into the fourth week of being away, it could get tough, and I remember wanting to be home. Time could go slowly. You play one match a day and you wait all day. Sometimes there were days off where we had to kill 48 hours.

But the only thing I would say with tennis, which is the bad part that I don't miss, is all the waiting and hanging around at the venue. Being an outdoor sport, you don't always know when you're going to play! There's a schedule that could say you're third match on, which could mean anytime. That's a difference between tennis and a lot of other sports, especially indoor ones. You know exactly when you will play, but in tennis you could be waiting around for days with rain. The nervous energy and tension that built from this was heavy.

I had an experience at Wimbledon where I was defending champion playing at 2 o'clock on Monday and we finished at something like 4 o'clock on Thursday afternoon. The mental pressure of all that was challenging, a lot of wasted time where you could have done so many other things rather than sit about in a locker room. As a top player at Wimbledon you can't just go and wander around or watch a match because of the crowds. And when it rains there are 30,000 people in the restaurants, all in the same place. The only place that's quiet is the locker room, and how much fun is it spending ten hours in a locker room three days in a row? That's just the way it is. Again, it's a lot easier today, now they have more things they can do, of course.

JW: Did you have a set warm-up routine you would go through before matches? Presumably, you wouldn't warm up too heavily before long matches?

SE: No, I think it's probably the same as what people do today in many respects. Except the warm-ups are a little more detailed; you see the players using bands and aids for all their exercises, which weren't known to us back then. The warm-up is similar though. Players probably warm up for anything from 20–45 minutes.

JW: You would stay on your own?

SE: Absolutely. Three hours before the match I would have something to eat, then go and do my thing.

JW: Can you remember the matches that particularly gave you the most pleasure or pride? The one with Michael Chang at the US Open perhaps?

SE: Still one of the longest at the US, I think.

JW: When you take yourself away from the heat of it all, looking back, do you think that matches like that were just wonderful to be part of, win or lose? The Jim Courier match, for example, where you won so well at the US. When you produce a level like that you must feel it's all worth it.

SE: When you're playing your best it's like being in heaven! The flow, where everything you touch turns to gold. It's a great feeling.

JW: You can't predict when it happens can you?!

SE: No, no. It might happen a few times in your life. You can pick out three or four matches where that happens. Sometimes it's a combination where you play well and your opponent doesn't, and that's perhaps when you have those big differentials. The US Open, the way I won it in 1992 was amazing, after spending 24 hours on the court during the two weeks. The way the second week went – where I won in five against Krajicek in the round of 16 after being down a break in the third, and then the quarters in five being down in the fifth against Lendl – I was pleased with that as an achievement. The semi-final was the Chang match, so winning the final against Pete Sampras the day after such a monumental tussle was something I'm very proud to remember. I didn't think I was going to be able to perform. In the morning everything was sore, and I had no energy. But as the day went on and I warmed up and ate something, I started to feel better, and once the first set was out of the way I was back into it. I started to feel good again, despite having felt like shit 12 hours earlier. Amazing how things can change.

JW: Becoming world number one was a big event.

SE: It was; it was one of the huge achievements looking back at the career, finishing the year as number one player. It's not a bad effort as you know. Winning a Grand Slam is monumental. Being the number one is even more difficult because it usually means you need to win a Slam at least and be the best consistently throughout the year.

JW: And for those five-hour matches, how did you train for them? Would you have to train for long periods to practise for playing those lengths of matches?

SE: I would always play a lot of matches. I didn't do a lot of gym work to start with. There would be circuit/strength-based work – push-ups, sit-ups, high-knee work. I was skipping a lot, doing sprints off court. I started to use the gym more towards the end of my career, but if I had my career again, I would have done the off-court gym work earlier. All the players are reaping the benefit of that now. But in order to get through these long matches you need to have played a lot of matches. It does get so mental between two players when you get into these long matches and it often goes in patches. Sometimes you feel like shit then suddenly you get a chance, a bit of energy back, you come through a wall, there's a momentum shift, and then you can get in the winning circle again. You're not feeling too bad, then you lose again, your energy level plummets. There are lots of shifts and it's very much a mental game, having to deal with them.

———

We talk a little more about peaking time for squash and tennis and reaction times and how they change as you get older. He says that reaction times in squash are crucial. Stefan asks how much longer I'll go on playing. As long as my body allows, I say.

Then a little boy of about two runs up to Stefan and hugs him. With no real option available, Stefan hugs the boy back and says, 'How are you?'

I ask Stefan, 'Is he a relative?' 'No,' Stefan says. 'I don't know him.'

Laughter and incredulity. How unusual and rare, for a random little toddler to find such warmth towards an unknown adult. Maybe the boy intuitively knew this was one of the great tennis players of all time. Or maybe he just thought he was a good person. Something that showed the boy, and Stefan, in a good light.

'I notice he didn't come to me for a hug,' I say.

SE: At 30, I could have played for another five years physically, but once your mind goes you want to do something else, I think. Before I quit, I was in the habit of just playing three or four times a week. I was able to play some of my best tennis in practice against Tim Henman and Greg Rusedski, and later on I could take top-ten players in practice. I was enjoying those sessions! I had nothing to lose, the body held up and I was fresh. There was a lot to say for that. I wasn't training that hard but I was playing enough to keep the momentum going during those last years. I picked up some speed in my last year or two doing that.

Stuart Pearce

STUART WON 78 caps playing for England at football. His was a major name in world football in the 1990s and 2000s, associated primarily with Nottingham Forest. He later managed the team, as well as Manchester City, England U21s and the Great Britain team at the Olympic Games in 2012. He managed England's senior team in a caretaker role for one match, and played under one of the greatest football coaches ever, Brian Clough. He's probably most known for his penalties in the 1996 European Championships matches, where England reached the semi-final. The backstory was that he missed in a World Cup penalty shoot-out in Italy in 1990. If the reader isn't aware of how the English media and public react to football matches played and lost (especially in penalty shoot-outs) by the national team, let's say they don't exactly sit on the fence, so there was scrutiny.

In the weeks, months and even years after Italy, Stuart will have had journalists lambasting him, people in taxi cabs and locker rooms countrywide discussing and deriding him, and will have received constant abuse at opposition football grounds all over the country. The famous photo after the first 1996 penalty shows how he explosively shed all that baggage once and for all.

We met in a cafe near Blackpool, where Stuart was attending one of his beloved punk music festivals.

—

JW: What do you think made you a world-class footballer?

SP: I think every top-level sportsperson has a different journey making it to that top level. Was I the most talented footballer? Probably not. But I think my background – an upbringing as an electrician, working in warehouses, leaving school with no qualifications and failing to get into the army – all of those things, added to the environment created by my family, really helped make me the footballer I became. The best lessons I've had have come through the adversity I've experienced. They shaped me as a character. Talent-wise I'm way down the pecking order, but with regard to mental strength, I rank higher, and I'm sure that was affected by not having it all on a plate.

—

Stuart always gets asked about the penalties, the missed one in Italy in 1990, but then remarkably the two strikes at Euro 96. It's one of the most admirable, exciting, inspiring sporting responses I can remember watching as a kid. He's matter-of-fact about it. Perhaps, as he says, it wasn't real pressure; no lives were at stake, but he had a whole nation watching him and he would either succeed and redeem or miss again, and fall foul of the nation, become the butt of every joke, again.

The guy had some mettle to do what he did. He could so easily have refused to take the penalties, as it was, he confirms amazingly, only a matter of volunteering. He stood up though, knowing the next morning's headlines and hangovers nationwide would have a distinct feel should he score or miss. If you think about it enough, those penalties have the potential to sort of change the rhythm of the nation's existence in the following weeks. If England are playing, lives revolve around the match, work patterns change, opening hours shorten, plans are shelved. Question of the moment becomes: 'Where are you watching the football?'

Better to stay matter-of-fact about it then.

Stuart Pearce certainly experienced an unmitigated level of scrutiny and pressure that perhaps no other person featured in this book has. He featured in a cultural or sporting occasion that came as near as anyone ever can to making the world/country almost stop still in light of its unfolding.

—

JW: Is to be mentally strong a talent in itself?

SP: There's natural-born ability involved in these things, but a huge part of it comes as a result of environments and opportunities you're given as a child. As a squash player I'm sure you will have needed the way in; playing squash isn't an obvious, natural thing to do. Playing football maybe is, as most kids often get the option to kick a ball about in the street at some stage.

My dad had a real work ethic. He was never a shouty dad, but he drove me in a quiet way. He knew I was a good footballer; he wanted me to go for it.

I'm not so sure, though, that you can learn mental strength. You can hone it slightly, but I think you seem to be born with it. In the end, I've worked with young England players and what you've got in front of you is for the most part it, I think. When push comes to shove you can see the ones who have that special desire and application.

Young players probably need to know or find out what they are good at too. I've watched kids copying Ronaldo, trying to emulate the free kicks, which they haven't got the technical ability to do. Instead they could excel at another aspect of the sport. Recognising this takes a certain cleverness.

Anyone searching for improvement and success in anything could do well to heed this point. Rightly so, people concentrate on things they are less good at, on improving their weaknesses or something they want to copy. It's certainly valid to try to emulate what others do better than you, but almost as important is the dedication to improving and honing the strengths you have. Some people forget this. Examples permeate through successful enterprises everywhere.

Having had a career in professional squash, I know that some players on the tour are better in certain areas on the spectrum, and if, for example, I were to be thrown into a general fitness test against the world's top 100 players I might come in the bottom 20. I have to work very hard at my physicality, not being a natural athlete, but thankfully there are so many facets to playing squash, some of which come easier to me.

Ramy Ashour is the most brilliant racket player I've ever seen, perhaps in any racket sport, and I love watching him play. During our careers together, people seemed to enjoy some of our first few matches against each other. They found them entertaining and exciting, but they were exciting because I would play with him, at his game. It made for fast, frantic squash. If I was going to actually beat him I would have to think of something different, because I wasn't going to beat him at a shoot-out, playing great, fancy shots; in other words, exactly what he was good at. It might be alright for the crowd, but it was doing nothing for me. I could never and will never hit a backhand nick shot the way he did, however hard I worked at it.

But I did start to find success against him and that didn't happen by simply trying to get better at what he was so good at. I had great confidence in what I could do and found a way by concentrating on what I did best. I could nullify his strengths and allow my own game to thrive if I was clever enough. When I counteracted his game well, I had wins, and interestingly those games were much less commented on by audiences for being as entertaining. I didn't care because what I had essentially done was to stop him doing his brilliant things.

So, in any field it's vital to play to the things we do best. This is certainly important in coaches, teachers, chief executives or writers. The coach of the rugby team has to find the players' strengths and use them as part of the team. The chief executive of a company wouldn't throw in their brightest and cleverest employee to deliver a public presentation to a room full of prospective clients if their weakness lay in public address, no matter how clever they are. A writer may steer clear of writing a novel if they are more suited to writing poetry. The difficulty and subtlety are in the recognising of this.

———

JW: You must be sick of talking about the penalties, but I'm interested in how you dealt with all that scrutiny from the public and the media, and how you kept composed through all that. What you dealt with was the ultimate in sporting pressure.

SP: It starts in 1990 where I stumbled into that situation as one of the penalty takers. There was no preparation and people simply put their name forward.

JW: I can't believe it.

SP: So, I'm on the field and I look around me. I took penalties for my club, so there was no way I was going to stand on the halfway line and let the others go ahead of me.

It's a long story, but we came back having reached the semi-final to open-top bus parades, celebrations. This wouldn't have happened anywhere in the world for having reached the semis. The rest of the squad were almost euphoric and Chris Waddle and I, who also missed, weren't. The following season as a group we were tired. Many of the squad had a poor season. Fair enough. But it turned out to be one of my best.

Every away ground I went to the crowds were hammering me, calling me German. I scored 16 goals and none were penalties. That season wouldn't have happened or looked like it did if it wasn't for that missed penalty. It seemed to provide me with the mental strength, the desire to improve. After Italy, after all the disappointments, you ask yourself 'why' so much more than if you win. The other players felt tired, but it was a relative success for them. It was different for me. The disappointment fuelled me to improve.

Six years later we stumbled into a penalty shoot-out, again with little preparation as a team, some ad hoc practice in training perhaps. I say to the manager on the field that I want to take the first penalty. He looks at me and says, 'Are you fucking sure?' I say, 'Yes'.

JW: This is all done at the time?

SP: This is on the pitch.

JW: So, the team had made no provisions for penalties?

SP: No. I took penalties for my club. I had practised alone. I knew I had done the work on my own to put it right. Other than that, there was scant team preparation.

JW: God.

SP: Anyway, I scored the penalties. In my mind, standing on the halfway line, and not standing up to be counted, was failure. Missing the penalty was less of a failure.

—

At this point someone comes up to our table and asks for a picture. Stuart is gracious and says this is no problem. He half apologised to me for the interruption and I said there was no need to do so. I gladly assumed the role of photographer. The young man was nervous and said that it's not every day that you see an England legend in your local farm cafe.

SP: So, happy ending for me on that one, less so for the team. After 1990 I did my thinking, and I knew I didn't want to go into a scenario like that ever again. I then took over the England Under-21s in 2007. The first thing I wanted to dispel was that this was a lottery situation. Nothing in sport is a lottery. If you think it's a lottery you're set up for failure straight away. As soon as the players started training two years out from a tournament, we would practise penalties after every session. We monitored every training session and took down stats on penalties taken by all the players, so we knew everything about every player. We collated the stats and worked with the clubs, and in 2009 my Under-21 team played Sweden in the semi-final of the European Championships. It went to extra time, then penalties. Everyone knew the order of penalty takers; everyone knew how much they had practised and prepared. There was none of this coming forward, offering at the last minute.

After extra time all I did was say, 'Gents, we have been practising for two years. It's all there.' The research we had done suggested the most important penalty was the first, followed by the fourth, then second, third and fifth.

Joe Hart was our goalkeeper, but he was our third-best penalty taker, so he was in second. Very few teams put their goalkeeper in as a taker because they have never thought to practise and find out if he is any good. But I knew my best five were taking penalties. So, even if we had lost that shoot-out there were no qualms because we had given it everything. It's never a failure if you've prepared as best you can and lost. When I looked at those England misses down the years, these players had no background in penalty taking. We were plainly just hoping it would work. You can't work on that basis. Is there any wonder we lost?

Everyone wants to talk about 1990 and 1996, but the one that gives me pride is 2009 when I've learned the lessons and applied them in my coaching. It gave me a nice warm glow, turning the adversity on its head.

JW: Have things changed now, in football, with regard to penalty taking?

SP: I don't think so. Penalty shoot-outs are 'down the line', two years, four years. A long way away. It may never happen – that's the mentality for many coaches. I'm assuming you wouldn't go into your sport thinking like that?

JW: At the time I couldn't believe that world 'experts' in football implied it was impossible to practise penalties. They kept talking about not being able to replicate the pressure of the situation! What high-level sporting atmosphere can you really replicate in training? It doesn't stop us all trying.

Despite that learning process, the 1996 experience must have been extreme compared to what many athletes (or anyone in any line of work anywhere) feel. It wasn't just the pressure from yourself or your team, but every eye in the country was on you.

Perhaps the England football team, the odd mega celebrity and maybe some select politicians are the only ones in that band who have to suffer this level of invasion and criticism of their work. They are most accountable for what they do, and people feel it's their business to have an opinion, because it's so public. Most people don't have this level of scrutiny to deal with. Taxi drivers, doctors, CEOs, chefs, architects – they don't have to deal with a public being so invested in what they do and often so openly critical of their work.

SP: You probably have to minimise all that and ask yourself questions like, 'How do you think it feels for the opponents? How bad might they be feeling?' People get obsessed with being under pressure. I try to transfer it on to the other team, and make positives out of the doubts they will inevitably feel. Chances are, statistically over my career I've scored 80 per cent of my penalties, which is good. The practice I've done over the years, that's good. It's all there. Let it happen. I suppose that's how I approached that pressure.

JW: Just to know you've done the work means you can let go and trust it. If you fail to score, then so be it.

SP: Yes, arming yourself to be stronger and more positive and confident. To be honest, you don't know all this when you're in your twenties or when you're a kid. As you get older and wiser it builds up. I can talk to you now with confidence. I couldn't possibly have analysed all this at 18.

JW: As a player you posted ads in the Nottingham Forest programmes for your business as an electrician, and didn't that earn you more than the football?

SP: I was earning £220 a week as an electrician, taking £280 as a footballer. I got signed for a big club, went to the manager, told him what I wanted, and he actually offered me a wage cut below what I was paid as an electrician. If I didn't like it I could be on my way. I had already handed my notice in to the council with the previous job so I couldn't turn back. I had no choice but to settle for it. Then I started advertising in the programme at that time. Fans used to ring me after games for a chat. A lot of the guys in the dressing room were doing things to earn money, not just me.

Players need to find a way of feeling difficulty or adversity and not have everything laid out on a plate. Football isn't encouraging this these days.

Today's footballers are supplied with everything they need because of the money that's involved. When everything is there on a plate you draw hunger out of the belly. The coaches today don't have the strength like Ferguson and Clough did.

It's a big world out there, and these footballers are so far removed from what an electrician has to do.

JW: Brian Clough might have struggled with today's footballer …

SP: Brian Clough was brilliant at managing players who were in danger of disappearing up their own arse. I was picked for England for the first time and I went to his office, and what did he do? Congratulations? He basically told me to fuck off! How you judge that, I've no idea. I suppose that was part of his genius. A coach probably needs to know who he's talking to, to know whether to deliver that, but Cloughie was so different, he probably didn't really care. The message was clear: keep your feet on the floor.

JW: How influential were coaches or mentors on you, and how important to young players do you think they are?

SP: If the coach gets it wrong, they can put someone off for life. I've had all sorts of relationships with coaches over the years, some more important than others. I played non-league football for years, under Allen Batsford, who had a real work ethic about him. We were non-league players, but he would keep pushing me, pushing me, in a good way. There's a nice memory I have with Alan. We were a non-league team, a million miles away from the top echelons of the game, and we went to a PFA awards dinner. At one point in the evening he introduced me to Kenny Sansom, England left-back, a legend with 86 England caps. I was in awe. There was the inevitable awkward conversation and then Alan said to him, 'This boy is going to take your place one day.' It was a bit buoyant, I was embarrassed, but three years later there I was playing in Kenny's position for England. Funny when you look back, but Alan was right behind me and helped me a lot. This sort of gesture or comment from him would lift me.

I learned important lessons in different ways at Newcastle when Ruud Gullit was in charge. It was late in my career and he put me in the reserve squad. I soon realised from talking to the reserve players that Gullit didn't even know their names. They thought the senior manager didn't care about them and that inadvertently taught me a great lesson. I knew then that if I went into management I would make it my business to take an interest in the young players.

JW: Throughout your career, how hard did you work? And how did you feel about putting in the work? Did you enjoy training?

SP: I've had a few injuries: one groin operation and two knee ops, broke my shin bone, and a whole catalogue of bits and pieces. That actually enabled me to play until I was 40. There were gaps with these injuries, the rests, the rehab time I had, where I could completely refresh. I then had it in my head that the game owed me five years. That was my mentality. I wasn't going to retire at 35, as was the custom.

I broke my shin at 37, rehabbed for five months and then almost immediately broke it again. To his credit, my manager Harry Redknapp backed me, and said my place would be there for me when I came back. It's tough to make that call to a 37-year-old, and it might have been a throwaway line, but hell, it gave me a boost. I was in tears in the dressing room and I thought my life in football was over. That following afternoon I was back down the pool rehabbing. If it weren't for his faith, it could have been over.

———

Injuries are just one of the setbacks that sometimes literally impinge on an athlete's career, and it's worst of all when they threaten that career. In June 2014, almost 31 years old, I had an MRI scan on my hip to try to get to the bottom of some pain I had been feeling for months. The scan came back, and the doctor told me that my career playing squash was over. As it happened it wasn't all over; I went to a specialist, had an op and 16 months later I was in the semi-finals of the World Championships.

The fact was, though, that until I saw the hip specialist, who deciphered the scan properly a week and a half later, I actually believed it was over. And that was a strange place to be. For 20 years, each day I had been waking up to the knowledge I would be pushing myself in order to compete in major squash championships, and suddenly I was looking for a job. I was in a cafe eating lunch at the time I took the call about the scan, and I stifled back the tears, left my lunch and went home to tell Vanessa. The day before I had been training for the Commonwealth Games of six weeks later and looking forward to another season of squash, and now I was crestfallen, and it was probably all over. I was in shock, really. Giving up your life's work of your own volition is tough on its own, but to be dispossessed of your squash faculties so abruptly when not even close to being ready was a shock at the time.

I certainly relate to the two feelings Stuart touched on through his injury: that desolate feeling that it could be over, and the fact that he felt that the enforced time away had helped him elongate his career. I felt exactly that. The injury kept me out for five and a half months, and whilst I was doubting how and if I could come back, in fact this had freshened my body and mind totally. While the other players were cranking out air miles and matches on tour, I was having a massive reboot, something at 31 I probably needed.

Rest and relaxation are a huge part of any high achiever's routine. Being a high achiever inevitably means there's tension and difficulty, bad feelings and stress involved, so it simply has to be balanced with downtime. Though I hadn't called for it, it unquestionably reinvigorated my appetite for the sport and for the hard work needed to get me back and to carry on.

SP: To come back to your question, the older I got the more set in my ways I became with training. I wanted to train intensely, and I did. Brian Clough trained us quite lightly, but when we did train, we trained bloody well, we had the energy to put in it. We would give so much effort for him too because he commanded such respect. When he was running training sessions, you could feel the intensity skyrocket from the boys.

A brilliant bit of coaching: he would have a tendency to stop training before you, as an athlete, wanted. He would leave you wanting more.

My training has always been as close to match intensity as I could get it. I never found it a chore to train. I wanted to win in training.

JW: So, going back to Brian Clough and his light schedule, and as a coaching principle, it's quality over quantity?

SP: Definitely.

JW: Athletes are good clock watchers. They like to build up hours of practice and training because it makes them feel good, rather than because it's the best thing that can be done.

SP: With modern-day teams, fitness experts are often saying the athletes have done too much, that they are in the red zone, and ask them to rein it in. They have got all this academic knowledge now but Cloughie was so ahead of his time. There were no spreadsheets or statistics, he just knew we had to be fresher for it. He used to take the team away four times a year on holidays. He always said it would do us good in the long run, and it did. After Christmas we would very often come good, having a bit more energy in the tank than anyone else.

JW: The formative years in squash are very important. How is it in football? The best players in squash often start very young.

SP: I don't think you can start any child playing sport too early. My daughter represented British Equestrian. She was on a horse at two. They all are. Look at Tiger Woods with the golf club – he was hitting the thing and he could barely even lift the club. I was kicking the ball early; you had a racket in your hand as a toddler. You don't get to the top of the tree if you don't get ahead early in these highly skilled sports. You learn so much at that young age. Yes, expose kids as early as possible, if they are wanting it, but the trick is not to burden them, and to not push their training too hard too early. It's easy to put kids off. The best parents and coaches should let them find out for themselves.

Denise Gough

IN SPRING 2016, on my way to a tournament, travelling out of Heathrow, I stopped in town to watch a new play, *People, Places and Things*. It was a fascinating piece of theatre. The place was just alive with electricity, a thousand people all at once utterly engaged by this story, and at the centre of it was Denise Gough, playing the character of Emma: addicted, tortured and clever.

This is the type of artistic performance I love to compare with sport. I talked to Denise about how she managed to balance so many levels of tone in two and a half hours. At the beginning Emma is wrecked, wasted and can hardly walk; at the end she's loyal, loving, sober and clear as she tries to salvage her relationship with her tough parents. The shades of light and dark were staggering to watch. Denise knew when to hold back, to inject pace, to raise her voice or to lower it, in a way that she could perfectly convey the complexities and contradictions, the dilemmas and difficulties Emma faced.

In many ways it's what I'm looking for on a squash court, to produce an artistic form of sport that can either interest a room of people or can win me points, games, matches. It's about knowing when to go fast or slow or to quicken pace, or which shot to play when.

She just got it. It's hard to explain from the point of view of someone watching, and according to her it's even harder to explain how she does it. Here, surprise surprise, she talks about years of failing, working as a waitress, being skint, working at her acting day in, day out. She thinks all this built her and made her. She didn't just walk into winning an Olivier Award (theatre equivalent of a BAFTA award) for Best Actress by accident.

You might not be aware of her (there might be time yet) but Denise is as captivating, exciting and moving on a stage as any of her more famous counterparts the world over; the ones you know have the fame, the ones who are force-fed to the public, but as with Alex, this is where the fame and the inspiration don't equate. She doesn't actively seek it either. She most importantly looks for truth in the characters she plays and the stories she gets to tell on stage or screen, and this seems to be what success means to her, whether that reaps a hundred or a million plaudits.

—

DG: You saw the play? Twice?

JW: Yes, came down to see it again. And I live in Harrogate. Good effort, eh?

DG: Oh, well done, you must have liked it.

JW: Don't worry, I'm balanced. Whatever that means. No stalking or anything.

DG: Good to hear.

JW: The reception it received was justified and widespread. Did you know the play was so good?

DG: It had a huge effect on me when I read it. I had actually been out of work for so long before it that I was thinking I might stop. I was circumspect about it and didn't necessarily think it had commercial success written all over it, but, the night before we opened at the National Theatre, the people from the treatment centre in Catford came to see it and, at the end when my character calls to go to a meeting, one of them shouted 'good girl' from the audience and I knew we had done something right with it. For the first time in my career I found myself not caring if anything came of it because we had already succeeded with a reaction like that.

It succeeded because in the end people want the truth on the stage. They really want that. I go to the theatre a lot, and there's a lot of bullshit where you know they are just 'performing'. And that's fine, but it's safe. I don't subscribe to it and I don't feel that's what I do. I don't know what happens when I'm on stage, I genuinely don't know. I think it's something other. It's kind of nothing to do with me. But it's my job to go to a place to tell the truth. Have you been to see Billie Piper yet in *Yerma*?

JW: No, but I saw you tweet about that.

DG: Oh my god. What she's doing is the thing that people want to see; they want to see the truth in the story. Eight hundred people every night want to suck that up. You can feel it, they really want this woman to survive, and that's a powerful thing. And if people are craving that, then there's a responsibility to do that stuff. I get so tired of people looking just so on stage, or deliberately not looking ugly, or doing ugly in a contrived way.

JW: Anyway, congratulations on a great performance.

DG: I had a reaction like yours to Billie's performance, getting so involved. After that piece I just had to sit in the auditorium for a while to take in what I had just seen. And it wasn't just Billie; the whole production was fucking phenomenal. And judging by reactions maybe that's what people were feeling for me and that's what theatre should be. It should be real.

JW: I see sport as being a lot about shifting shades and lots of subtlety: changing pace, changing tone, varying the play, switching the emphasis on all the shots and moves we make. I saw this in you and the way you varied the tone of your voice, and the way you captured the various emotions with each subtle inflection was clever. Do you think as an actor you work for this? Are you consciously working on subtlety?

DG: Don't you think that experience plays a huge part in this?

As an athlete you do it for so long and it just naturally seeps further and further into your cells over time; therefore, you can take it. I prepare and rehearse, get physically ready, then when I'm on stage something else takes over, and the instinct just takes me. So, I'm not sure whether I'm always constantly aware of how I apply subtleties.

It's why I'm uncomfortable when people who are not experienced enough take on huge roles. They can't possibly be able to do what needs to be done on a stage every night without that background. It's different in film but on stage it's endurance too, it's live and raw. You can't edit or redo anything there. You need the years of experience and training for that.

When I got the 'newcomer' award …

JW: You would have been hard at it for 11 years …

DG: But also, I couldn't have played that part ten years ago in the way that I did because I didn't have all those other women in me. It's like each game for you maybe gives you another muscle, another thing that you couldn't do before, yes? It builds and builds. It's like somebody who practises at the weekend going and playing a match at your level. No fucking chance.

I have a big thing about earning your stripes, and I see people doing these huge roles when they are not ready and they are hung out to dry because no one is telling them to go and play a small part somewhere first and learn and absorb from some top people. *People, Places and Things* for me wasn't just a result of 15 years of hard work but also 15 years of rejection, being broke, out of work. So, all that light shade and whatever – I've no idea where that comes from, just from graft.

Rudolf Nureyev was asked about how he lifted partners up with such grace and he couldn't answer it, because he said by the time he had thought about explaining it the partner would be on the floor. It's hard to explain these things.

JW: So, what about talent then? Are actors talented or have they worked hard? Or both?

And how young do most professional actors come to be exposed to the industry?

DG: What we have in our industry is all ego. You might have that in squash as well, I don't know, but basically if you can play a certain level you can win the rally, the match. We don't necessarily have that. Child actors can be surrounded by crazy people and it can go wrong because they start too young and don't have the right people looking after them. Also, at a young age a lot of their success can come from the fact that they are cute, sort of superficial, whereas as an athlete or musician, it's kind of undeniable if you can do your thing. In acting, it's a more shady area.

JW: The world-ranking list doesn't lie, but with you, success gets confused with fame.

DG: Exactly, yes, fame can be so corrosive. It's a by-product of acting. I've recognised it in the last year. I'm definitely more recognisable now, more well known within our industry because of that play. That's fine because having been in it for a long time I don't get carried away. But I've seen people become famous and they allow themselves to be made national treasures, giving themselves over to a public, some of whom are wanting you to fall apart. They find some weird pleasure in that. You've got to somehow hold on to the real reasons you act.

I've seen too many people not cope, and if this fame had happened ten years ago for me maybe I wouldn't have been able to deal with it, but the background gives me the wherewithal. Unemployment taught me the most. Acting is easy, being on stage and in work. That's the great bit. It's the other stuff that teaches you what life is about. It probably taught me that I'm not just an actress and I'm really happy about that. I have other stuff to rely upon.

You have to be very careful where you get your esteem from in our business because, unlike yours, people get away with it. If someone gets successful and they get carried away with the fame, their work can get worse. I don't want to be that, so I want to do everything to stay away from it, to make sure the work, the performance, comes first.

Also, my success in that play, and people forget this, comes from Duncan Macmillan's writing. I can only work with what I have and what I had was brilliant. It was great writing. People remember these big performances but it's very difficult to elevate yourself like that if the writing is shit. I've done a lot of trying to elevate shit writing, and to an extent bad writing can be hidden by good acting. I just know that his writing, the sheer elegance of it, helped me make that character.

So, it was Jeremy Herrin [director], Duncan, me and the cast in the end, all finding it together. And we had such a laugh.

JW: I've heard you talk before about your life away from acting, and how your relationships with your family are important. You've talked about how you try not to let work become so overbearing that it affects those relationships.

DG: I was banging on this wall, trying to knock it down, trying so hard and getting nowhere. The advice was to just turn around. I did and saw what was really there.

I turned around and the wall was gone because I focused on what really fucking mattered. I don't think that's taught enough. We're kind of told to 'want want want' it to the nth degree and that it should consume you and you need to sacrifice everything. While I think an episode or period of time with that mindset can be good, eventually it will kill me and prevent me from having healthy relationships and friendships.

We need healthy competition but why don't we see an actress giving an award to another actress? Why can't we celebrate each other? I loved Billie's performance, yet I'm led to think I should be in competition with her. I just can't fucking live like that – I tried it and it was fucking horrendous. I also have a sister who is an actress, so if I compete with other women then I compete with her! I don't want it. I don't know if there are parallels in what you do.

JW: I completely understand what you're saying about your perspective on success. It's not healthy to be all out, to let it all consume you. Like you, I did all that. I would put all my energy into winning 'the title', achieving 'the ranking'. I would actually come to hate the phrases because it created all this tension in me, in my life, when I even mentioned or thought of it. I was tense and nervous and irritable leading into these events, which I had built up. And why? Instead of being relaxed and concentrating on the performance, on the moment, the quality of the work, the enjoyment of playing squash, I got lost in 'success' and 'failure', which are not good measurements upon which to base your world.

I had a major surgery a few of years ago and I had this massive jolt. My career in squash was suddenly threatened and I might not even play another World Championship let alone win one! It transformed the way I thought about everything. I started to train less, eliminate the sessions I hated, spent more time doing things I enjoyed away from the court, enjoying time with my son and girlfriend. If I missed training, never mind. If I lost, never mind. Ever since then I've enjoyed squash and life more, and I've still won matches. But the winning almost became secondary and it set me free a bit.

DG: I know, and nobody teaches you this!

JW: No! Coaches, teachers don't do this and it's a vital, vital lesson that's hard for younger people to learn. Everyone talks about rankings and titles and awards and none of that really matters to me now.

DG: You get there, and you achieve the dream so to speak, and then what? I can't touch it, what does it mean? My dad used to always tell me that I'm somebody's daughter, and now I really, really get the point.

I feel like that whole award situation is a bit funny. Am I only like that for a year then? And then hope that next year's performance is better? As good as it is to be applauded for what I'm doing, I'm not doing what I do to impress people who give awards. If I start listening to other people, that performance becomes this unreachable thing. How do you follow *People, Places and Things*? I don't want to fucking follow it. It was amazing and I hope we might be able to revisit it again someday, but it's on to the next thing. The pressure is too fucking much. I don't think I'm made up for being competitive and for being the best. I went for a burger with my boyfriend on the night of the Olivier Awards because it's all a bit too much. All these people are going fucking mad over you and I'm happy that everyone's happy, but this is not the thing. If you've made all that your reason for doing the job, then it must feel scary when you get it and don't feel fulfilled.

JW: It changes nothing.

DG: It doesn't change anything; people think that it does. Everyone says everything has changed for you. Well I have more money so I can pay my rent without worrying about it. I have work for the next year or two so it's easier to get my foot in doors in the industry. That's all great, but in terms of what's inside me it doesn't switch any mysterious light on. The light was on already, and it was when I realised the light was on that things started to happen. The light is on whether somebody hires me or not. Nobody teaches you that shit.

I had things said to me, especially being female: 'You had better take that part because they might have their blonde-haired, blue-eyed girl.' Give me a break! We're taught that there isn't enough room for everybody, but there is enough room for everybody.

JW: What's this little bit of fame you now have like?

DG: Yeah. It's like something happens and they go, 'Oh my god, look at you! You can come in now.' And you think, 'Well, actually I don't want to go in. I'm gonna go over here.' I've been very fortunate to work with great people at what they do, and my interest is in keeping growing, keeping pushing in what I do, and I want to learn how to get really good on screen, which isn't my forte. I haven't flexed my muscles in that area so much. So, as I would expect somebody to do in theatre, I've been playing smaller parts for years, figuring it out, and now I'm going to try to do some bigger stuff. I'm not putting pressure on myself to impress though.

We live in a society that can give you love for a long time, and as soon as you fuck up they will realise you fucked up and I don't want that. I would rather stay in the background, shouting off every now and then.

JW: Do you stick by routines?

DG: Well, I try to meditate; that really helps. I try to do yoga too. In terms of the last show there came a point where I was just running on adrenaline and if I did a run of it again I would have to be far more conscious about it: have food plans and deliveries and work out a cleverer routine. The life is exhausting, it makes you a bit manic, and then actors sometimes have to take the edge off by getting trashed. The hearts and minds of a thousand people are pouring through you every night and I remember about a month before the end thinking I didn't know whether I could get through it.

JW: The high you must be on every single night. I've sometimes dreaded getting my head down after matches because it's so hard to come away from it. You can imagine where the alcohol and pills come in. You just can't simply come down off the high of the experience. The mind is just flying.

DG: It's insane! The sleep thing is always an issue for me. I'm a big thinker anyway. I wasn't sure how I could ever rid myself of the energy in the room. There were moments in that show where the whole room was focused so intensely on what was going on with my character, they were so invested in it, and I'm holding all that energy. Those moments in theatre are quite rare and so intense. It was an intense but amazing place to be.

There's this brilliant talk by Mary-Elizabeth Gilbert where she addresses the pressure we put on artists, athletes and people who excel at things. We like calling them geniuses. In Ancient Greece, though, they would say these people had genius but weren't actually geniuses. It supposedly just came to you and then it was gone. And it means you take the pressure off the body that's supposed to be channelling this thing. I related to this because if I think I own this thing, I'm going to feel like I have to do something to keep it going. This was helpful for me.

JW: Were there certain shows in that recent run of yours that stood out? We might play an exceptional or average squash match. Every performance varies with quality. Does that happen?

DG: Every show there for me hit the heights, it was almost the same. Even when I felt there was no way I could make it, she came down and did it. And off she would go, and I'm left there.

JW: Really? That's how it works?

DG: Yep, every time. I never had a show where it was a disaster. I would invite her in and tell her I was a bit tired tonight but we're here and I'm doing it, so show me. And there would be things happening on stage and I would be thinking what the hell is she doing? I'm not big on technique. People ask me what my process is, and I don't know. I rehearse as much as I can. I connect with everybody as much as I can. I'm not good at warm-ups or getting in zones. I don't really do that. I say a prayer and she does everything else.

I don't have to act like I'm making it happen because that character was wandering around in the shadows needing somebody to tell her story. She chose me. She was in the auditions saying no, then I came in and she said perfect. It feels healthier to think of it that way – it's nothing to do with me. I prefer not to go with that ego-led way of thinking.

But having said that, I work very hard. I've shown up. I've been through it. So, I don't have any problem accepting awards and great jobs, there's no faux modesty. On my first day at the National Theatre I was so grateful to be there and not really believing it, but I was ready. People were saying not to be, that I deserved it. I told them not to mistake this, I was ready, but I could never stop being grateful. People have to work at real jobs. I used to work as a waitress everywhere. Come on, I get to go in, dress up, tell stories and everybody claps for me at the end! Then pay me. It's ridiculous.

So, I'm quite comfortable with what I can do, and I know I'm ready.

Someone said to me last week that I was a good actress, and I said, 'Yeah.' He said he liked my modesty, sarcastically. But come on, nobody wins if I'm saying I'm no good by being all modest about it. You have to know what you can do. I've spent 15 years learning how to use these tools, so damn right I'm going to enjoy it.

There are so many people who get to positions and don't deserve it, and they are getting away with it, treating the sound person like shit. You know? Stop it! They need to teach you how to not be a dick at drama school. Seriously.

JW: So you're a world-class actor. You've said you put the work in, you've worked so hard. But can you tell me how much depth you need to go into in what you do daily? Do you have to analyse constantly? Once the play is up and running, is the director giving notes, constantly looking at improving his piece, like a coach in sport would do?

DG: I don't know really. It's weird. What was beautiful about working with Jeremy was that we were like children. I would get freaked out if I read someone's script and it was full of notes. How do you think about it that much? I try not to think about it! But I rehearse and rehearse and read the script.

223

JW: So, are you less methody then? You were saying that you do become the character.

DG: For me, the method has been a bit ruined by people who just want to make you see their homework, so those people who stay in character all the time and make it very difficult for other people to do their job by insisting they interact with them as their character and all that, I just don't buy it.

JW: Are you giving Emma a detailed backstory?

DG: I've done that work in the past. And I think maybe it can work but I just try to stay in the moment, and if the writing is good, then most of that stuff is done for you. I mean, at the moment I'm playing a character in a drama and I had to have a Skype call with the art department about what her house looks like. I thought, oh shit, yes! You have to know if she's messy, if she reads books. You have to be very clear on who these characters are.

JW: The hard work you talk about, is it coming from the rehearsal room?

DG: Yes, and it's coming from having years in and out of work, and not being able to go to family weddings. Sacrificing, that feels like work, that's part of the work, when you're living a life that is so transient and weird. I've just come from a whole meeting about the logistics of a sex scene. It's fucking bizarre.

I read the script but other than that I don't want it around much. We went on tour once with [director] Max Stafford-Clark. He asked me what I was doing on a line. I said I didn't know, so he said, 'Well, where's your script?' I didn't know; I don't carry it around. He does all this actioning, which I just find so difficult. Right there when I'm playing a character I'm not thinking, 'What am I doing to you?' We're human, we're having a conversation and I don't know what's going to come out.

Jessica Ennis-Hill and Alison Rose, with far right Derry Suter, far left Mick Hill and Toni Minichiello.

Jonah Barrington is driven to exhaustion by opponent Geoff Hunt as he drops his racket in relief at winning the 1970 British Open squash title in Birmingham.

Julian Barnes at a gala screening of the film The Sense of An Ending, *adapted from his 2011 novel. London, 2017.*

'Both Anna and I had defined roles. I knew what I needed to do for the six minutes.' Katherine Grainger (right) and Anna Watkins find their rhythm in the 2012 Olympic women's double sculls final, with the media an ominous presence on the banks of the Thames.

Alexander Hanson (right) with from left Stephen Sondheim, Catherine Zeta-Jones and Angela Lansbury in New York in 2010, during the run of Sondheim's musical A Little Night Music.

Away from the crowds and plaudits, Jonny Wilkinson practises, kicking goal after goal in an empty stadium in Toulon in 2009.

Alistair Brownlee (left) and his brother Jonny take to the floor after a back-breaking Olympic final in Rio in 2016. The brothers won gold and silver.

With his unmistakeable technique, Stefan Edberg unleashes a serve on Boris Becker in the fifth set of the Wimbledon final in 1990.

One of the best-known sporting images in history, taken at Wembley stadium in 1996, the picture shows that this was about much more for Stuart Pearce than the scoring of a goal.

Denise Gough with fellow actor James Norton.

James Brining.

Steve Redgrave (back) and partner Matthew Pinsent do what has to be done in dreary conditions, on the Thames in Henley, December 1995.

Playwright Simon Stephens in New York, 2016.

Rich Landau and Kate Jacoby, New York, 2012.

Despite both of us being on the cusp of big injuries Ramy Ashour and me had fun working together at an exhibition match in Dubai in 2014.

Total concentration: Ramy Ashour lines up a serve in a match in London in 2011.

Dominic McHugh (right), Malcolm Willstrop (left) and author up to no good in Nantes, 2019.

Dad Malcolm (right) talks to brother David Campion in between games during the 2008 British Open Over-35 Final which David won, one of his last big playing outings.

Vanessa Atkinson with the Qatar Classic trophy in 2004.

With myself and Barbara [actor in *People, Places and Things*], every night things were different. Her day would come on with her, my day with me, and things fused differently. You don't want to be giving the same performance. That's a real thing, to be able to perform in a long run, and yet keep it moving throughout the run. Some actors start off with one performance and that's it for the whole four months. Same, same.

JW: What's next?

DG: *Angels in America* at the National Theatre. I heard this thing the other day on advice for actors, which was to find parts or act wherever you can. I'm not sure about that. You can be picky, and if you're going to be picky know that you might be out of work. But it's the only power we have.

JW: Can you tell me about the instance recently with the big job you were offered at the Globe Theatre.

DG: Yes, I turned it down and then didn't eventually find any work until the day after the job would have ended!

JW: You speak really positively about *People, Places and Things*. Were there any moments in the process where you struggled, found it hard, when things weren't going so well?

DG: No. It was the most incredible, profound experience of my career. There's been one other part that I've really felt that with, which was *Desire Under the Elms* at the Lyric Theatre with Sean Holmes, and that was brilliant.

For *People, Places and Things* I loved working with the whole team. Jeremy, our director, is a brilliant director and funny guy. That for me is important because I don't want to sit around being serious all the time. We would fuck about then do a bit of work. He was trying to get me to do some work first, then fuck about.

JW: Did you get inspiration from the actors of your childhood? Did any performance or actor spark you into drama?

DG: I always wanted to go to drama school again. I was very young when I came to London and it maybe shouldn't have worked out; I wasn't from a family with money and I was self-destructive, and a seeker. I tell the story where I used to pick up fag butts on Shaftesbury Avenue and make cigs out of them, so when I walked up there later down the line and there was a poster of me outside the theatre that was interesting.

I try not to do awe so much though. One of my sisters is a heart surgeon, the other a doctor. My father and mother raised 11 children. There are other things to be in awe of other than giving a great performance on stage. Charlize Theron in *Monster*, fucking brilliant. But I don't like awe because it means when you meet someone …

JW: Like me today …

DG: Yes, a crazed stalker like you … We get elevated by being on photos and all of that stuff, but really? I had a young girl hand me a note the other day. I was in the middle of having a meltdown about my boyfriend and she was so reverent. I thought, 'Darling, if you only knew! I'm just the same as you, don't put me on any pedestal!' We all have work to do on our self-esteem. I don't like to do heroes in my business. It's what we do, sorry.

JW: No! It's an interesting take on it, but if someone is inspired by you, then they can't help but be admiring.

DG: I know we go to difficult places but if you're in a huge Hollywood movie and you drive the car and own the house, well done, but you've been looked after and supported by some brilliant people, so forgive me if I'm not gushing when I see you. I want to be a peer to everyone, and I think I get uncomfortable when people are like that with me and I can't really be like that with other people.

My father worked as an electrician for 50 years, where's his fucking award? We can dress it all up, we have to be careful .

JW: It's a public eye thing, don't you think?

DG: People were coming up to me who hadn't even seen the play and getting full on with me. Just because the attention was building, and the fame was building. One guy spoke to us, wanted to direct a film of the play, and he had never seen the play! You're buying into the hype around the thing. It's this mass hysteria that I don't like to engage in too much. Unless it's Billie of course! But even then, I say hello to her and there's huge respect, but I don't go around feeling I'm inferior. It's important to use the inspiration to empower yourself to get better, not to be all deferential about it. People can sense it. Am I like that with anyone? Possibly some of *The Real Housewives*! Brilliant.

JW: Any favourite TV shows?

DG: *American Crime*. Brilliant.

JW: What do you think to *Happy Valley*?

DG: Brilliant. Sarah Lancashire, brilliant. I don't watch that many English shows, to be honest. It's hard to see much when you're in the play. Everything else takes a bit of a back seat. You certainly don't get to the theatre much.

JW: Eight shows a week, that's a pretty heavy schedule. How do you manage it? How does the two-show day work?

DG: It's a tough day; I try to meditate.

JW: Do you get there a couple of hours before?

DG: An hour maybe, get a coffee. By the end I just had to get through the shows and life goes on hold a bit. When it finished, I asked myself where my life had gone! It's a surreal thing.

JW: It was quite a physical performance; you had physio treatments, right?

DG: I had a couple of treatments a week, some reflexology, acupuncture.

JW: Diet?

DG: It has to be a considered, a good diet, but I could do better. Next time there's a longer run I'm going to have to pay more attention, I think, and plan better.

JW: How do you travel around London?

DG: I would always get a car back from the National when we were there. I tried the Tube a few times but I struggled with the posters.

James Brining

I'VE SPENT many hours at the Leeds Playhouse over the years, and been manipulated and moulded by the stories that James has overseen or staged there. He's a Leeds lad and the theatre's Artistic Director.

Vanessa was pregnant with our first child when his production of *Sweeney Todd* played there in the autumn of 2013. I had tried to watch the film starring Johnny Depp some time before and didn't get it. I didn't finish it and found the music harsh. When I saw it was coming to the Playhouse, I wanted to make the effort again, so downloaded the soundtrack, leaving it on repeat during garden training sessions on sunny autumnal evenings. Slowly, as we were clamped in rickety anticipation, Vanessa gradually fattened, and the music started to stick. It was a challenging listen: sometimes discordant, sometimes utterly melodic, but it required time and when I gave it some I was near hallucinatory, in a controlled, pleasurable, legal way.

I would hear little lines of melody that on first outing weren't there, and it was the first time in ages I found myself listening and thinking, 'How has he written that?' There weren't really verses and choruses, yet it was structured subtly. The intelligence of it was bracing. And talk about light and shade ... this was it. In the theatre, James's interpretation/ production was mesmerising and creepy, and it all clicked, as only the fusion of music and drama can. The story, the words, the music, the production all coalesced to make this creepy, gorgeous work of art. I saw it twice in Leeds, once quite late into Vanessa's term, so I remember sitting at the back by the exit just in case there were movements, then again later, in Manchester at the Royal Exchange Theatre.

You know that curious thing when music takes you back to your life and elicits memories from a very specific time? I happened to discover *Sweeney* at an already heightened and precious moment, from which affectionate memories can easily be summoned, so to have this music to evince those memories further results in sensory overload. To me, that's almost too much to fathom. And I play it now and it takes me there. Puke, nappies, tears, hospitals, hope, anxiety, adoration.

There must be a sense of fulfilment for James when he's able to bring an audience to their feet, as they also did in droves in the winter of 2015/16 at his production of *Chitty Chitty Bang Bang*. They are afternoons or evenings out that are remembered by many, and to be able to leave that sort of imprint on people, to change the way they feel or think or react, to sadden or please them in some way, perhaps means he's done something right. I remain moved and grateful for his productions down the years.

———

JW: How have you managed to become the chief of one of the country's leading theatres? Do you call it success, and how do you find it?

JB: One person's success is obviously not another's. I do remember writing to the Grand Theatre and here as a school kid, cheekily asking for work experience.

If I'm successful it's related to me doing what I want to do. I love it, so maybe that's success. When I was at university I didn't have that clear an idea, other than knowing I wanted to make shows. Then, that meant doing it myself out of the back of a van with no money and learning from it. Since then, every job I've done has been about moving on and applying myself to the next challenge. It sounds like it's not very planned and it isn't.

I suppose there's a work ethic there that's helped me. I had an environment that perhaps helped me benefit from the opportunities I had: background, gender, material to work with. All that comes into play when anyone develops. My parents weren't into theatre, so it wasn't like I was born into privilege but I did have support to pursue things I wanted to.

JW: Did you go to Cambridge?

JB: Yes, studied English. There was no drama course there, but they have a host of drama societies. I went to Leeds Grammar School, which didn't exactly encourage creativity, but I got a free place to Cambridge – they had them in those days. I was wide-eyed and learned a lot, and it gave me so many opportunities to do theatre. It gave me confidence to use language and articulate and explore ideas that have stood me in good stead.

Some like to say that if you go to a certain school you get to a certain university, therefore you're going to do a certain thing. It's useful to say that, but it wasn't like I had come out of Cambridge with any more contacts or wherewithal than I went in with. It wasn't like I had built a whole network of people and was all set in the industry. After uni I went up to Newcastle in the back of a van on the dole, backed by the Enterprise Allowance Scheme. It allowed me to run my own business on £40 a week. Doing that taught me as much as three years at Cambridge.

JW: What first got you excited and involved in theatre?

JB: I did school plays. I went to university and did shows there, probably because somebody I fancied did it as well. But I think I started to love making theatre because I had done a huge amount of reading as a young person and I built this connection with story through plays, poetry and novels. They used to send you away with a pile of books to read in a week. It would be impossible and did at times become like a chore. What was exciting to me about theatre was that it was story that wasn't just in the mind but had the visual aspect, and it could come alive three-dimensionally.

And you may or may not recognise this in what you do but it's the collective effort of the thing that inspired me. Starting this process with so many people, making this thing [*Chitty Chitty Bang Bang*, with 250 cast and crew] that plays to half a million people, is seriously fulfilling. You're bringing people together to share something that can affect them profoundly. To make story come alive in a context where it's about human beings gathering – I'm happy to be doing that.

JW: You must see some real ability coming through this door. What is it that makes the special ones special?

JB: As an example, there were two actors I worked with up in Dundee whose processes were very different. One was an instinctive animal and in the moment, and the other was much more intellectual in the process, reasoning her way in and conceptualising things. I did a job with each and I aimed simply to get the best out of everybody, however they worked. Two brilliant actors there, working entirely differently.

JW: That's one thing about sport and clearly theatre, that there can never be one way of doing something, technically speaking. People seem to be looking to coaches and directors to have the answers, to give them a technique that will make everything perfect, but there are so many different technical players in squash that it's clear that there can't be one way to do it. Interesting to hear it's the same for you. I'm always a bit suspicious when coaches come in and enforce a very specific technical way of playing.

JB: No, there isn't a specific template, but hard work and application is part of the deal of finding quality. Some people who are hard-working don't quite have that thing; some actors are very smart and yet can't get their intellect away from the performance. There isn't necessarily an outright correlation between hard work and quality, but there are not many people who don't work hard who are successful and make it through these doors.

The level of detail is the key if we're talking about aspiring to reach a high level. I can remember times where we've spent half an hour on whether that [points to plate on table] should be here or there [moves plate six inches]. That might seem completely ridiculous but everything on that stage is a decision to be made. There's a reason everything is there, and there are countless decisions behind all an audience sees and hears.

Superfluous

When someone does something to the highest level, a lot of what they must be savvy about is simply chopping the superfluous. They simply must get rid of the rubbish, the stuff that doesn't help and that doesn't have a point. Finding the superfluous is a bit of an art. Everything James does on that stage is done for a reason. Every scene a director or an editor keeps in a movie must do or say something, or it must give the story some momentum. Every practice drill for Jonny Wilkinson is done cogently, not heedlessly. For a squash player, I have to make every shot I hit purposeful, therefore every practice routine I do I try to consider why I'm doing it and how it will help, or how I can do it better so it will help. When I practise a shot, I more and more ask myself why and what its purpose is. If it can't help me win rallies on court against opponents in big matches, I probably shouldn't bother with it.

An example it would be worth citing from my own experiences is that people often ask me at events whether I do running as my training, and the answer is no, because running as an exercise has limitations for improving anybody's squash game. Running isn't squash, running doesn't make me react to a ball the way I need to, and it uses completely different muscles. So why would I put significant time into it?

There's a reason behind why I play a certain shot at a certain time in a game. I might use a high lob to defend and give myself time or to break up a rhythm, because it needs to be there to help me. You can see the squash players on tour who know exactly what they are doing with every shot.

It's so, so easy to get your daily rituals done without purpose. It's so easy to train badly, to practise any old way, without ridding yourself of the superfluous. I've done it plenty as I've learned, and it has become so apparent with age.

This seems to me a universal concept and I think James has proved it by what he said. Whether you're a storyteller who must keep viewers or readers interested, or the squash player who needs to make every shot count to something, it will reward us in all our ventures to edit and to remove, to recognise the superfluous in what we do.

JW: Should artists, namely actors, be able to improvise, let go and express themselves?

JB: There are some projects that allow a freedom and fluidity but that in itself is a decision. The process by which that becomes a freeing thing and not a negative thing – or something that isn't properly worked out and prepared – that has to be carefully manufactured.

In Aberdeen I worked with a Russian director whose process was very different to a typical British director. His theory was that the actors knew how the scene started and ended, but in between that they were free to realise the character and just play it. Every move wasn't in place, but he was asking his actors to be truthful, to completely let the moment take them. That can be very scary for actors. Other directors might have every single move mapped out meticulously and that can cause its own problems. It can seem mechanical, and the actor might not be alive and truthful to the situations he or she is in. And passion and feeling and truth make thrilling theatre. So, there's a skill to all that. For me it's about detail and layering, but then finding a way of throwing that all away. It's maybe not about being so meticulous that it stifles you.

—

One of the reasons I was motivated to write this book was to discover whether my hunch about direct links in processes of people who reach high levels exists. Here is a neat comparison.

If I were to play out my squash career again, I would listen to James's sentiments about meticulousness that can be stifling. I would pursue, calculate, study and analyse as much as I could, but then I would try to let go of it more, just so I could allow myself to function impulsively better, just so I could tap into the creative aspects that are valuable for high performers. My coach Malcolm often talked to me at length about relaxing, having fun, messing about a bit. He tried to convince me it was part of the process too, and I perhaps railed against this; I was conscious of that sort of work being the superfluous stuff I alluded to earlier. I see now that there's a place for mechanical, ordered routine, but also for impulse, creation and discovery. This for an athlete could mean doing new practices, inventing games, training with different people, or just completing less-intense sessions.

On the other side of this, I know players who have everything analysed and intellectualised to minute detail all the time, and they thrive on that too. I would implode if I worked like that, especially now. Once the work is done, I have to somehow find a freedom, and I couldn't always make it as a younger player.

—

JW: Do you analyse, re-watch and dissect footage?

JB: Actually, having worked with a lot of choreographers now, they do a lot of videoing, watching, rewinding, making notes and then work from there. Good work is about the detail and that doesn't mean making every decision. It's sometimes about being unafraid to not make a decision. When you go in with all the answers you sometimes don't ask the questions you need to be asking.

JW: So you're not so autocratic as a director?

JB: Well, it depends on so much: who I'm working with, what show I'm working on. I hope I would adapt to what I'm doing.

JW: How much work goes into rehearsing for a production? Are you studying the play, researching and reading?

JB: I read the script a lot! Back in the day we would have a fortnight just working on the script.

Now time is less and there's more pressure. We can't afford to be spending that time studying scripts in such detail, but what I'm beginning to realise is that I've been preparing for the next show for the last 25 years. It sounds silly but the background is there. It's not lazy, but everything I've done prepares me for it.

And the new challenges I face are stimulating and enriching. The next show I'm directing is about performance poets and beatboxes, which I've got no clue about – I just apply what I do know to the project – and it's stretching me, always improving my knowledge of theatre.

JW: What gives you the most pleasure out of everything you do or have done? Is it those moments when the audience are on their feet, loving every minute?

JB: That can be fantastic. I remember doing a First World War piece, though, in front of an audience of a hundred and people were so moved by it. That gives me satisfaction in a different way.

It's funny – sometimes your feelings about a piece don't always chime with an audience's and you can be left a little flat. Some audiences have gone wild for stuff I've been less sure about, and they have been less excited about stuff I thought was life-changing. It's wonderful to see people inspired by the work, but if you know you've given it all you have there can still be an immense feeling of pride and pleasure about that, regardless of outside reactions.

JW: Do you remember people who inspired you when you were younger?

JB: I feel like I've been and am inspired by a whole range of people.

JW: If you aspire to work at high levels you have to be alive to influences everywhere.

JB: I love this job. I get to talk to all sorts of different people, from the cleaning staff, restaurant staff, the artists, the audiences, to the accountant.

Steve Redgrave

HIS ACHIEVEMENTS in rowing are unprecedented and he was Britain's most decorated Olympian until Chris Hoy took that title off him a few years after his last Olympics, but even the cycling legend couldn't claim to have had the same longevity. Steve had five chances to win five golds in five Olympics and he hit the level, won the loot, every single time. He held that highest of high peaks in one of the most punishing sports. Training day in, day out, hitting what would prove to be unfathomable intensities for most of us, he soaked up pain on a daily basis, and on the last leg of his Olympic ambush, he discovered he had diabetes, which made everything even harder.

To himself – confident, modest and unassuming – he's just a sportsman doing what he does. To many he's been a soaring inspiration: to athletes who search for guidance on their own way to discovering a peak performance, or to the numbers of people with recently diagnosed diabetes who need something to grasp as they navigate their own suddenly compromised worlds.

The man is clearly busy. There's no wonder scavengers like me want a piece of him, but he invited me into his home warmly and we embarked on an enlightening and lengthy interview. He talked freely, often taking his own route off my intended road to get to his own answer, which as an interviewer I love.

The overwhelming feeling at the end of an interview like this is that, yes, the medals and achievements count, but there's an extra layer to all that. It's the inspiration his efforts and performances have given to young kids who then take up sport, or the happiness he brings to people up against their own adversities, perhaps as they watched his boat poke its nose in front in the final at the Sydney Olympics in 2000, which do so much to stir.

———

JW: So, I'll start with the million dollar question. How do you win five Olympic gold medals in 16 years?

SR: This can't be a simple answer! I've been doing some motivational speaking recently and you can tell people are looking for the one secret; the fact is that so much influences someone on their way to winning Olympic titles. It's so hard for there ever to be a set template; every individual is different and reacts differently to learning, absorbs things at varying speeds, and it's different depending on the sport or discipline.

It's necessary to have some talent or aptitude and, more importantly, then honing it. There are few individuals who get very far with talent alone. In different disciplines you can nurture talent more than others.

For example, I feel like for the 100m sprint, if you don't have a talent for sheer speed, strength and power, then you can probably forget it, no matter how hard you work.

To look at the rowing ecosystem specifically: there are plenty of people around the world who row but it's not a huge sport, and it's considered a public school or university sport, quite exclusive. The net, therefore, is fairly small. Wherever there's a river or lake there will likely be a rowing club, but as you can imagine, the development of any youngster depends on this.

You have to go somewhere to row, perhaps like squash I would imagine. You can't just open your front door and put your trainers on and go rowing, so the geography is a defining aspect that affects a rower's development. With running, cycling or football you can almost gain instant access to improvement in these disciplines. No additional equipment is really needed. Kids can play football in the streets with pals, lots of people have or have access to bikes, and to run literally requires a pair of shoes.

In England we have an interesting advantage in rowing because the water doesn't freeze up in the winter. The universities tend to be on rivers or near water, so there's no surprise that universities have strong rowing cultures. There's talent out there walking every street, potential world champions in all sports and our mechanisms don't always find that talent. It's sometimes by chance they stumble into something. I probably did. I was lucky to be born here in Marlow, went to a comprehensive school, and the Head of English asked me to row. The Marlow Regatta happened to be the biggest one-day rowing regatta in the world at the time. All that meant to me at the time was a party, but the opportunity to find the sport was right there for me, in front of my eyes.

JW: Do you still know your headmaster?

SR: Yes. I've not seen him for a while. Out of 450 kids from three school years that were able to try the sport, a maximum of 12 people rowed. Out of those 12 in my era, three of us got through to the 1988 Olympics and came fourth or better.

Incredible to think how one small state school can produce so much, but these little pockets or hotbeds often form in the most unlikely places.

Around the time, I remember another state school that won the big hockey champs two years running, and until then they had often been won by public schools. It was clear that it was the teacher driving the system that made it happen, and of course this random school didn't just get good by chance. And as it turned out, the coach had played for England and knew what he was doing. The system was in place and suddenly this state school becomes a hotbed for hockey.

Going back to what made things work out for me – I was perhaps ahead of my time ability-wise. Into my later teens people started saying to me that I could be world champion. It was quite exciting, and the encouragement from the coaches made me feel special. I didn't enjoy school that much and to row you have to leave school premises, which was cool. It all helped to rouse my interest and motivation.

Early on I was doing quite a lot of single sculling and winning races on my own. This sowed the seeds, and the motivation kept coming. I started to think about being Olympic champion and to make goals real. I'm a big believer in setting goals and working towards them.

At a certain stage later on, success didn't come the way I wanted it to, and I realised what we were doing wasn't enough. I almost felt my name was on the trophy but that we weren't moving in the right direction. At this point I railed against British Rowing. We were part-time, the Eastern Bloc countries were all full-time and I didn't have that much ability!

So, in 1983 I changed my training and within a year became Olympic champion. We had been getting further behind the East Germans, and we needed to change to close the gap.

We had been training very intensely for shorter periods, producing lots of lactic acid and taking more time to recover. The Germans were doing more mileage, more extended sessions, with less intensity. So, I increased my volumes of work and yet kept the intensity pretty high – I like to think higher than theirs! Someone who wants to reach the highest world standard needs always to be alive to adaptation, looking deeper, and changing things if the need is there.

If you're Olympic champion you have to know that if you want to repeat it, the likelihood is you're going to have to be a better athlete. The sport moves in cycles, and the standards rarely fall. The year after the Olympics, athletes come off that level slightly, having wound down from it somewhat. The year after that the level is back up to where it was, maybe slightly above and it will keep improving in the two years into the Olympics. This is how purely physical sports operate. I'm sure skill sports like squash see improvements, but in timed sports you can measure it by a clock extremely clinically. So actually, if you've got your goals in rowing you can actually plan your training to hit the speeds you want to hit to reach Olympic level. It's quite clinical.

JW: It's interesting to hear you talk about the endurance emphasis when essentially what was required by you in competition was a six-minute intense blast. I would have guessed that the intensity of the efforts in training would have been a priority.

SR: Yes, but it's still a muscular endurance effort. A 400m sprinter can go about 30 seconds before the body starts seizing up, so from then on it's endurance. In a boat you can probably go flat out for 45 seconds. If you go too hard too soon in a six-minute race you will burn out.

We don't do much under an hour in training and not much over two hours, and we're still going out hard. It's still pretty intense, even though I'm saying the intensity decreased and the volume increased. For the first 20km session of the day we're holding about 120–140 beats per minute. For the average athlete the absolute maximum is 190–200 heart rate. For the average man then, that would be quite tough.

It was Jürgen's [Grobler – Steve's coach] input too – he encouraged these changes. You could often do more, but you were bored out of your mind.

JW: How did you deal with the tough sessions? Did increasing/decreasing the intensity help you to withstand it all?

SR: In rowing we work in a team, day in, day out. So, there were people to go through it with, which always makes that part of it slightly easier, but there are the sessions that are so unpleasant, and they are part of the deal.

When I started to get successful, I actually stopped doing heavy weight training and switched to more specific muscular endurance circuit sessions. My coach's theory was that if you want to be a great rower, why go and lift weights all the time? It makes sense. I can certainly see there's room for cross-training at different stages in the schedule of an athlete, but for a rower it's about moving a boat, and the only way you move that boat better is by getting in and out of it. There are ways of making the specific rowing sessions different and more intense. We can adjust our training on the water to improve different aspects: speed, power, endurance. But specificity is crucial.

Jürgen sometimes had us in the boat with an elastic bungee, for instance, which would make it tougher, a really specific form of strength training.

On the other side of this, anyone wanting to become better at something means hours and hours of repetition, and at some stage the brain can't cope; this is exactly where other forms of training can be greatly beneficial. You can train well and still mix it up, to preserve some mental and physical freshness. Essentially though, I do still believe that the more you do of the actual discipline, the better you can potentially be. It's a balance. But these circuits we did were absolutely horrible, and they were probably the sessions that made all the difference. I saw the other teams training and their strength sessions were more sedate. They would do a set, have a chat, wait a few minutes, then go on to the next thing. We would be fiercely competitive with each other and that intensity was right there.

JW: So, you wouldn't ever do extreme lifting, which would require longer rests/chats in between, to maximise power?

SR: We would do only a little bit of heavy lifting. It's not a power sport, it's a leverage sport.

JW: You didn't have much rest generally, did you?

SR: We didn't have many rest days. There's more scientific emphasis now, more monitoring and pacing out of the training sessions. Matthew [Pinsent, Steve's team-mate] and I wanted to get things done, so we would want to get there early and go. We liked playing golf, and Wednesday was a half day. So, we would go down and do two sessions before lunch. Or sometimes we would do one session, play golf and then do another. But these were our easier days.

Circuits were two or three times a week and we would get through between 18–24 sessions per week.

JW: That's a phenomenal work rate. It's interesting comparing your training to squash training, because sometimes in squash it's difficult to know which energy system to train. It's not as clinical or measurable; one day you can be playing on a cool court and need to move quicker for less time, the next you're on a boiling court where the rallies never end, playing for two hours.

SR: Yes, talking squash now, when I was at my fittest, I just wouldn't have been able to keep the intensity of my movement.

The amount of time the rallies go on for is incredible. When I played, we had 15-shot rallies and were knackered. What I was seeing was players almost having to try to recover in the rallies themselves! At the T they were having a breather. It was their only chance.

JW: How do you peak for certain events? It's one thing getting up to train every day to become great, which you did, but the key is being good on the right day, which for you is a few significant days once every four years. I always wonder how Olympic athletes approach this. There's no wonder they get edgy.

SR: We only race five or six times a year, which compared to most sports isn't that much. The theory initially was that you do the heavy weights and endurance work in the winter, and as things drew nearer you would make it more speed orientated, and that's what we tended to do.

When Jürgen came over he took the intensity down, built up the circuit training and muscular endurance work so it was more about the heart and lungs with the lighter weights, and we would only stop this two or three weeks before the season. This was done all year round and it made much more sense to me. Why not have the advantage all the time, and train with quality right up to the events?

Peaking is interesting. Earlier in my career with my first coach it was maybe a bit hit and miss. His ethos was that 'miles make champions' and I agree with him to a certain degree but, without some of the scientific knowledge, we would be liable to go into races not knowing whether we were on the button or a bit overdone.

When Jürgen came over from East Germany, we always seemed to be right at the right time. As a potential coach, in East Germany, their systems dictated that they be sent to study for five years as a precursor to even starting to be thought of as a coach. These coaches were so well versed in the science of sport.

We athletes had an assessment every six weeks, like a formal race of some sort, to see where we were. Jürgen could then form opinions from the tests – whether we needed more power work, more endurance work, whatever. The following races or tests needed to be higher and higher, then we would be tapering up to the major championship of that year. After the championships we would have three weeks off and start again. With Jürgen we almost always hit the button at the right time. Probably why he's so good.

With all the hard training that we do, the limiting factor can be the mind. It's easy to get stuck in the here and now. We think it's all so much harder than it was before. Well maybe it has to be! Training evolves. We used to think of having four hard sessions a week. Now we're doing 24! The mind can keep pushing if you let it. Athletes will keep improving and pushing boundaries.

It's about having the mindset that we're capable of doing more. It's about quality, yes, but to an extent, the more we can do the better we can become. In many respects we're a lazy race. We do just enough to get to where we need to be!

We need to look at and visualise what sport is going to be like in five, ten, 15 years' time. Are squash players going to be worse athletes? No, they will be better. Knowledge, desire, research will all keep improving, especially with more technology. It's just what happens.

JW: This whole idea reminds me of the Fosbury Flop [the now widely used technique in the high jump].

SR: Dick's actually a great example. He found a different way to everyone else. He wasn't great, or that much better than everyone, but he advanced that particular discipline. That's why I like the way Clive Woodward worked.

In 2003 he put systems in place by delegating. It possibly wasn't his actual 'coaching' that may have won that Rugby World Cup, but the whole system he put in place for those players so they could become world champions.

Clive wanted to outdo the other teams in everything they did. He would look at every small detail, from having the players fly business class, to changing shirts at half-time. He had the buy-in from the athletes too, and once you've got that the boundaries can be extended significantly.

JW: How did you deal with the highs and lows of competing in rowing? After an Olympic win, how would you find balance?

SR: It's a tough question to answer. I met Michael Campbell, the golfer from New Zealand, and we talked about this. His whole goal was to win a major, and when he won it there was this emptiness after having achieved his lifetime's ambition. He could have gone on to win more, but I'm not sure he had the drive ever again.

I wanted to win a gold medal, and it just came naturally to me to go for another. I enjoyed what I was doing too, and that was motivation enough. I didn't want to go and work in an office. At the beginning I was raw and hungry, and by the end of it I was old and had diabetes and colitis! But I was backed and spurred on by Matthew, the next generation whose coat-tails I could hang on to. By Atlanta we had become quite similar in standard. Up until then I had maybe been top dog, but he was beating me on tests. It was an interesting scenario, but great motivation.

After the high of winning you're certainly forced to re-evaluate things. Some athletes don't know which way to go. I always wanted to keep pushing.

JW: Like many world-class athletes you must have had some testing rejections and disappointments, not least when you became ill with diabetes and weren't sure whether you could continue.

SR: It was difficult to stay strong through all that. I think performance-wise, year on year, I was getting better, but perhaps my performance curve was flatter than the younger rowers, who were seeing much steeper improvement. But once I had committed to do something, that was it.

Around the time the diabetes initially surfaced I remember being out in South Africa on a training camp, and every session I was doing just proved that I wasn't the same athlete as before. It was that bad that I couldn't see how I was going to be able to carry on. There came this sense of pride at simply finishing the sessions. We were doing long road bike sessions and I would come in half an hour later than everybody else. I remember one ride in particular where we came out of the hotel straight on to a hill and I got dropped straight away and couldn't catch them up until a break. At said break I got off my bike to rest and the others were back on theirs getting ready to go again. Demoralising stuff.

I grabbed a banana and water, we started coming down the hill and I got a puncture. The van came down, we fixed it and Jürgen was in the van.

'Come on Steve, leave it. Put the bike in the back of the van.'

'No, I'm finishing this session.'

And I did. It was all sunny weather and beautiful views, but I was riding home going through turmoil thinking that was it. I was literally going to pack my bags when I got back. I wouldn't even make the team at that level, let alone win anything, and this was three years out from Sydney, in 1997.

I got back to the hotel and crashed on the bed. I thought, right I'll pack the bag. But I didn't have the energy. So, I waited and pondered a bit, and after a bit of time I became ever so slightly more positive, thinking that at least I had completed that session, and this afternoon I had got 20km on the rowing machine. I thought I would stick around and just do that session and then leave. So, I had talked myself round to at least doing the next session and seeing how it went. It's amazing how the mind can change things.

In the afternoon I was on the ergo doing this 20km session – awful performance again. The facts are that it takes less than about two seconds to complete a rowing cycle. I was so tired, and simply was saying to myself, 'You can do one more stroke. Okay, do that.' So I would. 'One more stroke, then you can stop.' This is all going through my head in fractions of seconds. The mind is telling the body what to do, urging it on, even though one part of the mind is saying there's nothing there! So, that was how I was getting through. Just one more stroke, two more seconds, the most basic bit of time.

It wasn't about any Olympic dream back then! I was absolutely miles off but kept getting myself those small bits of time and somehow kept finishing the sessions. The performances were depressing but there was also this feeling of self-satisfaction at having got through them.

Slowly, over weeks and months, the performance started to come back; we talk about light at the end of the tunnel, and the tunnels can get pretty dark, but there's often a little glimmer by approaching the whole thing in smaller elements.

What's good about all this is that we can relay this inspiration through books like the one you're writing, for instance. People can read it, see the difficulty I had to go through to succeed, and they can almost think, well if he can do it why can't I? I'm not just some one-off genius – that's not what's getting me through. It's brutality at times, and you don't have to be a genius to work hard.

I get letters or emails saying I've been an inspiration, and that's all good, but I was just doing what I needed to do to get better at my sport. I'm flattered that doctors use me as an example now, that things can be achieved with this affliction, but it was simply moment to moment.

JW: And the one doctor who showed you belief through all this actually lived close by.

SR: Yes, incredible really. Things are different now, but it was an unknown business at that time. As far as I could see there weren't a great many athletes making it with diabetes, and especially in a physical event like rowing. This expert doctor I saw lived about two miles down the road.

We had a three-hour meeting, and I was just waiting for the bad news, but it didn't come. He set out the plan, saying that we might have to make this, that and the other change, and that we had to work it out. It wasn't what I was expecting. I might have been looking for an excuse to get out at that time, but he certainly didn't give me one.

JW: How important are the formative years in terms of making it at the top level in a sport like rowing?

SR: I think the very best will have probably started with the sport not much later than 14 years. It's probably about the right sort of age for maturity. There are certain limitations with rowing, dangers going into water for instance, and young people need to be able to row a boat safely.

It's a sport you can come to a bit later because the physical aspect is so prominent. It's necessary, though, to have used the heart and lungs as a young person in order to develop at high levels.

They say if you can't catch, throw or kick a ball, or run, then you end up rowing. Rowing is actually a very coordinated sport and it's amazing how it seems to attract uncoordinated people! But there's a rhythm.

If a golfer has a basket of balls at the driving range, they find rhythm in that, and rowing is about rhythm. Then the matchplay aspect for the golfer takes that rhythm away because it's broken up, perhaps like a squash player, footballer, tennis player. Endless patterns of skill need to be honed and explored over years and years. A player must be reactive, and the ball is going to be in all sorts of different places. You're never ever going to play the same game, from the exact same positions. With rowing, it's essentially the same moves in every race. There are fewer variables that can throw you off and we haven't got all these complex and singular movements to make. It's for that reason that rowers don't need to embed all those patterns and skills early on as much as some sports.

Different disciplines and different levels of skill

One thing we can probably be confident about is that starting early in life to develop skills, certainly in some fields, is significant. We only have to look at how young kids soak up languages to know they have unbelievable absorption capacities, so asking the expert interviewees about this aspect within their specific area of interest has been very interesting.

Steve makes this point about different sports and he has described it perfectly. Running, cycling or rowing are certainly closed skill, extremely physical sports, requiring of the athlete very specific and repeated movements, often made in limited planes of movement. They are endurance or speed-based and the margins between success or failure are often minuscule. An open skill sport like tennis requires many very complex skills completed in very random planes of movement. Each game takes on a different and unique pattern to the last.

Tennis, squash, football, snooker and languages are disciplines requiring extremely specific detail and they will require very fine and unique skill patterns, built up over many years of highly specific practice.

Closed skills sports will require immense effort and training, but the in-depth practice and fine-tuning at a young age doesn't appear to be as necessary.

Several times I've come across players in their twenties who have been playing a couple of years and are absolutely convinced they can become a professional player.

Some obviously have no idea what being a professional squash player entails, and the lifetime commitment it requires. One player really got quite upset when Malcolm gave his career prospects to him straight. He took umbrage and wrote back something about proving him wrong, but he could be as buoyant as he wanted. All the passion, spirit, guts, determination and long hours in the world wouldn't have made him a world-class player, or even a professional one. Never mind 10,000 hours, 50,000 wouldn't have done it. Far ... too ... late.

The same principle applies here as the one regarding picking up language. Imagine a 16-year-old English pupil picking up French for the first time, and then announcing a year later that they will become fluent in the language. However hard they try, I'm not sure they will ever speak French like a French native, because they simply didn't start the process early enough.

I was hitting squash balls in my playroom at home when I was three. I was playing tournaments at six and seven. I was a regular on the junior circuit at eight. The exposure I had to the game from such a young age was considerable and I was lapping up experience and background by playing in junior tournaments all over the country, by playing most days and by having coaching. Look at all that time, and all at a time when my brain was at its most receptive, before I was ten. My fellow pros will have been following similar paths. So, when you've undergone all that background, you can surmise how silly it sounds when someone thinks they can turn up and turn professional at 18.

I'm taking this from memory, so the numbers and facts might be questionable, but in 2007 I was at Leeds Carnegie University gym training when I set eyes on a poster calling for the attention of people aged between 16 and 22 who liked sport, were tall, quite fit and who thought they might have an aptitude for rowing, cycling or basketball. It alluded to the London and Rio Olympics in 2012 and 2016 and explained briefly how national governing associations of these sports were looking to recruit athletes, to produce champions.

This was the first time I had come across this sort of advertisement for talent. It was implying that even a person with decent and nowhere near professional levels of fitness, but the right build, age and enthusiasm could find success, or even a place at the Olympic Games within only five years or under with the support of a world-class system.

Rebecca Romero became a cycling medallist at the Sydney Olympics and a rowing medallist in Athens in 2004. It's an incredible achievement, yet certainly doable in these sports, since they are defined more by the physical intensity than for complex skills.

It would be almost impossible to transfer from squash to football, or squash to tennis, or the other way round in that way, and win Olympic-level medals in both. And you couldn't, I don't think, appeal to university student athletes to recruit them to an Olympic programme.

Physicality can be built late on, and naturally develops later, and this is why I don't believe junior squash players need to be trained too physically too early. If they can do the practising of the skills and movements early, do the wiring, the physical strength can always be improved. The hours on court can be caught up less easily.

JW: The way you prolonged your career in such a physical sport, maintaining the highest standard, has been the sensational part of your achievement in many people's eyes. The mental intensity of training that hard for so long must have taken a toll. Were there sessions or days where you took the emphasis off the intensity and quality and just did training you wanted to enjoy, as a kind of act of self-preservation almost?

SR: Good question. Enjoy? Probably not. Especially with the illnesses, becoming older and with younger athletes pushing me hard. I saw a lot of my intensity in James Cracknell. We were racers, never wanting anyone coming past us at any time. It was always hard for me to do things by halves.

Matthew is a great racer, but it's not in his DNA to be quite so constantly competitive. You can't class him as lazy, but he only does what he has to do.

We were racing at Henley, paddling our steady three laps around the lake and a sculler was catching us up. Even though it was a warm-up I didn't want to be behind him; Matt didn't really care. We got to the end and I was disgusted that we had let a single sculler, a boat that's four categories slower, go past us. Matt turned round and said, 'Well, he is lightweight world champion.'

But he never left me wanting when it came to races. James had my traits, wanting to win everything. It's not a bad way to be, but I also subscribe to the fact that there will be races where you need to draw on every reserve, dig deeper than ever before, and in a funny way if you've pushed in every training session to your max, you sort of know where the boundaries are. Sometimes it might be good to not know the boundaries, or to at least have energy to dig deeper when difficulties arise. Recovery sessions, lighter sessions, more 'fun' sessions have become more important in training for sport in this modern age, but I was probably not very good at them when I was a full-time athlete.

—

It took me a lifetime to get to grips with finding this balance and making sure there was lightness and fun in training. Intense and focused application in training is absolutely essential, but whenever anyone does anything for six hours a day, six days a week for years on end, some of it just HAS to be lighter, with an emphasis on enjoyment and freedom. For me, on some days the tactics, the bloody process needed to be thrown out of the window and I had to tell myself to back off after a tough few days. I simply needed to just go on court, hit the ball wherever, go for extravagant shots, play games, maybe have a few laughs with training partners. I found it really bloody hard to do, especially not being the lightest of touches.

I didn't always cope very well with the thought of one minute ever being wasted, and I alluded already somewhat to this in Julian's interview. Every hit, every exercise, every sprint, I want to matter. What I actually had to learn was that in a world of stress and fight and intensity, finding a little time to waste away, time doing not much, giving yourself time to be a lazy arse, is time very valuably spent.

My coach Malcolm was very clever with this, and it was one of the most important lessons he taught me. There was never much doubting I would ever shy away from work; the challenge for him as a coach was to get me to do less work or do more fun work. He would have us put the rackets down and introduce different games in sessions, or play doubles, which would still be a form of training different enough to rejuvenate whilst still tapping into hand-eye coordination skills and general fitness.

Nowadays, sport scientists talk a lot about recovery sessions, and this was what this was. In whatever we do, unless we're the prime minister or the head of the CIA, we all might make room to ease off on the intensity or change up what we do. In the case of an athlete, it helps to freshen the body and mind, so that when the hard work needs to be done it can really be done. It's particularly important for athletes because the intensity of their daily routines are often so intense and difficult, requiring high levels of application and concentration.

What I'm talking about applies everywhere where anyone works themselves full tilt. Office managers like David Brent talk about building morale within companies, and while his guitar interludes may have been dubious, his ideas about toning down the intensity are right on. Despite the dodgy term, 'team building' activities are always given hype in work arenas, but the principle is the same. Doing the same work, the same session, the same anything day after day will burn anyone out eventually. It's probably a bit of a wayward glance for me to compare all this to Steve Redgrave's training schedule – I'm on one of my tangents again – but it's echoed for many of us in whatever we do.

—

SR: James could get frustrated if we took a lead in a race only to then hold back and win within ourselves, so we would talk about keeping these few gears available.

There's a race that springs to mind that I had with my first partner, Andy [Holmes]. We broke the world record two weeks before it and found ourselves racing against two younger guys, U23 champions, who weren't expecting much.

After a strong start they began pegging us back, putting pressure on. I remember thinking I had nothing to give and we had 750m to go. We were never going to win as far as I was concerned.

Andy shouted to go, and I couldn't. I said to myself, 'I'm going to put in ten strokes and I'm done.' As it happened, we must have hung on for long enough, me thinking we had no chance, and we just drew away. You could see their faces, thinking that we were Olympic champions, but they couldn't recognise how much trouble we were in. I was about to break, but our experience took us through. It was a great lesson.

It also taught us about coming back down off that high of breaking the world record. You might be world record holders, but it doesn't mean you suddenly win everything.

Chris Hoy

CYCLING HAS enjoyed a surge in popularity in the last decades, certainly in the UK, and much of this undoubtedly stems from the incredible success of British Cycling recently. Chris Hoy was at the forefront of this British brilliance in the globe's velodromes.

So engrained in the British sporting landscape are his achievements in world cycling that it seems pointless really to recite them here.

I didn't spend much time with him, but as everyone has always said, he was humble, modest and kind. He encapsulates the type of sporting hero our kids desperately need to be seeing, in an age where they are often impelled to sit on football stadium terraces listening to hostile crowds berating antagonistic footballers and slagging referees. Hoy lacks all of the obnoxiousness of an archetypal sporting hooligan, but has twice the dignity and, ironically, no less aggression.

He confirms to us all that a champion can be classy and dare I say nice with it.

I feel very fortunate to have been able to interview, for this book, two of Britain's most successful ever Olympic athletes, in Chris Hoy and Steve Redgrave, the latter whose record of five golds the cyclist surpassed in London in 2012.

JW: How did you become an Olympic champion cyclist?

CH: I don't think we can assume that talent is everything and that you're born exceptional. I would say, though, certainly with cycling, that you have to have the right physiological parameters naturally to be successful. If you want to be a basketball player, you're better off tall, and if you want to be a cox in rowing, you can't be six feet. There are boundaries for some sports but beyond that it's hard work, application and the commitment that are the biggest factors.

It's mostly the successful people who have the drive and commitment, funnily enough.

JW: Having done it all now, is there anything you feel that was apparent as a child that formed you or made a difference? You seemed to do a lot of work without coaching. Was it important that you were doing the hours quite freely as a young athlete, not getting too analytical or serious?

CH: Maybe with technical sports it's more necessary to have significant coaching input earlier, but the closest thing I had to a coach was my dad.

One of the biggest things about sport and kids is that they all grow, learn and respond at different rates. A ten-year-old might be naturally heavier than his mates in school, which therefore would be conducive to being better at rugby earlier than the others. A young runner might run faster because he has natural strength earlier, and because the coaches don't see weaknesses, technique may get ignored.

I was actually the opposite when I was younger, naturally smaller than the others in my rugby team, and I had to work a lot harder just to keep up physically. When I did catch up physically eventually, I was already used to working a lot harder just to keep my head above water. This helped me.

Difference in rates of development at a young age is a huge factor and a difficult thing to understand for parents and coaches. What my parents were good at was letting me enjoy sport and not comparing what I was doing to the others.

JW: So, was the early exposure important? How early would a pro cyclist have started as a kid?

CH: If you're looking at an event like the time trial, pursuit or track, where the actual skill element is less, then I think you can get there quicker, arrive at it later. Someone like Rebecca Romero had done a lot of cycling before she switched to cycling from rowing, so it was possible to switch because she had developed that endurance engine so extensively. The potential was there to be able to produce a lot of power for long periods. It wasn't like it was a completely new skill, not like she was trying to take up golf! It's different. In cycling, the biggest skill, if you can call it that, is the ability to suffer pain. That's the biggest challenge to overcome. There are just no shortcuts, and every single time you sit on a bike you know it will be difficult, whoever you are.

JW: And you did a lot of sport as a kid?

CH: Yes. I wasn't the biggest, strongest, tallest, best, and I always remember having to work harder. The pain of physical training just became part of it and rowing certainly helped me. That was a great form of discipline. The close-knit group of the crew was a good thing to be a part of, like track events in cycling. Every single session, you're inspiring each other to work harder. It was good to have that.

JW: How significant was the external analysis, sports science, psychology and data analysis in your career, all of which are readily associated with the performance of an athlete in this modern age?

CH: The key thing is that you're sure all those things are helping you; they shouldn't just be there for the sake of it. Before these services became available to us there was perhaps some guesswork involved and maybe in some sports there still is. Cycling is a clinical sport based on specific facts and figures, and we wanted to make sure the guesswork was taken out of it.

One of the biggest turning points of my career was when I went to university to study sports science. I decided that if nobody was going to tell me how to train then I would learn for myself. I wanted to learn the theory behind training for sport and how best to design my own programme. Years later, when I could benefit from the expert advice, it wasn't then just a matter of doing what I was told. I wanted to know the reasons behind why we were doing a certain session or designing a programme in a certain way. Having that understanding from the study meant I could commit easier to the advice.

JW: Do you think you were doing things in a more thorough and professional way than everyone else?

CH: My outlook throughout was just to do everything possible to be the best I could. You never know if you've done everything right, but you give yourself the very best chance. You have little control over what rivals are doing but if you've worked and trained the best you can with the knowledge you have, raced as well as you can and still come second, you shake the guy's hand and move on. But if I had wasted time and taken shortcuts and failed I would never be able to forgive myself.

JW: Can you talk about the balance of quality and quantity of work? And has this balance changed over the years?

CH: Every athlete is different and has different responses to training at different stages. Some athletes may need to train more or less than others; some need to have people around, some prefer working it out alone. The significant thing going into London was that I could still hit the numbers; the one-off efforts were as good as ever but repeating the efforts day after day was more challenging. I don't think I was recovering as quickly as I was in my twenties. I had to accommodate the requirement for more recovery and I really had to make the most of the time off I had. When I was younger there was the temptation on a training camp to go out and do something, to get away from the training, but I realised later on in my career that it was important to use the time in between sessions to really rest. I had to make sure I had done everything possible to be ready for the next session. That was a big difference that came with age.

JW: Do you feel some athletes get a bit obsessed with totting the hours up?

CH: Absolutely. Sometimes, if my times dropped below a certain level, I would be forced to just pack up and go home and this was an incredibly difficult thing to do because if you're not going well you naturally feel you want to do more to correct it, but the clever thing is to know that's exactly the time to stop. That input would likely come easier from the coach. They have a clearer perspective looking in and that's when they have to know the athlete they are working with and be very astute. That was the best thing about having a coach.

JW: You would have had to go through some horrible, painful sessions on a regular basis. Did you have a way of mentally dealing with these?

CH: For certain sessions there was a nervousness that was similar to what you would feel pre-race! You wake up and it's not funny. 'Here we go again, this is going to be horrible.' But I always recognised what it was going to do for me. There's always this perverse enjoyment of them – I knew and was motivated by the fact I could gain an advantage over anybody by doing them. I didn't think anyone was going to push themselves as hard as I was.

JW: How did you manage to perform the way you wanted to, at the peak of your powers, for those specific days in the Olympics?

CH: As the experiences build you learn from each one about how to taper, when to back off the heavy sessions and generally how much to do leading in so that you're not over- or under-worked. A coach might have a basic template regarding tapering but then it's also about considering the individual. Experience is a big factor here and there's no set way.

You want to make all the effort count, but it can be detrimental to over-analyse, especially as leading into competition you find yourself with more time. It's best not to overplay it, to make it as ordinary a time as you can. So, on rest days, a psychological ploy would be to turn the situation on its head, let myself just do whatever, to think along the lines of being normal, doing the things I normally would do. I would tell myself that it's not the end of the world, which it isn't. At the same time, it's a massive opportunity. I try to reinforce to myself that the work is done. Having put all the work in, I've done all I can, so it's time to let it happen.

JW: And psychologically it's about focusing on the process rather than the end result?

CH: Absolutely, yes.

JW: Did you visualise?

CH: I was always running races through my mind. I had a clear picture of how I wanted the race to pan out. Visualisation not only enables you to rehearse and reinforce what you want to do, it helps you avoid negative thoughts and stress, which can't creep in because you're focusing on something specific.

JW: How do you come down after a performance? Do you sleep well, and do you deal well with highs and lows?

CH: It's so difficult to switch yourself off after a race, to not replay it over and over, but you have to find a way to recalibrate and look at what's happened and get moving on to the next stage. As for the Olympics and how you come down off that, well it's nice to party and do the things you haven't been able to do, but it can feel a little empty as you try to get yourself back into training ready for the next four-year cycle. Many athletes have struggled mentally and physically to get back into competition and training but I did okay. There was actually a realisation for me that it wasn't just about a gold medal, it was about the daily routine. Nothing really changes and gold medals don't mean you're happier in your life. I realised that I get as much adrenaline from the actual process itself: the training, planning, the teamwork and being in the gym. All that matters too.

When I got past all the highs of winning the gold medal, I really wanted to get back into the routine with some purpose. It's one of the changes that I find hard in my life now, that I don't have that discipline of training to look forward to the way I did. I do get to have greater variety perhaps now. An athlete's life can be one-dimensional, where everything is incessantly geared towards how I do on a bike. I can do things I couldn't do then, though; I've just become a dad, so that might not last!

Simon Stephens

SIMON WRITES unremitting, sometimes violent and exciting plays for theatre. They feature a wide range of characters from cab drivers, teenagers at school, rock stars, children running away from home, to blokes in pubs swearing. You probably don't go to one of his plays for a comfortable night. Together with his actors, he shows us stories and worlds of hatred and decay, difficulty and despair, yet sometimes with comedic pay off, which renders them far from morose or depressing.

He wrote the play based on the novel *The Curious Incident of the Dog in the Night-Time*, which ran at the National Theatre and in the West End for three years, and on Broadway for nearly two. Aside from the plays, he has written a fascinating book of diaries about his work in the theatre, which gives a tantalising insight into the craft. He describes his enjoyment of collaboration with theatre artists and the difficulties he discovers in rewriting and tuning his work, with the help of others, to make it sing.

He has recently ushered some of the most lauded playwrights of this generation into an entertaining podcast series for the Royal Court Theatre in which he intelligently interrogates his fellow playwrights, digesting every word they say. He's effusive about their abilities and explicit in his admiration, leaving any ego at the door and demonstrating a willingness to learn rather than compete with or envy them.

He's a fascinating and compelling presence when he speaks. He's a natural (or maybe it's practised!), almost disarmingly eloquent orator, and such command of the spoken word is often an unusual trait among writers, who can often withdraw into themselves and remain introverted. When Simon talks, the words fizz and the swearing isn't infrequent, and with not a boring word or sentence, he's honest, generous, profound, respectful and sometimes scathing. I've been on one or two of his talks and teaching workshops and could tell he would be a cracking interview.

His laugh is soaring and infectious, and his range of vocabulary at times impressive without being contrived. His is a weird dichotomy because he writes serious plays drawing on darkness and violence, and yet to talk to he's exuberant and happy and cheeky. I'm confident that even if you have absolutely no interest in plays or drama, then unless I cock it up, this interview will give anyone delicious information and anecdotes they can either learn from or simply just enjoy.

He's moved by music, and he sometimes puts specific tracks in his plays. He draws on the arts and sport for inspiration, reads widely for cues, and talks passionately about Manchester United. He's alive to the problems and issues that are draining and propelling our landscape in 2017, and observes and absorbs what life has to show him. This general open discernment of the world can only help to create the stories.

For someone so lauded and respected in his field, he's humble, respectful and eager to bring you into his world, and to perhaps follow a path that you might show him. He's keen to hear about others and their lives and experiences, and to enlarge his own by doing so.

I was the fan in our exchange, and yet he managed as we talked for an hour and a half to ask endlessly about me, to engage wholeheartedly in the interview and sound enthusiastic about it. Interviews can be awkward and tiptoey. Not even remotely so here. Simon has a natural conviviality that makes such an occasion feel liberating and joyful.

—

SS: So, what are you up to in London?

JW: After listening to your words of wisdom, I'm going to see *The Ferryman* [a play running in the West End] this afternoon.

SS: It's an astonishing piece of writing. Sometimes you read something and think you want to give up, it's that good. It had that effect on me. Do you get that at squash?

JW: You absolutely do. I watch other players and think, 'Hell, can I really reach the same standard as this?'

SS: I have the psychotic need to be liked. I end up asking the people I'm talking to all the questions. So, stop me if I lose myself. So, the squash ... you've been world champion!

JW: A world team champion three times.

SS: You said you've got kids?

JW: Yes. I was really interested – reading the things you've written about having children and how it's affected your plays and your writing. Do you think things that happen in our lives outside our specialist field, without sounding trite, help to encourage that always? I know many people think or fear that having children can diminish ambition or output.

SS: When you have children, you get a perspective on things, and realise what's important and that it's not necessarily puncturing the desire.

That Cyril Connolly aphorism that the pram in the hallway is the enemy of creativity, I think, is pernicious and not true. I wouldn't have been a fraction of the writer nor have written any of the plays I've written if I hadn't become a father.

JW: As a parent you discover a new landscape with a desperation and profundity you've never felt before! Feelings and emotions are heightened because of them.

SS: The other thing is the combination between an intense depth of feeling and an intense displacement of feeling, which is interesting for a playwright. What a playwright is doing is not putting themselves on stage, they are putting somebody else on stage, so the agony of parenting is that you've got this intense feeling but you have to let them live their own lives and fuck up. If you try to intervene too much you just damage them. The characters in drama have to live separately from you too, and you've got to imbue them with the same sense of love. It's not autobiography. If people write with too much autobiography, then they are not playwrights.

I think becoming a father has been a defining thing, and being in a marriage, a family. The oscillations that arise within the relationships you have with those closest to you are so strong, and it's the one thing no one ever talks about.

JW: Do you talk about that openly?

SS: I'm probably talking to you about it more than anyone else because it's the first time I've met you! [Laughs]. What does Vanessa do?

JW: She commentates for TV and puts a lot of time into our children.

SS: What I'm probably getting at is that my wife was an art teacher and she stopped doing that, for the kids. If you're world champion or your plays are getting produced it's a bit more sexy than going home to put the rubbish out or buying the milk. You're like, 'I've been opening an important play! [Giggles] I can't do the recycling! I've been in New York.'

JW: Do playwrights tend to deteriorate with age or get better? Are you limited with time in that respect, like an athlete is?

SS: My wife and I talk about snooker. We wonder why they shouldn't be good when they are older; it's not physical is it? Maybe it's the same with playwrights.

There are moments where I'm hanging out with my kids when I think, 'Sod the writing, let's just take the dog to the park.' But then my sense of the fragility and the ephemeral nature of the writer's career make me think, 'I've got to write.' So that threat does give me more drive. I think that comes from a sense that if I'm not writing I can lose my ability, my status as a playwright. I think I'm slightly worried about not being able to write a good play one day.

JW: Does the writing just have to get done so that you stay happy and fulfilled? I know if I want to get sad, I just have to not exercise for a couple of days.

SS: I don't know what training's like for you but there are two engines for me. It's my job. The dynamics of my family is conventional. That's just how it has worked out. My wife runs the house, it's down to me to earn. However much food I give the kids, they will continue to eat it. I also wonder whether I didn't have that. It's interesting at the minute because *Curious Incident* was so successful that it takes the edge off that a little bit. Would I still have the drive to write without that motivation? Well, if I didn't write or make theatre in some way, after about four days I would start struggling. When I'm on holiday I can switch off and rest, but when the holiday's finished I need to get going.

So, you're an actor?

JW: Yes, away from squash I act. I love it. You wrote a fascinating book of diaries. How did you decide not to write about your family?

SS: I suppose they are kids, aren't they? This was just about the work and that's how I wanted to keep it. So, you've written books? Any plays?

JW: I've written two plays … awful ones.

SS: No, don't do that. That's great. It's good to have done that!

JW: You've got to get them done, however bad. You wrote seven plays before you got one produced?

SS: Yes, and the advantage is I've lost some of them. The third play could be in a box in my attic!

JW: And at the time they will have been very, very important to you?

SS: Massively important! I thought they were everything at the time. The very first one I wrote at 17. I've talked about going to a comprehensive in Stockport. It didn't have the oomph of a public school, where you might be shit but at least you will end up as a lawyer. You were just rubbish. [Laughs] One of the things I did a lot, though, was read a lot and listen to lots of music to get out into my imaginary world. It was the kind of school where if you admitted to loving reading or literature you wouldn't get too many people concurring.

I remember doing *Wind in the Willows* at school and playing the second ferret. I loved it! The kids worked with the parents, the cleaners, the costume and the backstage to get the show moving. It's still the thing I find exciting about coming to rehearsals today.

I soon wrote a monologue with another character. My play was a dramatic staging of a Tom Waits song. It was very bad, but you have to write bad stuff to someday find the good.

—

I remember as a young squash player of 20–21 wanting to be the best a bit too earnestly, and a few years down the line I saw much more clearly that at that time I just wasn't ready. You also realise then that there was too much riding on it in your own head and that those experiences you thought were life and death were merely apprenticeships. I prepared hugely for big events when I was younger thinking that this was it, that I was there, only for the results to sometimes be disappointing.

It wasn't about building to the future – I saw myself as the world number one right then. It was a rapacious, all-consuming thing. I look back now and understand that the years of work and the experience and battle hardening needed to be soaked into the bones. If only I had known back then, I could have been a bit more measured about it.

But then to eke out every inch of improvement, perhaps you need to have that determined ferocious mindset when you're young. I'm drawing a parallel with what Simon is saying here about his first written plays, that maybe your first ten efforts at a script mean the whole world to you, maybe you think they will be that good that they will be instantly taken on and staged by a world-class theatre. The likelihood is, how can they be? These are often just your practice runs, unless you're somehow very special or harbouring some superpower. The real difficulty is that you've got to be mentally strong enough to accept that these efforts are not good enough and to try and try and try again.

And perhaps, similarly, you need several world champ-ionship defeats before you might be unusual and lustrous and lucky enough to nail it. The greatest athletes and achievers are somehow able to stay clear about the fact that the continuation of effort will one day accumulate, and they seem to know to remember that the work they do now might not win them a world title or yield a West End commission now, but that same work might well do someday, a long, long time from now.

—

JW: You went to York University?

SS: Yes. You can completely reinvent yourself when you move away. You can be someone different. I'd written this play and I took it to the drama society and said, 'Do that man. It's a proper play, my play,' like I was Liam Gallagher. And they did! In a tiny little theatre at York University. It remains one of the most important theatres in my life. Still today there are aesthetics that I developed in the work I did there that I still draw on now.

I had entered into a world. I was interested by the gang mentality, by the notion of something I had imagined myself, being made real by other people. By the time I had left university we had taken a couple of shows to the Edinburgh Fringe, so I just committed to writing.

JW: I heard a story about you not being able to make it to the National Theatre for a meeting because you couldn't make the train fare.

SS: I went to live in Edinburgh, formed a band, kept writing plays, met my girlfriend who is now my wife. I was a DJ in a mobile disco for a bit in rough pubs. Everyone wanted me to play music I didn't know. I wanted to play the Happy Mondays and Stone Roses, and everyone thought I was a c***.

There was this 18th birthday party and none of her friends turned up, just 20 people. Her mum told me to take some food because there was so much left. I had no money, so I took all my food for the week.

I was also a door-to-door salesman for Betterware – that was grim. Then I got a job in a cafe above a bookshop, working 4.30–10 five nights a week. I had hours either side of it. I would get up at ten, write for three hours, go to work, come back and write more. I sent this play to Jack Bradley, literary manager at Soho Theatre Company, and I can't remember much about it except that there was a sex scene with paint. He asked me to come down and we could do a workshop on it but I couldn't afford the train fare. Back then, even sending a script out was expensive in terms of getting it copied and sending it in the post. So, I couldn't go down.

I then got a job at the Riverside Studios, stopped writing plays, discovered Charles Bukowski and started writing very bad poetry, some of which still does exist in my internet dropbox. I set up a poetry night just so I could read this poetry, and an amazing guy called Andrew Braidford liked the poems and asked if I had any plays for his new writing festival. I wrote the play *Bring Me Sunshine* on the back of that. We got a cast together to read it and he wanted to do it, got a director and did a production at the Edinburgh Fringe. He invested £5,000 of his own money. It was fucking amazing.

JW: But you had already been up to Edinburgh with plays?

SS: Yes, a couple of my plays had been put on at the Edinburgh Fringe. I produced one myself there, to audiences of about four. I vividly remember people leaving. People walk out of everything I've written.

JW: Yes, that's a good thing.

SS: Yes, it is. But they normally walk out if they are offended. You don't want them walking out because they are just piss bored. These people were walking out because it was just shit and the football was on. They were a bit apologetic about it.

I was proud of that show. So, you go either of two ways, and one is to ask why they are walking out. How can I make this better? What can I learn? How do I tighten it?

Then on the last week, we got a five-star review in *The Scotsman* and an editorial in *The Stage*. They were saying this was an amazing time for playwriting: 'David Harrower's *Knives in Hens*, David Greig's *Europe*, Mike Cullen's *Anna Weiss*, Mark Ravenhill's *Shopping and Fucking*, Enda Walsh's *Disco Pigs,* Simon Stephens's *Bring Me Sunshine* mark a whole new generation of playwrights.' I'm in that list! By that stage I had really committed to not quitting, and the last week we sold out every night. I was like, 'Fucking hell, come on!'

I went back to London, was still working at Riverside, and my girlfriend, now wife, decided to have a baby. I knew I couldn't raise a family on a bartender's wages, so I retrained as a schoolteacher and got a job in Dagenham. Interestingly, one of the things about working in this bar after midnight was that I could get free taxis or travel on the night bus, and as the only sober person in a city of deranged drunks, I put all this material together into another play. I wanted to excavate the fear of parenting. All new fathers have a fear of killing their own child. It's like, 'What if I drop them?'

JW: Yes, that's true. You're walking down the steps holding them, playing it out. If you faint or trip, the child could die.

SS: Exactly! The play became a play about a taxi driver, trying to atone for having killed his own child. There was a sequence of people travelling in his cab, leading up to him saying sorry to his ex-wife. It was a play called *Bluebird* because he drove a Nissan Bluebird. I sent it to the new artistic director at the Royal Court Theatre [England's renowned theatre for new writing].

JW: This was before an agent took you on?

SS: Yes. I was just sending plays to theatres. On the day Oscar was born, I got home, and the Royal Court rang telling me they were going to do the play. Kind of remarkable.

JW: Were you doing a lot of writing as a young person? Were you into the craft purposefully or inadvertently then?

SS: I was always writing for fun, always reading, from very young. I hated being at school, so I got away in my imagination through books.

JW: How do your kids react to your plays, if they have seen or read them?

SS: I remember going to see *Punk Rock* with Oscar. I was sitting on a train with him while he was reading it. He would look up at me going, 'Fuck!'

JW: And what do you say?

SS: It's really exciting. I love it. Nervous. And after the end he looks at me and says, 'Did you write that?' It's like, whoaar! It's really thrilling. The first time they went to see *Curious Incident of the Dog in the Night-Time* they were just telling everyone around that I was the writer, and now the play is on their school syllabus. I was talking to Oscar's mates and they were doing these questions: 'How does Stephens present Christopher's sense of loss in the play' – I was like, 'I don't know!' One of them gave an answer and I was like, 'Fuck, yeah.'

JW: That must be quite strange.

SS: It's great though. Have you got film of you winning world championships?

JW: Yes.

SS: The good thing is they mainly just take the piss out of me. I think underneath it they are quite proud.

JW: My son comes to watch, and he will sit for three minutes and then he's off, or he's more interested in the other players. In the theatre industry, you're surrounded by all these special artists who are very good at what they do. How much are they all just talented and how much of it's about them dedicating themselves to a craft and working hard?

SS: What do you think about this?

JW: I'm a bit dubious and reticent with the word 'talent'. The number of hours talented people seem to do is too much for it to be innate or god-given or whatever they say. It borders on the offensive because it implies there has been no work, determination or persistence involved. Usually 'talented' people are simply the ones who spill the most blood working hard.

SS: I always think about Gary Neville. He was by no means the best footballer in the school teams, but he worked and was so tenacious. In the end he's the most successful England right-back ever, captained England and won the Champions League. Then there are the 'talented' ones who fall away because they can't work. I don't necessarily think I know enough about genetics to confidently answer the big question.

But there are forces outside our control that mean the application is afforded to theatre or poetry or song writing or novel writing, or fucking squash playing. There's a reason why, when I was a shit tennis player as a kid, I didn't carry on playing tennis for ten hours – but instead I went home and wrote. I wasn't in control of that. In its simplest terms it was just what made me happy, but the reason it made me happy was how all the tectonic plates of my life that I don't control lined up. I then just did it all the time. When you do it a lot you get better.

JW: I would watch Wimbledon on TV then pick up a racket and go in the garden and replicate what the players were doing; I feel like that stuff was the really important stuff, rather than any structure.

SS: And the other thing is, a great irony that I talk to beginning writers about, is the notion of being a writer. There's something sexy and thrilling about 'being' a writer. For me it was probably that distinction of coming from Stockport to now being asked to do two days in New York. That's quite sexy!

The more I do this job the more I think the noun is irrelevant and the verb is what matters. It's about the work. It's not about being a writer, it's about writing. But I think you need the noun in the story to earn the desire. But in the end, it's the process. What's complicated is that the narratives that surround being a writer are actually pernicious and potentially destructive.

There was a time in the 90s when professional footballers hadn't had the media training and they were really interesting, which is odd because they were all inarticulate and not particularly intelligent. They hadn't learned the cut phrases, but what was fascinating was their inarticulacy in the face of something around which more narrative was being written than anything else in the world. It's constant storytelling.

But watch a footballer talk about it and they are actually not that interested in the narrative. They don't care about winning the league or being the first-ever England player to do whatever. They seem to think about putting their head down, passing the ball and getting to the other end of the field. Don't worry about the fucking noun, worry about the career and do the work.

The agony of being a writer is that you, for instance, James, start at 34, and there's maybe part of you that thinks, 'Fucking hell, Sarah Kane was dead when she was 28 and she changed the face of British playwriting.' You might think you're too late but you've just got to be tenacious enough to ignore it and to just write. This mindset is what's more important than any talent.

In the years when nobody was putting on my plays and people were leaving up in Edinburgh, which coincided with Sarah Kane and Jez Butterworth [lauded playwrights in the 1990s – Butterworth still is today] at the Royal Court, the frustration of that took me so close to quitting. I was really proud of the play though, I had worked hard on it. I thought about it, but then thought the day after I decide to quit was bound to be the day I would get the email or phone call – if only I had decided not to quit. You can't stop, you've just got to keep going and searching for improvement.

JW: And now you've achieved what you have, you're established, you have a reputation in the industry, does your outlook change?

SS: The fascinating thing now, if I were to objectively look at my career, I think it wouldn't be an unreasonable thing to say that this person was a successful playwright. But I've never really relaxed. I very rarely get a moment when I go, 'Look at this, I've fucking made it!' Now the anxiety is that I may have already done the best stuff. If the next one's shit they are going to reject it – this is the start of my downfall. But it's probably a good thing to feel that.

JW: It gives you the drive. You've done a lot of teaching. In squash a lot of people want the magic fix. Coaching is highly regarded, sought after, perhaps too much in certain areas of the world. Isn't a lot of it about just getting down to hard work, or is coaching crucial?

SS: I do think it's possible to teach playwriting, but that still can't substitute the actual practice a pupil must put in.

This is how I think playwrights can improve. For five years I read a play every day. I don't read a play every day now, but there was a time when I was reading a play every day. If you can read that much, you're going to learn. You can access the books nowadays. And when reading a play, I wouldn't always read for fun. Sometimes life's too short not to! But I would say not to analyse the academic side. I always say to not read like a fan, nor like an academic, but like a thief. Read the play and see if there's something you could take. You could keep a diary, and record these things – it could be a line of dialogue, image or a cultural decision. It's a better language in which to think about playwriting rather than wondering what it is the writer is trying to present.

JW: So, the study guides are no good then?

SS: They are shit, don't bother. The best way is to simply ask, 'What are the good bits?' And then, 'How do they do it?'

—

I learned so much from studying plays and books in English literature classes at school and I felt it opened the doors into seemingly impenetrable texts.

As Simon talked about his disdain for going overboard with the study guide, I was reminded of my own reactions to people who get too theoretical and academic about squash.

At events and exhibitions people have sometimes approached me to talk in massive technical detail and asked about how I play this or that shot, how I change my grip or what specific string tension I use in a racket. I often just bumble my way through a pitiful answer or tell them how sorry I am that I can't provide a riposte that at least makes me look like I know what I'm talking about.

Perhaps people are making things more complicated than professionals would and this indulging in theory can be overdone, and I urge them to guard against the theory being the replacement for the actual doing of the thing.

In my case, the moves and techniques are nailed into the subconscious because I've been repeating and developing them constantly since I was a young child, so I come to play and it's there. I'm not often thinking in academic terms about how it comes to be there.

As a writer, Simon doesn't seem to get as bogged down with the academia as the academic does.

He's perhaps advising burgeoning writers who want to write well to look at the plays they admire and to discern very simply what they like about them, what moved them and then to unabashedly steal it, use it, copy it. Learn from it, re-watch it, use it.

This could be a simple way for theorists to approach learning a sport. Watching the best rallies of your favourite players and stealing their ideas and copying them is one of the best ways to improve. It's not a bad idea to watch players who do it less well too, then attempt to understand why it is they do it less well.

It's a pure, unfettered approach. It isn't there to burden anyone by great waves of complex thinking, which I've found can make the issues cloudy. Sitting in a room theorising over a book about squash or talking for three hours to a coach about the perfect way to hold a squash racket could be of some benefit, certainly for players who are motivated by this sort of work, but it might be good to also remember the axiom which states: 'The essence of style is simplicity.'

—

JW: So, when writing a script try to find what might be effective dramatically and entertaining to audiences?

SS: Yes, it's entertainment but you need to dig into the technicalities. Another good approach is to take a great scene and think how the writer could have fucked it up.

If you want to write, doing amateur theatre is brilliant. Keep doing that. If you're in a company that's doing plays as good as the ones you're doing, do as much of that as you can because what you will find as an actor is that there are some lines that are effortlessly speakable and somewhere you've really got to get your mouth around them. When they are effortlessly speakable you know the writing is good.

You will realise that what makes great, speakable writing comes from the thinking about the spelling of the word 'playwright'. As writers, our work isn't linguistic, it's structural. And the structure for me always comes from the tension between desire and obstacle. Which is why it's like squash.

JW: The construction of a rally in squash is the same: push and pull, desire/obstacle. In tennis, Roger Federer works out his angles and shots within rallies meticulously to overcome the obstacles, the responses of the opponent. And when you say writing is structural but not linguistic, squash too is about creating a structure. One beautiful, sexy shot doesn't always win rallies or matches, but the subtle construction of all the rallies in a match can do.

SS: Yeah, yeah! I tell you this: one day I'm gonna do a workshop and all I'm going to do is show them the 2008 Wimbledon Men's Final between Nadal and Federer, when Nadal had never won and Federer was on the point of winning the most titles. It was five hours long; they were both at the top of their game. And every point was dramatic.

JW: It was.

SS: And you could feel the audience change allegiances all the time. If Nadal won, they wanted Federer to win.

If Federer won a point, they wanted Nadal. That's great playwriting.

JW: Opposing forces …

SS: Because it's people in plays or tennis matches who really want something yet have to come across obstacles and negotiate them. And it's in that negotiation that character is revealed.

The one thing that most beginning playwrights don't understand is that it's not about language, the words, fancy speeches or jokes. It's the defining thought, I would say, of 90 per cent of first and second and third plays. Often beginning writers are kind of making sense of trauma. Normally when people experience trauma, the question is why is this happening to me? If you work with a therapist, they will encourage you in trauma to subvert this question, not make it about why this is happening to me, but instead why I might be doing this.

To me it's been invaluable to think about what my character wants, what's stopping them getting what they want, and what they do in order to get it. That will be in your metabolism as a sportsman. What do I want? I want that point! What's stopping me? This opponent and the way he or she plays. What do I do to get the result I want?

JW: Often, where squash players or athletes struggle, is that they think too much about the winning, the trophy, the title. What they might be better off doing is thinking about what they need to do to get it and be very strict about it.

SS: It's reminding me. You watch interviews with Ryan Giggs talking about that goal he scored with the shirt off, and he's got nothing to say about it.

JW: All the years of practice allowed him to make it happen almost automatically.

SS: If he had thought about winning the FA Cup or the team being the first to win the treble, he probably wouldn't have scored that goal.

JW: The podcast has been brilliant. Your book of diaries was great fun to read.

SS: That means a huge amount, man. Somebody asked me who the diaries were for and I said that the book is for me 20 years ago when I was starting out. The image of the professional writer when you're not one can be daunting, so I just wanted to relate what happens to those trying. Sometimes it's great, sometimes it's really shit and confusing.

JW: The highs and lows you experience come across in it. It seemed that you never thought that you solved every problem, you were always leaning into directors, actors and other theatre artists to give you that advice and you were very open like that. It's not autocratic. It's not like you ever thought, 'This is my play, and it should be presented just how I've written it.'

SS: Yeah! Are you like that with your coaches?

JW: Yes, I listen more now to people than ever. You never know where the next bit of information might come from. It might even be from people who know nothing about squash! They might say something that just hasn't occurred to me. Sometimes you get garbage thrown at you, but it's happened where I've taken something and thought, 'Maybe they have got a point there.' The more I carry on the more I struggle with autocracy from coaches and players who have certain styles, and who want you as a player to do it their way. Improvement, I feel, comes from conversations and thoughtful calculations between different people. It's a conversation and work that takes place continuously between myself and my coaches, which it seems is how you work with directors.

I read your comments about Katie Mitchell, who has directed your work, and how she's a great watcher of an audience in preview shows [warm-up shows with audiences]. Presumably then, she's watching them to tell her things about what they are or are not enjoying about the play?

SS: But also it's really hard and you get it in parenting. I don't know if you've had it yet. And there are bits where you fuck up, you really fuck up. My negotiation with my kids about how much screen time they are allowed, I often end up handling badly, and so you need somebody to stand back from it with fresh eyes and tell you you've fucked up, to tell you the writing needs a tweak. I cherish this relationship with other directors and actors and am always open to it.

Rich Landau and Kate Jacoby

READERS MIGHT have no interest in the chosen worlds of some of the characters in this book, yet one thing as sure as taxes is that for humans food might be the ultimate art form, the one thing each of us can invest in and do so daily. It moves, excites, depresses every single living being of us to some extent, under certain conditions, on a daily basis.

We might recall certain meals, the smells around a table at a very specific time or on a significant occasion. Many of us have been lucky enough to be able to recall the discovery of a new food or combination that's life-changing. Eating food is so elementary, basic and primal, but perhaps most of the rituals that come with eating can amount to some of our very favourite bits of life. For some, of course, upsettingly they may be their least favourite. Food evinces memories of happiness, sadness, disgust; and great meals are our favourite movie, or the song we can't stop playing.

Philadelphia has been the host city for the US Open Squash Championships for several years. I'll always have fond memories of autumnal ambles around Rittenhouse Square in between sessions and matches. Of all the places squash has shoved me, Philly is the best for non-carnivorous eating houses, and during my early visits I found a restaurant called

Vedge, which served high-end food made only from plants, with no meat or dairy produce coming from animals.

There's a horrible stigma attached to being vegan, so like Rich and Kate I try not to mention the word. I would rather say I don't 'want' (rather than what most people tag on me – that I'm not 'allowed') to eat animals or what they milk for their babies, but that's just too long-winded. Non-vegans think a vegan is all about dry lettuce leaves, green tea and wearing bandanas.

We've all been brought up to think eating animals is normal, and most cafes and restaurants on our high streets are dominated by foods with animal products, so no wonder then that people find veganism a difficult concept. Tradition has a far stronger pull than alternative, or even logic.

Actually, stopping to consider the thought of a piece of meat once being a living animal that had most probably been tortured for us to eat turned me off. Cutting out dairy produce was harder and tends to be so for most people, but the dairy industry still takes advantage of animals and has to by its nature make them feel some form of pain.

Every restaurant has a veggie meal with dairy produce available, but it's harder to find meals without. It's a tough step to make when it's all we know. I remember visiting Vedge and thinking for the first time that people will never tell me again that vegan food can't be the ultimate in gastronomical pleasure! Apologies for that pompous phraseology. It's just that mainstream chefs don't know it or haven't realised it. The known chefs of this world, those of the supposed highest order, barely even attempt to cook wonderful vegan food, so there's no wonder we feel it can't be done. Rich and Kate have proved it can.

Rather than crusade here, I'm merely lending context to the brilliance of Rich and Kate's cooking.

Vedge's food was just sublime. I remember eating there alone and I had to put the knife and fork down and say words aloud to myself in between bites. To myself! I mean, how pathetic! All I wanted to do was to tell everyone and serve it to people who smirked and questioned what they believed to be such a bland diet.

This was a completely new, original, colourful way of cooking that could kick pizzas and dairy-addled ice cream out of the water. And without the guilt of knowing that you would be separating a calf from its mother at birth. To think of enjoying great food that is made compassionately and considerately. At Vedge it felt so bloody indulgent. Vegan food is undoubtedly so good now in 2021, and nowhere near as elusive. Back when I first went to Vedge, though, things were different.

Doing the same things or eating in the same places all the time when I'm playing is criminal in a city like Philadelphia, but with Vedge I'm hopeless, and this ethos goes right out of the window. One year I went three nights on the trot, and they must have been wondering what the hell I was up to.

Kate and Rich and their restaurant give another, perhaps surprising, context to this book and I'm so happy to bring them in on a conversation about how brilliant, awesome (to hell with it, we're talking America here) standards are achieved.

Food is, of course, there for us to function, but it can astound and transport and there's room for artistic balance. Cue the eye roll again, but you only need to watch people eating in a busy dining room to see how it both comforts and inspires.

—

JW: I love Vedge. I think it's stunning. What you do with ingredients most restaurateurs never think of using. It makes me think that every restaurant I walk into now is so predictably the same as the next one.

RL: Thanks, we really appreciate that.

JW: Can you tell me about your first forays into this industry?

KJ: We were very self-taught. I hosted at one other restaurant before we met and that was it. Rich bartended in other restaurants. He opened a place, a small kitchen called Horizons, in 1994, and he was doing it because he wanted to do it. There were so few examples of plant-based cooking to learn from, so he went for it.

RL: I always cooked at home and I've loved thinking about and working with food my whole life. I liked the taste of meat and giving it up was purely for ethical reasons. When this conflict surfaced I wasn't about to turn to sunflower seeds, kale and wheatgerm; I had to have really good cooked food.

I taught myself how to put all these meaty flavours into the food I was missing, and that was the foundation that Horizons was built on. I did bartend a lot in my early twenties and one of the restaurants I worked at were really ahead of their time, doing California-based cuisine. It blew my mind because not only were the flavours so fresh and vivid, but the food wasn't tortured and they didn't do a million things with it. I spent a lot of time in the kitchens there and I saw how you do this and that, where you keep that, how you prepare food, where it's stored.

I was, I guess, learning how to set up a restaurant and gained significant experience there. I started cooking for friends and family, then did catering. It soon occurred to me that I could sell this stuff. I opened Horizons, where nothing was over five dollars. I was expecting college kids coming in to sip on some coffee, but it wasn't like that at all, and people from the business parks were coming in suits and ties, families too, and I was amazed at how fast things started to happen. My goal was to reach out to the people who didn't really understand the food, and people really responded.

JW: So how old were you when you were doing all that learning?

RL: I was doing the bartending and learning in my early twenties, and I was 26 when I opened the restaurant.

JW: But you would have cooked from early on?

RL: Oh my god, my whole life.

KJ: But that was more at home, though.

RL: Yes, only at home. The first thing I remember as a kid that flicked a switch was visiting this old Italian family, first generation off the boat. They barely spoke any English and I walked into this kitchen and literally fell to my knees. They were making this fresh tomato sauce from tomatoes in the garden and the smell blew my mind. That summer I started to grow my own tomatoes at my parents' house and it became an addiction. I had always imagined in my mind this rustic garden cooking, elegantly presented, without any animal products, and that lady showed me. That's been my north star ever since.

JW: Did either of you have teachers or mentors?

KJ: Rich was my teacher.

RL: I had no one to teach anything. You could go down to the natural food store and they would tell you how to ferment your own kombucha and all the hippy-dippy stuff, but there was nobody really cooking tasty plant food in restaurants.

KJ: I think a lot of the training that was available early on was about natural cooking establishments, and they were very much health-orientated. They weren't so concerned about flavour. We were always more interested to approach cooking from flavour first, and this is good anyway because plant-based cooking is cholesterol free and lower in saturated fat naturally.

Above all, we want the food we serve to smell, look and taste really good.

JW: You said you didn't necessarily want the 'vegan' tag hanging over your restaurants, is that right?

RL: Most people associate vegan food with what is sacrificed. They see it as an apology or an excuse. They see it as what we're taking out of the diet in order to be more healthy. We're all about taking nothing out and instead giving you all the flavour you've always known from plants and spices and sauces, just without the animal flesh, which will hurt you anyway. When you flaunt the vegan thing, a lot of people don't understand it, so they run a mile.

JW: The food is such high quality that it can't be an accident. Was there a lot of practice going in? Did you study? Were you reading and researching a lot?

KJ: People ask about this a lot, about the inspiration. I think the level of complexity in the food is just from time spent cooking in the kitchen. We both strive for consistency, but then in amongst that it's important to revisit something later and recognise that we can do something better to move it on. Our methods and techniques we figured out for ourselves. As Rich said, there wasn't much to go against or model ourselves on in this area.

We've tried to travel as much as possible and spent a lot of time in the Caribbean and Central America; the most vivid travel inspiration was our first visit to Japan, where the delicateness of the food was so inspiring. It completely changed how we felt about sourcing our vegetables, and in terms of our stocks and sauces. We learned about simplicity.

Another big trip was to Morocco. We didn't come back and start cooking all this Moroccan food, but there were certain techniques of theirs we used, like the use of herbs and the layers of spices. When we travel, we go to amusement parks and do other things but we're always eating and thinking about food – whether it's high-end restaurant or street food – and constantly absorbing everything we can.

JW: There's a dish on our table as we speak. How much are you reviewing recipes and foods during the day?

RL: Every day, it's constant. It's what I do, I eat! They just made me one to test the product today. Yes, constant testing, evaluating.

JW: Do the examples come from your chefs now?

RL: Yes, they made me one to try. There was a new batch of seitan-marinated mushroom steak mix and I just wanted to make sure it was good. It's a solid recipe but I need to make sure. I have to work out a lot!

I want to expand on what Kate said about influences. I don't want this to come off the wrong way when I say this but I didn't do a lot of reading and researching. A lot of this came naturally to me, which is why I was very confident I could do it. I just cooked and cooked and it worked.

There was one cook and his situation that really helped drive me into what I wanted to do, and that was Graham Kerr, or the Galloping Gourmet, a British cook. He worked with so much butter and cream, cooking the most unhealthy food you can imagine. He was out there celebrating this classic French cuisine, and in the 80s his wife had a heart attack. He thought he had almost killed her with the food, so he created a show in the early 90s where his whole philosophy was to take what he used to cook and completely clean it up, removing all these products and putting back colour, flavour, texture and depth. The whole philosophy of removing bad stuff from a dish and putting back better stuff chimed for me. I knew it was where I needed to go, so if I was going to take the meat out, I had to make sure they were never going to miss it. He was inspiring.

JW: It's good to hear, and I wish some of our well-known chefs today would take a leaf. It's all the same old indulgent stuff. You rarely see a cook on TV try to bake something indulgent in a different way, without the same old butter and lashings of double cream. You feel like it's a cop out.

RL: I know. But people still don't think plant-based indulgences can actually be indulgences.

JW: I'm going to start drawing parallels, so bear with me, but in squash the changing of pace and texture in a rally is a huge thing. In the modern game players can't be one-dimensional. They have to change pace and vary what they do with the squash ball. Is what a chef does with a plate of food a bit similar? It seems that every plate is full of foods with different textures, cooked at different temperatures, different colours, spices and flavours that pair up with each other. It's a lesson in construction. Without sounding too much of a dick about this, is all this intentional?

KJ: I think there's an aspect in many things, whether it's playing a sport or being a cook, where when you reach a high level it becomes more of an art. You have your own personal expression. If you stand out in your field, you're artistic, and if you've been doing something a long time, you're growing and changing as a person. We talk about musicians and how the music changes and evolves for every album, those who still have that same distinctive sound yet who change and move over time.

A lot is about how you're able to adapt as you're changing, as the people working with you change, and then the audience you play to changes. However good anyone gets at a high level they must move with all that, while keeping in mind what the strengths are. You're always paying attention and doing things that stimulate you, but at the same time you can't lose sight of what you've done before.

You know what the signature move is, you know what your classic is, what your go-to thing is, but you riff off it. It's like Jimmy Buffett playing 'Margaritaville' at one of his concerts: there are things that got you where you are and it's no use taking them for granted, but holding yourself back from moving forward is no good either. We've always been afraid of doing the same. You don't want to get locked into only doing the same thing.

—

As I'm writing up this interview I'm in New York City. I had a practice hit with Ramy Ashour, fellow squasher from Egypt, the ultimate players' player, along with the brilliant Amr Shabana. I've banged on about both often enough but let's say I'm a fan. Ramy appears later in the book.

He turned up as a young kid on the professional tour in around 2006–2007, spurring a curiosity in squash circles, and at which time I remember his contemporaries all watching him and collectively breathing long sighs mixed with gasps of genuine amazement at what he was doing. The amazement was at what he was managing to make a ball do with just a graphite frame, and it was intoxicating. The sigh was that every single one of us probably knew we would never be able to recreate or get anywhere near to what he was doing, graphite frame or no graphite frame.

So, I'm practising with him here and we're doing a fairly run-of-the-mill practice routine. One of the shots in the routine

I notice he's playing completely differently to the way I've always played it. He's actually practising it from a completely different angle to what I would, his objective different to mine. His is to hit a winning nick shot, mine is to go with the percentage, safer option. His consistency was amazing to watch, not so much fun for me to keep retrieving. I suppose the point here is that, yes, Ramy is amazing, blah blah blah, but apart from all that, I'm sitting here at 34 years old, practically ready to retire, thinking that I could maybe adapt something from what Ramy has taught me about this shot.

I've clearly been practising that shot in a very regimented way for many years, probably, when I think about it, with the same people. Can I be open now to working in a different way and changing things? Playing it differently? Maybe it's too late, but it's interesting nonetheless. Obviously, this aspect of Ramy's might not work for me or my strengths as a squash player, but I have to be open to it being possible.

One of the hardest things is that we know practice and repetition will really, really help us to improve, but aside from this, for people to really do something exceptional, to be that unique and brilliant, they may need to have the capacity to try different methods of working, to explore different opinions, and take on new, unusual or unlooked for inspiration from anywhere. This is what successful people do.

In all aspects of a life, it's so easy to do the same things, get so carried away by the comfort of routine. It's so easy to have the same meetings, with the same people, in the same venues, eating the same foods, checking the same websites. We all do it and need it to a degree, but to choose change and variation can be brave. To opt for chiaroscuro is unknown, but it's exciting and daring and surprising. It replenishes us, moves us to different spheres and it sometimes confuses or surprises those around us.

RL: As far as the creation of actual dishes go, I want to sell them on the very first taste. I watch the dining room and I don't want them quizzical or curious, I want them to love the first bite. There should be no grey area.

I don't really look at the plate and think, 'We need some crunch, let's throw sunflower seeds on.' I'll say two words that we use at all three restaurants as cues: 'Shiny' and 'juicy'. I feel like shiny dishes look the best and then juicy – things mustn't be dry on the palate. The dish has to make sense. When you take the bite, we chefs should have done the work. I don't want the customer trying to figure out what the hell kind of message it is I'm getting across. Simplicity is the key.

JW: How much work goes into what you do? What does the day and week look like?

RL: It's gonna make you tired. We're up at 6.45am with our son for breakfast.

KJ: After that we're checking in with emails and shift notes from the night before from the restaurants. When they close at night, they will write up everything that happened. Things that were good and things that weren't.

JW: The chefs?

KJ: It will be the front and back of house managers. They will do the rundown of how the night finished up. Sometimes there are some fires we need to put out in emails.

JW: And the fires could be with staff, punters?

KJ: It could be anything: a problem with a piece of equipment that broke, someone losing something, complaints, problems, there might be compliments from customers (hopefully!).

We try three days a week to exercise, then we'll be working from home for a period of time. Typically, at lunch we'll first go to Vedge then make our way back to V Street, where we might taste food. I'll meet with our pastry chef and his team at Vedge and it might be just checking a menu change, planning a private party menu. We might be testing some new mushrooms we just got in or talking to one of our purveyors.

RL: By that time, we're off to pick up our son again and we have an hour with him, some coffee, and help him with homework. If we have a babysitter that night, we're back off to the restaurants and we make rounds. Sometimes we'll have a family night at home. Once in a while we'll go out.

JW: How often are you in the restaurants now during service?

RL: It varies, two to five. It depends what's going on in terms of menu changes, staff changes.

JW: Are you cooking now?

RL: Not as much any more. We oversee and teach these guys to do it. I did learn something very important: I cooked until my early forties on the line, perhaps a bit too long, but even though I was very proud of the way I cooked on the line at Horizons, I was only ever right here at my stove and my space. I couldn't watch the salad guy, I couldn't watch the appetiser girl. I couldn't supervise and manage the other aspects, only what I was doing. Also, by moving up I can create opportunity – people down the line are wanting their own shot! So, I stepped back and let people move up into other positions. I found I was actually a better teacher than I gave myself credit for. The food evolved so much more because I was able to oversee it. I could teach someone to do what I was doing, that's where we are now.

JW: So you will dip in, look around the stations.

RL: Exactly. I visit each and every station in every single kitchen almost daily and I can tell right away who has been working there, how old the radishes are, I could tell them the one thing they were forgetting. I'm a lot more valuable to what we're doing than me just cooking. When I cook will be when we develop recipes.

—

And this is an echoing of all the best overseers of big operations. The expert manager or leader is the expert delegator. Their brilliance comes from the way they subtly and cleverly choose and train people in many different areas to help the cogs in the wheel. The captain of a ship won't be putting coal in the engine or serving food at the cafeteria; the director of a film won't be dictating every costume nuance; the head coach of a rugby team may have his defence coach working on the specifics of a back-foot counter-attack; the CEO won't be spending every living moment cooking the books.

    I've found it as a squash player, and in fact I'm constantly leaning on people to help me with all aspects of being a squash player. How would it be possible for me to run everything that relates to me getting to a tournament fit and well? I might be the one who can pick up the trophy and give the cheesy grin to the cameras that are all turned to me, but I couldn't have given myself the physio I had to have, or provided the carefully balanced strength sessions which my trainer set me week in week out.

    The best coaches in the world are not the ones who know everything, they are the ones that know plenty but find out the rest from those who do. The great leader recognises and admits a weakness, asks for help and is open to learning and developing. They never ever can say they have every answer.

—

JW: Will you always be involved with development of recipes?

RL: Oh god, yeah. I love to cook. I don't want to be not doing that.

JW: Can things become diluted when you have more restaurants?

RL: We're conscious of it and afraid of losing the quality when we enlarge out.

KJ: We care about the details, and we are not losing sight of that. A restaurant on any given night is about details being perfect so nobody notices any of them and punters can just go in and have the best night of their lives. From the lights, feel of the room, temperatures, to how the plates land, the silverware, everything needs to be seamless.

But we're conscious that as we started to have multiple locations things changed a little. Now I might go to a restaurant and not know the table number or there might be a new dish on one of the menus that I haven't been involved with. I worry about that. It's up to the two of us to make sure that however our role changes there's always someone doing a really great job of what we want doing, the same standard as we've maintained before. They need to have spent enough time with us so that they know the common vision.

It's very much about having the right people, preparing them rigorously, before we can expand any more. We don't ever want our guests to ask what happened or to tell us they used to like it better when … It's a blessing and a curse I suppose. We'll have regular customers who see a front of house manager and they are their favourite person in the establishment. They don't know me at all! The great thing is that they love the restaurant and that's a compliment for us. We've translated and they have executed our vision and it just frees us up to do what we've wanted to do from day one, which is get this food to even more people.

JW: The process behind recruiting chefs – is that ultra-rigorous?

RL: It takes a while before we can really trust them. It comes down to knowing what our vision is, for quality and consistency. We spend as much time as we can with them and some just get it. We try to develop this inner circle of people that we can trust. The guys at the restaurant here today, I'll spend time with them, lots of time, and I'm not going to talk big-picture management or moving to DC someday. I'll talk to them about making the perfect vegan cheesesteak today, and we'll spend time talking about how to perfectly dress a salad so the customer can taste the greens and the dressing at the exact same moment and not one way or the other. So, the more they get that and the faster they get that the quicker we can go on to talk about other things. This is the psychology of managing people. These are the nuances of running a restaurant that most people don't know or talk about.

Building our chefs up is the priority and it depends on who they are, what they have done and how long they have been with us. Their capacity for understanding is important, adapting to and taking on what we're trying to do.

JW: So, what traits do you see most of in all the chefs you work with? Why do they make it to that level? Is it talent, hard work, maybe a bit of both?

RL: Both. They need to work hard, that's more important than the talent. If they are looking for a free ride they are told to find another restaurant.

JW: Do you see many levels? In squash, you see it in young kids. They have just got an aptitude for anticipating a squash ball or finding a space, and there are literally millions of levels of ability.

KJ: Yeah, definitely.

RL: Yes. Sometimes some chefs can be very, very good at one thing, and less good broadly speaking, so you might keep them in that one spot doing their strength. They might be happy at their stations, doing what they are best at, not aspiring to be anything else, and that's fine. I don't want to push the wrong people in the wrong directions. If they can cook amazing food in a certain way and they want to keep doing that for me then I'm certainly happy. I won't take them outside of the comfort zone if they are not ambitious. Then there are other people who come here, and they will do whatever they can to learn and they want to be kept in mind for the future. They are crying out for opportunities, and these are perhaps the ones you spend more time with.

JW: How much reviewing of a 'performance' do you do? And like a writer would take notes from an editor, and a squash player from a coach, do you have feedback? Do you listen to customers?

RL: Credibility is important. Some people want what they want, they expect restaurants to be there, to cook something very specific for them, and you can only take that with a grain of salt. Certain criticisms and complaints you can only do so much about: 'Why don't you have organic, gluten-free something or other that doesn't have any soy, sugar, salt and fat?' These comments don't help us run a business; it's purely what these people want for themselves. Then there are comments that are really constructive, like: 'I do have to tell you that the fries were a little dark the other day and I want you guys to succeed, so just a friendly reminder.' I'll listen to those people all night long.

KJ: We've been doing this a long time now and we've got people who used to be regulars when we were out in the suburbs 20 years ago. They have seen us grow and I value their support so much. It makes us feel a million bucks when they continue to come in and love it.

I think we're mindful of industry makers and breakers. We have a local food critic in Philadelphia, Craig LaBan, and he's fair, I think. For us he's like God; he motivates us to be the very best we can be so that we get the best rating. We've read and studied and analysed what he likes in a great restaurant and we've always used him as the benchmark. We got four bells, which is the best you can do, and he gave us a great write-up, but now we want to keep it. It's valuable to have an industry professional out there whose work and judgement you respect.

Then with the internet you've got all kinds of people writing Yelp reviews or blogging about you or putting something on a Google review. These are the ones you can't spend too much time worrying about, because as Rich said, you don't know who they are, you don't really know how to judge their opinion. Are they a troll who has been hired to try to take you out of business? If you listen to actual customers who pay you, or established key people in your industry, they can help you.

JW: Will you try out a new dish on a group of people or particular person before putting it out there?

KJ: We try and try and taste food with our staff. If we have an idea for a dish maybe Rich will put them together and coach the staff and ask them to come up with something. Then we will try them together and give them feedback.

RL: And there's this language or vocabulary that everyone uses here, if you will, of flavour profiles. We ask whether it's a Vedge dish or a V Street dish, we will know where it sits. You go to a French restaurant, and if the chef is talking about enchiladas there's something amiss. The dishes have to make sense. There's a certain flavour profile that we're looking for in each restaurant. Each dish has to be not just a dish that's there to get to the next, it's got to be a winner, so we keep our menus very small for that reason. We have

15 dishes on at Vedge. It's important; I don't like big menus because they are just throwing stuff together from one big ingredient pool.

JW: It's interesting how clear you are on the theme of the restaurant. There has to be a story or a structure behind it almost. Being able to play one particular shot in squash doesn't make you able to construct effective squash rallies and win matches if the other shots are weak, so your whole rally has to coalesce, like the menu!

Everyone loves a label, genre, or box too.

RL: There are a couple of interesting phrases that spring to mind. 'Casting a wide net' is one and 'trying to be all things to all people' is the other. They couldn't be more different. 'Casting a wide net' is to try to impress as many people as possible, perhaps downplaying the vegan thing, and hopefully they will come no matter what. We need to get the meat eaters in here, so casting a wide net is what we try to do. 'Trying to be all things to all people' is a restaurant trying to have spaghetti, sushi and enchiladas on the same menu. No, no, no. It's greedy. Do something and do it right.

Ramy Ashour

SOME OF the memorable occasions in my sporting career have occurred while sharing the court with this fellow. He first and foremost is a warm soul who as a world-level competitor manages to balance cut-throat aggression with respect and sportsmanship. He will take every inch of metaphorical and literal territory ruthlessly on court, but by dint of an artistic game rather than unwieldy gamesmanship.

The fact that he was like this armed us both, I think, with a feeling of genuine ease during our matches. I found him hard to play, of course, but there was a freedom to it. I knew I could walk through the court door with him and just play the game, without having to think about what baggage would be involved, which in a sense is liberating.

His ability is unquestionable and unbelievable, his style adored by everyone who knows squash. He's a player everyone wants to watch. It's sad that he has had to endure injuries perpetually over the last few years.

The interview took place in January 2015. Ramy at the time had undergone treatment for body issues he'd had since the summer. He played one event in the autumn of 2014, the World Championships, and won it. His last previous event had been the British Open in May. These two were his only events of the year. For much of the interview we discuss the context around this period.

Ramy is an effervescent, illuminating talker and I've tried to convey his spirit in the transcript, rather than sanitise it with my 'structure' as he calls it. What he says isn't always threaded together, and he can go off at tangents, answering a question in his own way. It's a little like his squash, and all the more interesting for it.

Folks, if you're talking about genius, then you won't come any closer than this.

—

JW: Can you tell me about the recent injuries you've had and how you've dealt with it whilst trying to play high-level squash?

RA: The details of the mental struggle dealing with injury were all in the article you wrote in *The Guardian* recently: the boredom of waking up in the morning wondering if it's going to improve and knowing you can't train, and thinking that you just want to get done with the day. You're trying to get by. So, when I read it, I thought how it told me what I had been through.

JW: It's all the doubting that's tough with injuries. Not knowing where you stand.

RA: I had been having so many problems over the summer and I went to see a guy in Delaware. He said he couldn't help, that there was something more than physiotherapy to this thing, so he hooked me up with another doctor, Brian Shiple. I had a 30cm tear in the hamstring, so it's wow, a bit of a shock. This was 4 or 5 September 2014. It took him 20 minutes to tell me about PRP [Platelet-rich plasma]. You have injections – your body heals itself. There was a bit of doubt. I went to my brother Hisham and we agreed that I had tried everything else, so it was worth a go.

JW: How many sessions of this?

RA: Two or three injections. I was on crutches for three days. Then after a month I took a second lot.

JW: So that settled you for the Worlds in Qatar?

RA: Yes, for the Worlds I was okay.

JW: And was all this related to the arm thing? [In the final the main problem Ramy seemed to be having was with his arm.]

RA: Oh man, no, that was just different and weird. Don't ask!

I started doing rehab 20 days before the Worlds. I had the last PRP on 24 October and was on crutches for five to seven days. Then rehab. First match was 16 November.

JW: Were you actually training?

RA: I had been, a lot of the summer was good, but it was in and out. Around this time, though, I was just doing everything I could: upper body and pushing my heart however I could. After the crutches, I started walking normally, then had three best-of-five practice matches before the Worlds.

JW: So, what were you thinking at the World Championships?

RA: All I wanted was to be a normal athlete, to play – and if I lost, so be it. Sometimes I was thinking I just wanted to go and lose. Part of me wanted to win but then I was also telling myself to just relax, that I couldn't win having not played. You've done so much in your career anyway, forget it! Then the other little voice would say just go and kill yourself, don't be so negative. You could win!

I just didn't want to be injured again and have everyone feeling sorry for me, giving me advice and saying they hope I come back and all that. I'm sick of it, I don't want to hear it.

The funny part, right before going to the Worlds, the hamstring felt okay, but I was feeling something in my knees.

And then a doctor I saw was saying I needed more injections, so I got hold of the doctor I knew, who told me that was ridiculous. He said to just get out there and play. It was a complete mess of a time.

To win was a dream. I never thought it was going to be this time.

JW: I think squash people were amazed by it. You had zero competitive matchplay. Even if you had been able to prepare freely without matches for six months it would still have been almost impossible for most players without matches.

RA: That's one of the things that I've found out that was quite beneficial. I was always on my own. Two sessions, morning and evening alone. I was just training for boredom. Training to get bored. Ten more minutes … get bored. It wasn't 'sweating' hard. It was 'boredom' hard.

JW: Were you always training at low intensity?

RA: I was on my own trying to do this fast weird stuff with my hands, but yes, a lot was just practice and low-level work. It was an intense time though, being alone, training alone, wanting to be injury free, the World Championships ahead. I would try to have fun at the weekends, and I was just thinking about squash.

I would sometimes get down and start thinking about my academy and that I might have to stop playing. I had done well out of squash and maybe that was it. So, when you talked about going to the job centre in the article it was ringing bells!

JW: That time-limit factor for an athlete isn't too easy to deal with.

RA: No, it got to the point where I had to just stop thinking any more about it. Let's just put one foot in front of the other. Anyway, hopefully this latest treatment can help.

I've been bored though. The worst thing is trying not to eat. I love food so much but I've just got to stop. I can't go and do any work to run it off. I've been trying for one meal a day. I would then eat all I wanted.

JW: I used to do that when I was off, miss meals. I would snack a bit. Three big meals a day and I would have put weight on.

RA: So now I'm doing core and upper body. It's not enjoyable. I think for me the only enjoyable time is at tournaments. Training times I have to seek motivation. I find it hard. The motivation to get through the sessions. I love tournaments, you have one match every day. One match, there's motivation and hope there for you. Training – there's none of that. You have to create the motivation.

JW: Was the move to NYC about the injury or did you want to move here?

RA: It was the career, the academy, and trying to help my squash get back on track with the surgeons here.

JW: Are you going to watch the event here this week?

RA: Yes, but I'm exhausted talking about the injuries. It will be the same stuff and I'm not in the best frame of mind for it maybe. When you're injured you don't want to bring everyone down, but I'm not in the most positive frame of mind. You get the same question a million times and it's very nice of everyone but it gets repetitive.

JW: So you're walking now? Walking, eating and rehab exercises?

RA: Mum's buying me too much food, coconut oil, nuts, everything. I don't need any more mum! Lots of movies. I'm using the Compex machine to stimulate the muscles.

JW: When you're out of the game injured now, do you watch the TV coverage of squash?

RA: Yes, I've been watching some of the events.

JW: What does that do?

RA: I enjoy it. It's good to get watching again, though I realise how much I miss it.

JW: I get asked about why the Egyptians are so good, especially so young, far too often. Can you give me something to say – how do you explain it?

RA: Well, they do work hard. They are pushed hard, that's for sure. I started playing around six, and they started pushing me when I was nine. The first tournament I played was the Scottish Open U13 at nine years old. All the kids at my age collapsed – way too much. But in another way, it serves you in being strong.

JW: Do they push them in terms of practising hitting great shots, or physical training?

RA: We train like any other juniors in the world. It comes from somewhere else. Someone started doing all this skillful stuff and then it becomes a ritual and tradition. The young kids copy it then.

Back home you've got to figure out things all the time. That's Egypt: there's bureaucracy, and you have to have sneaky ways of knowing people. The rules on the streets, for example, are sort of there but not really there, or if they are, nobody follows them. So, what happens is you must find an opening to get ahead. Anyone who's been on the roads in a car in Egypt will know. You can't wait in line; you take the opening. So, squash is a bit like this, you find the opening in squash and you go for it. It's part of the Egyptian way.

JW: Well now I know. For the benefit of England's squash future the government needs to slacken its traffic rules!

RA: Everyone asks us! We don't really know but I think there's something in the culture. It's like the man breaking down in his car on the street. It's hot, there are millions of cars …

JW: He probably doesn't have the AA …

RA: God no! Nobody helps him, but he HAS to find a way to make the thing work! So, he does it. We tend to find our way around things, however sticky the situation. It's not systematic. So you're forced to adapt. You're not learning patterns and systems and thought-out routines all the time.

JW: So, coaches are not necessarily talking to kids about hitting nicks and playing amazing shots, they are just letting it happen.

RA: No, you just do this, just do it. Just hit the nick. The training is hard, they are doing a lot of physical work, and that helps them to get so good so young, but it can be exacting on them so young.

I tore my ACL when I was 15. I was maybe training too heavily. Sports science wasn't very good. I was getting bigger and was running. You've no idea, James; I was running when I was young, running and splitting to the sides. Every day as a kid. It was heavy. We used to go on court and do these fitness drills and you had to keep going. I wouldn't say that it was a scientific approach. If you dare to stop, you get hit with the racket. You would get slapped.

JW: The coach would be in prison if they did that in England or the US.

RA: Yes. So anyway, I don't feel like we do practise and train any better, but it's a cultural thing. It's in the way we talk as well. You guys in England, you talk very structured. I love this and I want to do the same. But when we talk, it's more all over the place, it's frantic, and more disordered.

JW: You have amazing racket control and ability. Do you think then that you have a talent that makes you that good? Do you feel like hard work or other factors have helped you get there? Don't be modest.

RA: I think God gave me some help to do these things. To be able to see the nicks and feel the courts. But I've never relied on that. I know I have to put hours of effort in to keep the talent bubbling away. My brother Hisham is one of the most talented players I know, squash-wise, but maybe that work ethic wasn't quite there as much.

Mum was strong. There was always a solution, never a problem.

JW: I wonder whether we'll get to play again? [For context, I was injured at the time of the interview after hip surgery.] We had some good matches. The one in Chicago last year I thought was very good.

RA: You hit an amazing shot into the nick in that match. I played a cross court, but it was the reaction. The shot and the reaction were amazing. A bit like mine with the guitar in New York, with Greg, except my shot was okay, my reaction was great; yours had both!

You know when I think of these things, I just feel so sad. So sad that this game doesn't get what it deserves. We deserve a lot more people seeing this game, and the beauty of it. We are not being done any justice.

JW: As you say that I'm taken back to that world final again. I was sitting in a bookshop cafe watching it while I was injured. I was standing up watching the rallies, I couldn't sit down. There was some ridiculous stuff in that fourth game and the rallies were that good I remember taking notes and writing down the ones that were so good so that I could remember them. It was such a moving experience to see sport played that way, and there I was in this cafe, and everyone else in there was chugging along with a novel or newspaper, or working or studying or talking to each other about rubbish, with no idea that these magical sporting moments were happening. Joey and PJ were beside themselves on the TV commentary, and I just wanted to tell everyone there in the cafe all about it!

RA: I know, I remember it all. I was having all this treatment on the weird arm condition during the match. The doctor was telling me I was fine. I had all that. I started thinking so much and I'm trying to think about the body and the squash, and the head was just all over the place. I couldn't focus. Then the arm pain went and then came back, and I thought that was it. I couldn't really lift it. The physio was trying to do stuff. I went back in the court, the arm killing, it's all chaos and I'm thinking, 'Okay, maybe I've won twice and maybe that's my lot.' Then I'm like, 'No! I'm here, I've been all the way through this. He's two-one up. Whatever I'm feeling, I'm going to kill myself now. Whether it's surgery on my shoulder after this, or if the arm drops off, I don't care.' This was the time to leave it all out there.

I can't wait to get sweating again; so I can eat more and not worry so much.

Dominic McHugh

WHEN WATCHING and coaching me through matches, my dad Malcolm often eschews his official coach's seat on the front row and sits further back in the audience for a view he prefers. Later he will tell me how he got chatting to somebody, and one such person a few years back at Canary Wharf was Dominic, an eye surgeon and squash fan. Since their meeting we've become friends.

I remember a hit I had with Dominic one Sunday in London when he told me how much he was looking forward to it, and how he needed it to take him away from his work that day, and naturally I was curious as to why.

That particular work involved giving a patient bad news. The treatment hadn't recovered the patient's sight the way he had hoped it would. Here it struck me that we were dealing with real stakes, real pressure, not piddling little squash matches. And sometimes I think I feel dodgy before a big squash match.

Dominic, like so many others, holds futures in his hands with what he does, and it was through his admiration and love for squash that we met. It felt strange to me that, from what I could see, he received very little acclaim or outside validation for the impact he makes, yet we professional sportspeople for some reason did and do. We simply hit balls around a court and people clap and cheer. Then it's we who write the books and make the films.

—

JW: How do you come to be where you are today?

DM: They do say that going into medicine is a vocation or calling and I wanted to do medicine from the age of ten. My uncle was a GP and actually still is aged 88, still seeing patients. I think he gave me the first spark and I really couldn't think of doing anything else. If you analyse it, I had an interest in science, but I also liked interacting and talking to people, the Irish in me. Medicine combines art and science, interacting with people and applying knowledge. You look at a patient's history, ask their symptoms, how long they have had them, the nature of them; you examine the patient. My job as an eye doctor might be to test visual function, for example, the peripheral field of vision, and after we've got all the information make a diagnosis to treat the patient.

In many ways that made life quite easy for me at school. I knew what grades and subjects to do and I knew about the universities to apply for to do medicine. I had a very set target in mind.

Happily, I managed to fool the dean of the medical school to offer me a place at Middlesex Hospital medical school.

The course itself is then lengthy, five to six years of study. You learn about the human body from the top of the head to the tips of the toes and all in between, about the physiology and how the body works, the dynamic processes that keep you going. After you qualify you get to do a year of what we call house jobs – the year after school, where you gain experience, before you can really set up your plate independently. Then you become registered with the General Medical Council and decide what to do. You can go into general practice or one of the many, many sub-specialities within it.

I didn't know what I wanted to specialise in, so went to Norwich to be an orthopaedic surgeon. I enjoyed the practical aspects of the surgery. About a year after, someone said to me that a good orthopaedic surgeon is as strong as an ox but only twice as intelligent. So, I went into brain surgery, which was fascinating but incredibly hard work, 24/7. The patients were often critically ill, and even after an operation the mind develops severe problems within a minute, so it was total vigilance. I enjoyed the work, but it took over my whole life. The next step then was ophthalmology, which in the end was right for me. I took to the fine-detailed, intricate work. With an eye you're essentially operating on something the volume of an egg cup for hours at a time, so it's very delicate microsurgery.

It combines wider elements of medicine because the eye has many connections to the rest of the body. You can look in the eye and diagnose diabetes or a brain tumour. I've been very interested in research. For example, I spent a couple of years researching a kind of laser for treating various eye problems, to get an MD doctorate. To this day I still do research and publish papers. Linked with that's my interest in teaching. I'm now a consultant at King's College Hospital, and we work with undergraduates and trainee eye surgeons. A big element of our work is to teach and also lead and coordinate research, so it's a combination of enthusing juniors and also helping develop the specialty with new treatment techniques and new ways of investigation. And it has been very exciting to be involved in this because it's not static and is continually evolving, which means I can't just sit back. I need to constantly keep up with my investigation, keep up with new treatments and incorporate them in my practice.

It's a full life but very rewarding.

JW: How do you keep sharp? Do you read and study, learn from others?

DM: Every year we have an appraisal by a colleague who will see what we've done over the previous year. That period has to have included a certain amount of time attending seminars, lectures, symposiums on our own specialties, where we learn about new techniques or where our memories are refreshed on established techniques. We're obliged to demonstrate that we continue to read medical journals in our specialty, and that we've contributed something ourselves in terms of research and publication. And every five years, and mine's coming up later this year, we have what's called a revalidation, where our registration body, the General Medical Council, has to be assured that we continue to have the skills and capability to maintain our registration as a practitioner. Without this, we can't work as a doctor. I think, as in any line of work, if you stop developing yourself and keeping up with the latest ideas, you start going backwards. If you stand still, you're going backwards and could be a liability. So, it's very important you're kept up to speed.

JW: Will you analyse a surgery that you've done and then go away and practise what could have been better?

DM: In terms of my day-to-day work, I do three or four clinics a week, operating two or three times a week. The surgery I do is a combination of more general work, cataract operations, specialised work in my own sub-speciality interest, which is the retina. I've been operating now for getting on for 35 years without any big breaks.

Unlike a professional squash player, I don't go into a separate operating theatre to spend two or three hours practising a particular technique with a scalpel. I do nine or ten operations each week and that maintains my surgical edge. It also gives me a chance to teach my juniors. Tomorrow I'm doing a teaching operating list with one of my juniors who I give an operation. I then take my junior through the second operation by supervision. They might do an operation from beginning to end or I might let them do an element of it, and I can take over more complex parts. Or the junior might ask me to take over and I'll scrub up and take over. That's the way we teach, in a semi-apprenticeship style, which we have to this day.

Doing this job, because it's rather delicate work, it finds you out quickly and you can't bluff your way through an operation. Maybe in some areas you could bluff your way somewhat but in surgery the moment you pick up the scalpel people will know whether you're the real deal or not. I make that point because the more senior one gets the more you have to realise that nothing's forever. And the instant I feel my hand isn't as steady as it was or I find that I'm struggling with operations I was doing with ease the year before, then it's time to move on. It's important to recognise this in any line of work – you must somehow have insight into your own capabilities and what you can and can't do. It's the easiest thing in the world to operate than not. Some of these operations are very complex and you've got to have the self-awareness to know if you're no longer up to it.

JW: That's interesting. I feel like at 35 years old that I've known more than I've ever known about the squash court, the geometry of it, the tactical strategic decision-making aspects. But on the other hand, age is supposed to be catching up with you and your body is becoming used. I feel that now I'm at my absolute optimum in terms of squash knowledge, I want to really make the most of these years because I've worked so hard all my life. So, I know retirement is creeping up, yet I'm at the height of my powers in some respects! Once I let go now, it's gone.

DM: That's a very good point. In surgery, a natural career can probably last into the sixties. Few people go beyond mid-sixties. I'm 62 now and I know that inevitably time's arrow only goes in one direction.

JW: Sixty-two, I don't believe you.

DM: But here's the thing. Even if my job has a big practical element to it, I don't have to get my heart rate up to 190 for two hours to do it, whereas in elite athletic endeavours like squash, if you make your mid-thirties that's very good. Inevitably though, you don't have 45-year-old world champions. So, it's life and it's a bit unfair but because there's a strong intellectual element and less a physical one to certain professions, you can go on longer.

The oldest clinician I know of is, I think, 103. He sees patients in Wimpole Street, but he's an allergy specialist. You are not going to have a 100-year-old surgeon, but I suppose we're getting better at defying age and it doesn't have to be the only marker.

JW: Can you talk a little about the standards in what you do. In sport there are thousands of levels of player. How many levels are there in your world? Are there world-class surgeons, mediocre ones?

DM: Well, if you can get to be a consultant surgeon in whatever speciality, then that gives you a certain kitemark, as it were. In order to become a surgeon, you have to pass rigorous exams beyond your basic qualifications, and you become a fellow of the Royal College of Surgeons.

You have to do the fellowship exam plus a certain number of years of prescribed training, so beyond the five to six years of medical school there will be another seven to eight years to become a specialist. In my case it was about 19 years from walking into medical school to becoming a consultant. From the start of looking at the body in an anatomy room to a medical consultant, 19 years.

JW: That's what it takes? That's incredible.

DM: Yes, I took a few side turns too – time in orthopaedics, time in neurosurgery. But all that was money in the bank because it taught me basic surgical skills. With brain surgery the brain is heavily connected with the eye, so I was able to see areas of the brain where vision is affected by certain conditions like tumours and so on. I also took time off to research for a doctorate, giving me the chance to publish papers, which meant I could get a better job in a better hospital. Because of my academic interest I wanted to work in a teaching hospital. But it was a long spell of concerted effort to get here. The point is that they say you become competent in 10,000 hours. Whether that's true or not, I've no idea, but I've done many thousands of hours of surgery not just to become a consultant, but also since then to maintain and improve the level.

It just hasn't stopped. So, in the UK if someone is a consultant it means they have done the best training. When I was doing a fellowship, I think the pass rate was 10 per cent. They don't hand these things out like sweets. There will no doubt be huge variations of abilities and competence within the group but by and large you can expect a good deal if you see a consultant.

In a teaching hospital there are juniors and I sometimes get asked to do an operation by a patient. I say I'll do my best but that it's a teaching hospital and it may be that my junior will do the operation under my supervision. Otherwise, how can they learn? The consultant can't do everything. They have got to take my job at some stage. In private medicine the patient chooses the doctor, who has to be a consultant. They make that choice. But whether I'm working in the NHS or privately I treat all my patients the same. There's no difference in terms of the quality of care and amount of time I give them. The only difference is you get to choose the doctor; in an NHS clinic you might see a different doctor every time.

So that's the long answer to your question. Consultants should be very highly trained by the time they get to be a consultant. And because of the appraisal and revalidation process, they have to keep on developing throughout their career to maintain and hopefully improve on their skills. And junior doctors do treatments under supervision.

JW: When you're doing surgeries, do you have bad days?

DM: Yes, but if the bad days make you feel like you're not going to do a good job, then you postpone the case and get someone else to do it. For example, if I've got a streaming cold and I'm going to sneeze halfway through the op, that clearly wouldn't work, and neither do I want to give everyone at work and the patient my cold. But I think this is something we all experience. We all wake up in bad moods, have personal problems, we all don't feel 100 per cent always, but you find ways of putting things aside and getting it done. I sometimes feel happy to let go of any issues through my work if things are not quite right personally. It can be therapeutic and can allow you to let go of the problems, whether it's the letter from the bank manager or whatever.

JW: People go on and on about sportspeople and the pressure. It seems to me that you people have to go through much more pressure but never get applause or adulation the way athletes do for being in an Olympic final. That experience you told me of that Sunday must have been quite something. You're dealing with people's lives, their sight can be dependent on how you treat them, your performance so to speak. How do you approach a big surgery then, where the stakes are so high?

DM: You're right. There are some complex operations where there's a huge amount riding on it, where you're not particularly looking forward to it. Once you've done it you're relieved and you hope you've done some good for the patient. In general terms any job that's worth doing is associated with pressure. If it's not, then it's boring. It stretches, engages, enthuses. You have to put 100 per cent into it. When it becomes stressful it gets difficult and probably indicates an inability to handle that pressure. The psychologists say the best way to approach any kind of challenge is to try to reach a state where you're moderately wound up about it. If you're too laid-back or too wound up, you can fail and mess up. But a moderate degree of tension can be good. An optimum level.

If I see a patient in a busy clinic, that patient could be one of 13 that morning, but I know for that 15 minutes I'm the most important person in their world. They are expecting me to help them. I must never forget this. For that 15 minutes I have to make them feel they are the only person in my world.

I had a patient last week who was 32 weeks' pregnant, with a detached retina. She had lost vision in one eye, so for me the challenge wasn't just doing a detached retina operation but to do it on a pregnant lady, which added another level of complexity to the problem. She was huge and had trouble lying flat for the hour or two of the operation, but we couldn't give general anaesthetic. I discussed it, worked it out with my anaesthetist and staff, but the operation went well and the next day the retina was attached.

So, it wasn't the thing I most wanted to do out of choice by any means at 8am on a Thursday morning but I had to do it. Unfortunately, not all operations go well despite best efforts. Some things are too tricky with what we have at our disposal, so we have to tell the patient. We have a duty of candour where we have to tell them what goes right and wrong and the reasons why. It's their eyes, their health and you can't sugar the pill. You have to inform them of the situation.

JW: This must be a tremendously hard part of what you have to do. This isn't about the studying and the medicine and textbooks. This is you as a shrink, having to tap into deep emotion and difficulty.

DM: Yes. When I was a medical student, we did have an attachment to psychology but it wasn't practical. Most of what I learned about interacting and communicating with patients I've just had to learn on the job. Quite often I've made mistakes along the line. The important thing is to recognise it and learn from it. The only surgeon who has never had complications during surgery is one who has never done an operation. It's impossible to avoid them, but with experience you start to see ahead. I can often watch a junior working and be able to take a step ahead and foresee a complication, so I can step in and take over. That's on the basis of having seen it all myself. That's one branch in the future you recognise to avoid. Everyone makes mistakes; you just have to learn not to make the same ones again.

JW: So just comparing what you do with the athlete – will you come out of a surgery having performed less well? And will you then analyse and look at where things went wrong and what you can do better?

DM: You really do need to debrief afterwards, yes. I do ask what I could have done differently. I remember 20 years ago doing an operation and I remember most of my surgeries, as you probably remember your matches. You pick up on patterns and if something goes outside that pattern you know that and remember it, so if I'm doing an operation now I'll think, well, if I did this then that could happen because it happened ten years ago, so I'm not going to do that. You might realise things like making a cut in a certain area with the scalpel didn't work, so you try another, something like that.

And with, say, the treatment of an infection, pneumonia, you might prescribe antibiotics and that's that, but with surgery there are an infinite number of variations within a set series of techniques. There are subtle changes and variations on how you do your operation, which can make things better for the patient. And that just comes with experience.

JW: Can you give an example of this? Not that I'll understand it but ...

DM: Yes, well, if I did a cataract operation the eye goes milky. The lens itself is contained in a very delicate bag called a capsule, and the important thing is not to break the bag when you're breaking the cataract. The idea of the cataract operation is to remove the cataract from the bag leaving an empty intact bag in which you put in the plastic lens. Now you take out the cataract by putting in a special probe, which vibrates at a high frequency and dissolves the cataract, turns it into a liquid and you can just suck it out of the eye. The important thing is, though, not to push the probe too close to the capsule because if you do the probe will not only dissolve the cataract but also the capsule, and once you've dissolved the capsule ...

JW: Is the capsule the bag?

DM: Yes. The capsule has got to be intact to contain the plastic lens implant. If it's got a tear in it, then the implant will fall to the back of the eye, which isn't great and causes all sorts of hassles. So, there are different techniques I've developed, which means that when I remove the cataract the tip of the probe is nowhere near the capsule. The way I can do that is by using another instrument, which pushes the substance of the cataract towards the probe, which is held in place. If you imagine, let's say, a football or balloon, and you put something into the middle of the balloon but not the wall of it. So, to bring the cataract away is safer than chasing after the cataract by pushing it towards the edge where the capsule is. That's a very basic example of trying to minimise the risk of complications by adjusting my technique. It's actually technically tricky and very few of my juniors master it, and they will go back to traditional techniques. Certainly, though, it works for me and it minimises my complication rate. So that's the kind of thing.

JW: When you go home you must be on a bit of a high. That feeling of relief. You must be working to extremes. It seems that after a squash match we have outlets. People ask how we did, people write reports, there's publicity and people are involved, yet we are not saving lives or sight. Do you have any outlet, anywhere to turn after a particularly extreme surgery or one where emotion has played its part?

DM: Well, as an example, last Thursday I started operating at 8 o'clock in the morning and finished at six, ten hours straight of surgery. And while you're doing this, because you're focused, you don't realise that it's taken quite a lot out of you. It's only when you get home and pour your scotch and soda that you realise how tiring the whole thing is. If I finish work at a reasonably civilised time, I have dinner, relax and unwind, sleep well, then I'm doing okay. But if I'm doing emergency surgery until nine or ten at night, then it's very difficult to unwind. Sleep is tricky because you're still in peak mode of arousal for your surgery, and it's important for anybody to have seven or eight hours' sleep, particularly if the whole process starts again early the next day. You must be rested.

I remember one of my seniors when I was a junior told me he did 12-hour shifts and he just couldn't sleep. He would be up all night drinking coke and watching television. Then he had to shave and come into hospital the next morning. He retired early and went off to live in relative peace in

Somerset. But yes, it's very important after long surgeries to unwind and relax, even though, as you say, I don't get rounds of applause at the end of it, like some people in their squash tournaments.

JW: Do you work at relaxing or does it come naturally? Do you have to make sure you put in a day's rest during a week? You have a responsibility to turn up to work but you're dealing with pressure situations if you're not rested.

DM: My mother always says that the McHughs always live long because they get plenty of sleep and they never worry about anything. It's probably true that we're like that. So not worrying doesn't mean you don't care but you perhaps have an ability to put your problems into a box, and I think I'm like that. I don't take my work home with me.

JW: It's not easy to be like that.

DM: My view is that whether I worry about something or not, I've done my job, I've done the best I can. But worrying about it is not going to help anyone. The second thing I think is to try to have some order and structure. Meals at the same time, not too late, bed at 10.30, good quality of sleep. Total blackout. No checking messages, no caffeine. Sleep is so important. It's the best free medicine known to man, and if you do work hard and have a stressful job, the sleep is crucial. But I wouldn't be still here doing it if it got to be too much. I've had colleagues who have reached the end and found they had had enough early. The nature of general practice: administrative hassles, not enough resources, paperwork that gets in the way – all this presents challenges and they have had enough. Even though I spend most of my waking hours doing my job, I still enjoy it and get something from it. I feel like it's contributing, and if I wasn't happy with my job, the stress would come through sleep disturbance and inability to unwind. I think it's because there's an enjoyment and I feel good about doing my job, which gives me contentment and personal fulfilment.

And the other building block in this is to be able to do something completely different, which is why playing a game of squash is an absolute tonic for me. It's pretty diametrically opposed to microsurgery, except maybe your subtle drop shots. An hour of squash for me is another great period of free medicine because it acts as physical and emotional catharsis.

It's a privilege and blessing to be able to play squash at my age. If all I had left was to slump in front of the box, then it wouldn't be great. Hopefully, squash can help keep me energised so I can keep doing this a little longer.

In closing the book, I speak to three people who I'm lucky enough to class as family members. Malcolm, David and Vanessa. I did travel and work and push for the interviews in this book at times, but it would have been silly of me not to have made use of the knowledge, expertise and understanding that lay on my doorstep.

Malcolm Willstrop

I WAS introduced and coached the game by my dad through his work as a coach, and his involvement in squash undoubtedly set me on my way. His expertise and knowledge then helped me right through it at every stage. It's very hard to not make clichéd statements at this juncture but I couldn't possibly have done what I've done in squash the way I did it without his help, and I don't know how else I can really express this.

He's a completely singular character who isn't going to be everybody's cup of tea. He can upset and frighten people (he will look askance on this), such is his presence as a person and coach. His voice booms over the balcony of courts one and two at our club in Pontefract and everyone knows their place and that they have to adhere to the standards of discipline he sets. He's so completely unfiltered and honest, which is sometimes bracing because it's so bloody unusual. It's probably caused problems in his time, as unfortunately anyone who is ever completely honest in life always finds out to some degree, but it is, nevertheless, him.

On the other side of it, and because of the honesty, Malcolm may come across heavy, with his philosophies on behaviour, but unlike many coaches and teachers he never holds back praise when it's warranted. When he likes what you've done, you get to know about it, and you feel a million dollars.

At 37 and having worked with him for so long, like with many of his players, the barriers have eroded and we're good pals. And he's really quite a soft soul underneath, who is happily prone to romanticism, sentimentality and who talks about fate and having good feelings about situations.

—

JW: Do you have a system from where you're always looking to find talented individuals as a squash coach, or do you not think of it like that?

MW: I think essentially I'm trying to make the sport available for children for them to simply enjoy, to partake in a healthy sport, and out of that there will emerge some talented children. I'm sure that applies in singing, acting, music, whatever else. So, if we deal with the number of children we do at Pontefract on a weekly basis, talented children will emerge. Then the important thing is to recognise the ability and encourage and promote. There's a lot involved when you're dealing with kids who have high-class potential. They themselves need to know at a sensible time what potential they have, as do the parents. Telling them is crucial, in fact. It might be the only time any teacher or coach has ever said they are good at something, and, if it is, this can light a fire inside them, give them confidence. Not enough teachers do this if they see something in a child, and I don't know why; it can give them such a lift!

The system, though, really is to get as many children involved as we can enjoying the sport and the social aspects of the club. That's first. Then hopefully they might play for a team, a club team, a county, some for university, some might go on to play for their country.

JW: So how does a little town in Pontefract produce player after player? How do you equate that with talent?

MW: It's probably not about the water here. Wherever you go, there will be talent. I worked in North Walsham, a village practically, and Cassie Jackman, who became world number one, emerged from there. Wherever I've been, talent has been there. A lot will go undiscovered, but then if you can create an environment where talent can be realised and fulfilled, it has a chance of coming out. It's good to see children fulfil themselves if they want to.

I had a lot of experience coaching squash and other sport and you build a team of people and create a situation and environment where children can prosper as people and squash players. That's what Pontefract is.

JW: Could there be more young players of Sam Todd's ability all over Pontefract then, with his talent, but who don't have the environment and the work ethic and the coaching to bring that all together to make a world-class player?

MW: Sam is the best player in the world of his age, so he's very unusual, but there will be players of very high capability who are undiscovered and who are not playing the game anyway. Then there will be those who have the capability and the environment but who won't have the backing and support they need. Some end up not having the inclination anyway, however able they are.

JW: So the talent we're talking about isn't just the talent for hitting great squash shots, they need a whole array of talents: talent to work hard, to have good backing, knowledge, mental strength.

MW: Absolutely, yeah. A lot of factors, you've hit on some there. Like hard work. You talk to any athlete – why are you good? I work hard. You talk to anyone in life; they will put a lot of it down to hard work, but so much else must come together to make it all happen.

JW: These are all like mini-talents in themselves.

MW: And when you've got all that together, you've got a chance of fulfilling it. In Sam's case, his dad Mick owns the club, likes the game, he gets the right parental support. In the case of a coach, you don't want the parental interference to be overbearing, but happily we don't have that here. We want support but not interference. The parental thing is crucial and very delicate.

JW: So, when you have all your groups, do you see lots of kids who have a lot going for them but who just don't make the next move because they are lacking some of these things? Are there some who are world-class possibilities but they just don't make the next steps?

MW: I agree with the whole hard work thing, but people who make world number ones like Sam are rare birds and there will be very few of those. Underneath that line will be people who are good enough to maybe play for counties or their country, which is terrific.

JW: And what stops them then going further?

MW: That's maybe where the talent comes in .

JW: Or could it be the requirement to really push on with the work or the lifestyle of being a squash player?

MW: Yes. I had a young player as an example recently who played for England, became number one in the country at their age and chose to pack the game in, which was difficult and astonishing for me, when so much was in place. But if it's not right for them, then it's their choice. It's repetitive and gruelling and bloody hard work to keep pushing to the very top, and most people simply won't want to do that. But it was such a shame in that particular case; it was such an opportunity and so much work had been done.

When kids specialise in something it's a very difficult line to tread. It has to come from them, that ability to keep seeing it through. They have to innately want that, perhaps that's a talent.

JW: You're brilliant at producing all players, but young players just keep emerging from your system. How do you keep them happy, motivated and training strongly and well but with enjoyment? How do you do it?

MW: I have a general life philosophy. Mine is based around fairness, good behaviour and enjoyment. My kids have to be disciplined and respectful. In the end it's about people. It's about playing good squash, winning, seeing good results and people achieving, but in the end my deep-rooted concern is about people. Those fundamentals are very important, and they will help to produce the player. If they are fair, respectful, if they work hard and are disciplined, that's the basis. I work to help them find self-discipline too, so that when I'm not standing over them they can do the work themselves. That underlies all the work I do. I want decent people; I don't want to work with people who are badly behaved or think they are better than they are.

JW: Another part of your philosophy seems to be about working in groups, often with all players and standards integrating with each other. Today we had a group session where we've laughed and interacted. I could have gone and done a session alone that was hard and good, but that element of interaction is such a part of what you give players. That enjoyment factor, the variation.

MW: Interesting thing yesterday when we did our junior session: four-year-old Annabel greeted three-year-old Betty as they came in. 'Hello Betty!' I thought that was lovely.

JW: And that makes you happier than the shots …

MW: Absolutely. I'm not interested in what she's doing on the court! Those two children engaged. That's enough for me.

JW: And do you think that then keeps them interested in the sport?

MW: Absolutely! They see their friends.

JW: So that's part of what you're doing …

MW: They are looking forward to playing or practising, but they are looking forward to seeing their friends. And I think the adults are the same. In the end it's got to be about people and trying to – not that I'm a brilliant person – inculcate through the sport good life principles and being a decent person. I do think about it because if people do behave badly I'm on to them. Quickly. At the club we don't have that; we discourage those people from coming. We want people who are respectful and can work together.

JW: And you can be quite heavy on people if they get it wrong. Some people can't accept it and leave, but most people come back for more, and they stay with you. People come more! Even though you scare them.

MW: But people like discipline. When we have the children in from the Pontefract Foundation, I sit them down and tell them how it is, how it will be and give them firm basic principles. We don't like too much noise, listen to the coaches, be polite to people in the club. I think they like that. Once a child knows where they stand, they have a good framework to move forward.

JW: How much time do you spend talking in depth about technique with your world-class players?

MW: I think I talk about technique all the time in a general sense, but it's more general. I'm offering general instructions from outside the court. Keep the shoulders relaxed, slow the swing, delay the shot, left foot lead. On top of that I want that player to be themselves. They are all different, but there are perhaps some fundamental principles.

JW: But you didn't go on with me much and try to dissect the way I hold the grip and the mechanics of the swing. We never did any of that.

MW: Hardly ever. I find lots of people are very keen to know where everything is and spend so much time over theorising. I don't think it always needs to be that specific.

JW: And, taking myself out for a minute, considering all that, your players actually seem pretty technically superb.

MW: I think I'm always on about technique generally during the sessions, but then you all found your own ways. I don't specifically say you should play in a certain way or have a certain technique. You pick up from what you watch too, and then my practice sessions are there to help you bring your own expression, through the repetition of hitting balls in different ways.

There's no one way of doing things. The French players, Thierry Lincou and Gregory Gaultier, had very square-on stances and positions. I would never outwardly teach that, but it clearly works, and coaches would be silly to ever be dismissive.

JW: Do you learn from other coaches? Do you have outside sources of inspiration?

MW: You can't stand still and you need to be progressive and welcome new ideas. You have to listen to other coaches, and in other sports, but you should choose wisely. Jonah Barrington, I've learned from so much. I remember snippets of his. He once said at a clinic that when a practice breaks down, begin again with purpose. To this day I always tell my kids to begin the practice on the right footing. It's a small thing but brilliant. Geoff Hunt mentioned once that it was helpful to swing from the hip and not the arm. Great piece of advice, and players in this scientific age are encouraged to incorporate the core muscles and not do isolated movements, so he was talking about that a long time ago. I love horse racing, and I heard a trainer recently talking about bringing their two-year-old into racing by not rushing them physically, but he described how he allowed them to strengthen and grow into themselves before being asked too many questions. That can apply to young squash players.

Latterly I've become close to Richard Agar and Tony Smith, world-standard rugby league coaches in the Super League, and I can't tell you how much I've learned from them over the last few years.

I'm very open-minded but I'm critical and clinical about who I listen to. I'm not dismissive but you're not going to meet myriads of people who can help. Closing your mind off is no good either. Sports are changing constantly, so if you don't, you will get left behind.

JW: You have an intuition for bringing players along, not pushing them too hard, not overworking them but slowly building their experience first. You're very discerning in terms of moving your kids up the league systems at Pontefract, for instance.

MW: It's what we were just saying about not overdoing it. I run five teams in the Yorkshire League. One I keep for the younger players to filter into. So, there will be two or three responsible adults with them. I never put them in until they are socially ready. I had one player who was ready in terms of standard but I wasn't certain he was up to it socially. He was good enough but he didn't play. He's come on a bundle recently so I called him up and told him I was impressed with the way he's conducting himself with adults and that when the leagues resume he will be playing. The parents will have been wondering why they are not in, but it's social. That comes first.

JW: With physical training for your kids, you don't make your sessions torturous and hard and intense. You get kids playing and competing, and you delay any specific hard fitness training for later.

MW: I've done bits of physical training with my players but the loads were never heavy, and it wouldn't have been arduous, certainly not at a young age. We used to go out in the summer down to the racecourse and do intervals but it would be 30 minutes' intensity and then done. Now we have experts who understand physical training, who help the players, so it's obvious then that these people know what they are doing in terms of detailed training programmes for players. But if I coach young players, I'm never ever going to work them to the bone. They want to find the sport, play the sport happily and socially, and you will lose them physically and mentally if you push them too hard.

JW: How do you still get so motivated after all these years, and why do you want to keep doing it?

MW: I think there are always new children, new players that you can help develop. It's exciting to see new kids every year. I've got little two- and three-year-olds on the court now enjoying it, knowing that they might join me soon, or Jayne (Robinson, coach at Pontefract) in another session in the week.

JW: You have worked with world champions, high-level coaches, club players to beginner level. What is it you want from or for your players?

MW: I'm very happy that the work here has produced coaches like David Campion, Paul Hornsby, Andrew Cross, Kirsty McPhee, Neil Guirey and Paul Bell – all national coaches. They have made a good living from squash, I'm proud of that. And of course, I'm proud of the players who've gone to the very top. But when you start with the kids it's good to just give them the enjoyment of the sport. If my players perhaps go on to play in their university teams after working with me, then we've done something good. That for me is important because they might be away from home for the first time ever, they can meet people, work with a team, do something they are good at and it gives them a start immediately with people with common interests.

JW: And you have players at the lowest levels whose improvement you always talk about.

MW: I'm not attached to elitism. I want to encourage the game for everyone. I had great pleasure recently working with three of my older men, who put a brilliant session together for their standards. I walk away from that elevated and I hope they do too.

Vanessa Atkinson

I'M LUCKY enough to live together with Vanessa and our two little boys. In 2005 she became world women's squash champion in Malaysia and held the number one position at that time. She now commentates on the professional tour for SQUASHTV. We talk about her attitude to being a professional and I always really admired how she never seemed to let her desire to be a top squash player become this injurious presence in her life. She was able to find a balance there, and she has always been such a calming and rational influence on me as she moved away from her own career and helped me with mine. The many chats we've had over the years about our 'work', that she always made time for when she probably had more pressing things to worry about, have always cleared the muddle.

—

JW: On the week of the World Championships, what does a world champion do to win that title. Are there routines and rituals? How did you feel going in?

VA: I had just come off a big training stint with Neil Harvey in London, so I was really fit at the time, and my mindset was to be much more patient than I had ever been. I was playing a different style, volleying everything and being much more conservative. And I think that worked well for that event because I was up against the Grinham sisters and Nicol David, who were really quick at the front. Even though I was an attacking player it didn't often work against them and I had run out of steam. I had also come off the back of winning in Qatar, which doesn't always work, but I think it did in this case, giving me confidence. I had also opted not to play a tournament just before Qatar so I could really train well before those two tournaments, so I was fresh.

JW: Were you stressed, relaxed at the world champs? Did you feel pressure?

VA: I think I was quite relaxed, because even though I was one of the favourites I wasn't world number one or top seed. I wasn't going into it thinking that if I didn't win it would be the end of the world. I had lost to all the others plenty of times before. I just knew I was among those who had a chance. It was just a question of having a good run.

JW: Is there a routine on finals day?

VA: I can't remember! I think I was excited, a bit nervous at that point because it was the only time throughout the event that I would have been clear favourite. Natalie Grinham had an epic match in the semis and would have been tired, so at that point I felt it was probably mine to lose. But still, I don't remember feeling really bad nerves and I don't know or can't explain why that came together in the way it did.

JW: I think you're really interesting to interview for this book because you reached the pinnacle without getting bogged down or overburdened with squash. It wasn't the end of the world necessarily to you, and there's an overriding tension that a lot of world champions have, which can be unhealthy. They have to succeed. You strike me as an athlete who did become world champion but were never necessarily like that.

How did you find the balance of working really hard, hard enough, but also happily going out for a few drinks or missing the odd session and it not being the end of the world? Did it help you to be that way?

VA: Maybe it did in that situation for the year I won the worlds but it wasn't always something that helped me because I probably could have worked harder earlier. There was definitely a flip side to being relaxed and I didn't always put the work in consistently enough or approach it as professionally as I could have done. So even though it never boiled over to the kind of intensity you sometimes struggled with, I also could have been more successful had I been a little more focused and ultra-dedicated.

I think that week it did help, because I think I had done the work previously, but I didn't let the pressure get to me. But overall, I would say my mindset wasn't necessarily a good mindset for an athlete. There are lots of positives to it: it was probably a healthier state of mind as a person and it probably made it easier when I stopped playing, but overall I probably could have been more successful if I had been a bit more professional.

JW: We should just say, we're making you out to be a bit of a slacker here. You did immense amounts of work and were really dedicated and committed. I think we're maybe just pointing out that you weren't necessarily that sort of general stereotypical world champion we often hear about who has to sacrifice everything and work themselves to the bone and live like a monk. That wasn't you.

VA: Exactly.

JW: When did you first play squash?

VA: I first picked a racket up at nine.

JW: Were you playing regularly then?

VA: From about 10–11 I was playing more regularly. That's when we moved to Holland. I played a few times in England, then we moved, found a club there and my parents realised I liked it and got me a membership. I steadily got more serious and started playing more tournaments.

JW: Were you talented would you say?

VA: No. I was good at all sports as a youngster. I was good athletically, bit of an all-rounder. Not necessarily a natural ball and racket player. I used to run and try hard and that was helpful. Before puberty I was tall and gangly.

JW: And competitive?

VA: Yes, I was competitive. I loved competing.

JW: So if you can't remember necessarily what you did specifically on the week of the World Championships then, what would you say, having actually done it and been through the ultimate sporting pressure, if players asked you how you deal with the pressure situation on court?

VA: Maybe think about what works for you. Don't always follow the prescribed route. So, for me in that instance taking myself away and being completely isolated just wouldn't have worked. I was with my friends and fellow players Jenny and Karen, and we were chatting and socialising in the evenings, rather than being in the room and thinking about the matches. During the day it was the same – I didn't spend much time on my own. If you're naturally quite intense and prone to getting nervous maybe being on your own and in your own head alone isn't the best thing; it wouldn't be for me. Some people maybe would prefer it, but for me it was always about distraction. I've talked to you about that book, *The Inner Game of Tennis* [by W. Timothy Gallwey] and I knew that I was able to perform if I didn't overthink things. I needed somehow to just go on court and block that voice in my head. This worked for me because my voice tended to be quite negative.

JW: So, do you remember how you would do it? Would you just reduce it to thinking about each shot you would play?

VA: No, I would honestly try to think about nothing. And the way the book explains it is to make the focus really, really small, so it's looking for the seam on the tennis ball [the book is about tennis but can be applied quite universally]. So, I would maybe look at the ball, or even the yellow dot! I'm not saying I was doing that in that match necessarily, but I was playing with that idea in mind. We tell people when we're coaching to watch the ball, but I was literally just concentrating on watching the ball. Even in between rallies just following the ball with my eyes helped me and it's amazing how if you focus on one thing your brain isn't able to focus on anything else. There's no room for you to be thinking that you're 5-2 down because hopefully you're just blocking all that out. I needed to be not thinking about anything. My whole body would move better, I would hit the ball better and it would all just happen. As soon as I started thinking it was always bad.

JW: Now that you're the age you are and you look back on it all, what would you say about it? Did you enjoy your life as a squash player?

VA: I did enjoy it but not all the time. I don't know … I feel like I would have done everything differently, but at the same time it's such a redundant way to think. I would be doing it with my 44-year-old head; it's such a slow maturing and development and that's the way it had to be. Because it didn't come naturally to be ultra-disciplined and to do all the repetition, which I found monotonous and boring, then I guess you've just got to be happy that you did put it together and get the best out of yourself even if it was just for those few years. I could easily have not done that as well.

JW: Would you say you trained really hard and smart but maybe wouldn't have done lots of extra? Did you just do what you had to do?

VA: I think it was just a bit in phases. I worked really hard at times, but the consistency was lacking. I would never do all the extra bits that you did, and I was crap at looking after myself, and these days players are so on to that. That's one of the big things I would do differently. I just never thought I would end up paying for it the way I've done with my back. I was never injured, got away with it for so long and I got really complacent.

But I was never lazy in sessions and I would find the bottom of the well. It wasn't always thought through and I didn't plan as well as I should, but then I knew players that I would train with who would have their whole week written out but only do the training half-heartedly. I got help with that from coaches I worked with at times and when I had someone pushing me the training was great.

JW: And if you were coaching or advising young kids now, would there be any things you might say as they were getting into their squash?

VA: All kids will be different, and I guess finding out what works for each individual maybe is a good idea. The coaching is important in this sense. Some kids might need that extra help, that extra push, while some kids will need to stop doing too much. You and I would have been polar opposites when we were younger, so we couldn't possibly have had a coach who would treat us the same. So, I don't know what I would say to kids, but the coaches have an important role – they need to be intuitive and look at each individual.

JW: And would you be happy after it all to have your own children doing what you did?

VA: Oh god, yeah!

JW: Any dangers or things you would be worried about?

VA: Well yes, but I don't think there would be a thing in the world that they could do where there wouldn't be risks or difficulties. That's just life. I wonder a bit when players complain about being a squash player, not earning loads of money and therefore not necessarily encouraging it for their kids. Not that many ever do, but I just think how lucky we've been and what a great life we've had, and still have. You're getting towards the end of your career and I'm long past it but we're still getting so much joy from squash and being around squash.

David Campion

MY BIG brother and I have had quite a journey in the sport. We went from playing He-Man and Skeletor together in the front room of our North Walsham cottage, to winning world championship finals together, me as player, him as England's national coach. He used to tickle and torment me until I couldn't breathe for laughing when I was five. Then 20 years later he was putting me through gruelling court sessions that had a similar effect on the breathing, without so much of the laughter.

Alongside Malcolm, I've worked extensively with David throughout my career. He has worked his way up to lead the England Squash coaching programme and has been fastidious and studious with regard to learning about the principles of coaching and playing the game. He was himself a breathtaking squash player whose career was constantly ruined by injuries. He studies and reads books constantly, never settling for anything, a real scholar of the game.

England Squash is in a transitional cycle perhaps right now, and he talks here about the extensive work that goes into nurturing the next generations of England players.

—

JW: So, I'm interested to talk to you as England's national squash coach. I know you're very interested in all this, and you've read a lot. So how do you describe talent?

DC: It's a very interesting subject. There are certain implications for genetics in sport. Rowers are usually tall, basketball players need to be tall, etc.

In every sport, genetics plays its part. Things do probably depend somewhat on innate capabilities, but for me it's about environment. I don't know ... you could probably claim we start with basic innate abilities, but again, where does that come from?

When you were two, we used to play tennis and chuck balls at you and run around throwing and catching all the time. You were picking up so much fundamental movement literacy, so when you started playing squash, when you were walking, it looked natural, but maybe the environment you were in affected that. You were born into a sporting family, so it's natural we would do that stuff with you, and who knows how much you took from all that stuff? I would suggest quite a lot!

You were at the dinner table in your nappy and there would be squash players always there who would come to stay with us. They are probably talking about squash, and while you're throwing food around, all this stuff is going in. No one's even realising it.

Then you go down to the squash club because your family goes there and you're thrown into it. You were watching squash videos, Jahangir Khan on *Grandstand*! No wonder you can then hit the ball pretty well at six years old – you've been ingesting it.

Tiger Woods was the same. By six years old he had seen so much golf through his father, then all of a sudden he's an 'amazing talent', but then is he an amazing talent or was it all about his environment? It's impossible to understand or to ever know about innate talent totally because you can't start scientifically testing kids.

JW: In your position, are you scouting, or do you concentrate more on the work with the coaches in the regions? How do you approach bringing young people into squash?

DC: I think we maybe need to start thinking about lowering the age of our competitions. We need more under-nine events, I think. At the minute there are very few, and the lowest age group really is under-11 for competition.

Squash is an open skill sport. It's different to cycling or rowing where the variables are diminished and it's more about physical and athletic ability. With racket sports there are so many variables and technical aspects that you're going to be better later if you specialise younger. I don't think you necessarily need to specialise late, that's a generic idea. If it's monitored and coached correctly, then children can concentrate quite specifically on a sport in a healthy way. And I should say it doesn't need to be their only sport. They can play other sports, do other things and still somewhat specialise. For a sport like squash, such a highly skilled sport dependent on quick decision-making, the people who make the top at world levels will do the sport from early on.

It's something we could maybe do better, but essentially those early starts come from the clubs all around the country.

JW: Yeah, perhaps, but you work really hard and extensively with your coaches though, so that they can bring youngsters into the sport, in their regions.

DC: Yes, we do. We have a great network of coaches who we work with all over the country. There are eight regional coaches, then all the performance hubs and centres that we work with. Those hubs often have professional set-ups, like yours at Pontefract with Malcolm, and they are successful at delivering players. We have communication with them all and they are doing frequent talent hub sessions on a weekly basis to try to encourage kids. So yes, maybe as national coach I'm not going around 'scouting' as such, but where we try to affect the system is by working with coaches and bringing their standards up as much as we can. The kids in all the different regions all over the country will be accessing these coaches before us, so these coaches are crucial.

JW: We've just come out of one of England's strongest generations in terms of squash. Take me through what happens to produce the next generations and how hard it is to keep producing these players! You've got some really promising teenagers, and some senior players who are on the cusp.

DC: The challenge you have is that we've just come out of having the best group of English players ever: that group of Nick Matthew, Laura Massaro, Jenny Duncalf, Alison Waters, Daryl Selby, Peter Barker and yourself. The expectation is therefore so high. That was a great generation, and it's very tough to replicate that on a conveyor belt. People ask where the next players are, but I've been hearing this for 20, 30 years. The generation prior to that – Cassie Thomas, Linda Elriani, Peter Marshall, Simon Parke, Del Harris, Chris Walker – was a great group too, and at that time your group were on the junior squads, and not many people were thinking you lot were necessarily outstanding prospects. People then were asking where the players were! But your group went on to surpass that previous group!

JW: We were there just building, but it takes time …

DC: Well they came through, didn't they. In abundance. Jenny reached two in the world, Alison three, Laura and Nick became world champions and world number ones, you were world number one, Peter Barker top five. Then all the Commonwealth medals. Absolutely outstanding.

I think our system is as strong as it ever has been. We have a wider scope now, definitely, in terms of sharing information and learning.

JW: And there have been three British Junior Open champions in the last three years, which I don't think was happening when we were juniors, so things look promising.

DC: I think it's worth saying at this point that sport is cyclical and you can't expect to produce the best-ever group in the immediate cycle following the previous best ever! It's unrealistic. Those were the targets, we set high targets, sometimes we could do with realigning those targets! World champions and world number ones don't come along every day. We've got some really good professional players now. What we don't have is one that looks like they are a Nick Matthew or Laura Massaro, but they are there or thereabouts. The interesting thing is that not many people at all were predicting Laura and Nick to make world number ones when you look back. But they got themselves up to 20 in the world and they developed and changed and adapted to become world beaters.

JW: You think and talk about psychology a lot don't you?

DC: It's a huge part of playing the professional game well, dealing with pressure situations. We talk a lot about concentrating on the processes rather than the results, right? I think it helps the players to get the best out of themselves if they can focus on what they are doing in the rally rather than the title or the score or all the other external factors. Often it comes down to getting through a training session minute by minute. At that point you can't be thinking about standing on the podium. You're getting through each repetition, eking every last drop out of yourself. The same applies in a match: at 8-8 in the decider you need a clear vision of what shot you're going to play next and what tactic you're going to play. It's no use worrying about your greater goals or the 'what ifs' at this stage.

JW: Spot on. How do you improve yourself as a coach?

DC: I read a lot – autobiographies of successful people to get an insight. I liked reading Damian Hughes's book on Barcelona. I like to talk to coaches in squash, I learn from Malcolm and have done all my life. Outside of squash, I've learned from Tony [Smith – David, Malcolm and I went once to watch his teams work in Warrington].

JW: You've worked with cricket a bit?

DC: Peter Moores. One thing I learned from both Peter and Tony was how they tried to work with players to allow them to buy into the training, not to just prescribe training. They wanted to help the player understand why he's doing something or where the coach is coming from with a certain theory. The athlete might not always enjoy the work I might prescribe as a coach, but if they understand the validity of it and what it will potentially lead to, then they can be more motivated to do it.

You didn't enjoy those tough sessions we did in Halifax. You wrote about it, but you knew there were certain things you needed to do to compete with some unbelievable players. There was work you needed to do that you didn't enjoy doing but you understood the benefits it would give you. You didn't just train for the sake of it because I told you to. You knew every move we did within that work was going to help you in the throes of the toughest matches.

The coach-player relationship is crucial and they both need to be on the same wavelength. There's maybe more room for direction when players are young, but as players get older it's more about the coach influencing and guiding rather than telling. Then there's an open framework for the players to bring their touches. Malcolm does exactly this, he gives the player room to develop and isn't massively prescriptive. He gives simple instructions, and the player works from there.

So, I hope I'm not too prescriptive. Good technique, of course, is a given, but I don't always say it has to be a certain way. The top ten in the world in the men's and women's games do things so differently.

Perhaps the questions to ask are: can they put the ball there or here? Can they achieve a certain shot or result? If not, then that's when we need to look at the technique. That's the way I look at it, maybe slightly inside out.

JW: What do you enjoy the most about what you do?

DC: Squash is in my blood. I love the sport, love watching, looking at how and why players win and lose. I probably talk too much about it and bore a few people, but anyway …

Also available at all good book stores

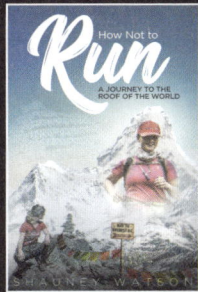

9781785314537

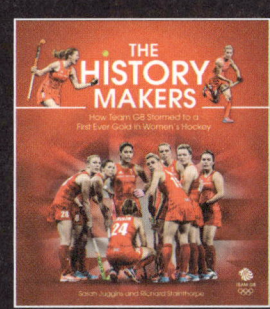

9781785313301

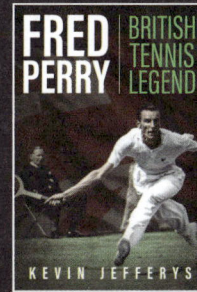

9781785312908

9781785314452

9781785314544

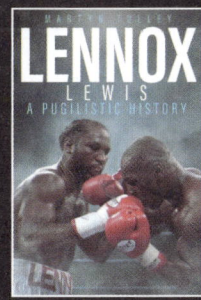

9781785313295

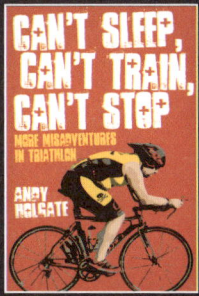

9781909178335

9781785314513

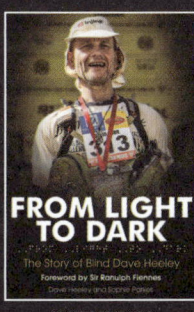

9781785312298